SHE'S GEEK!

women write about
science, technology
& other nerdy stuff

edited by
annalee newitz
& charlie anders

SEAL PRESS

Published by
Seal Press
An Imprint of Avalon Publishing Group, Incorporated
AVALON 1400 65th Street, Suite 250, Emeryville, CA 94608
publishing group incorporated

Library of Congress Cataloging-in-Publication Data
Newitz, Annalee, 1969–
She's such a geek : women write about science, technology, and other nerdy stuff /
Annalee Newitz and Charlie Anders.
    p. cm.

ISBN-13: 978-1-58005-190-3
ISBN-10: 1-58005-190-1
1. Women in science. 2. Technical writing. I. Anders, Charlie. II. Title.
Q130.N49 2006
508.2—dc22
2006021117

Book design by Kate Basart/Union Pageworks
Printed in the United States of America by Malloy
Distributed by Publishers Group West

»»»» contents

growing up nerd

high tech

in the lab

geek, interrupted

continued » » » »

games

superheroes

»»»»introduction

Annalee Newitz & Charlie Anders

The idea for this book began to percolate a couple of years ago, when we attended an annual conference in New York for activists and subversives interested in computers. Annalee and Wendy Seltzer (a contributor to this anthology) were about to speak on a panel about civil liberties. We looked out over the crowd of hundreds of geek progressives who'd gathered there, Charlie among them, and felt proud. These were our people!

That's when a guy got up to introduce the panel. Instead of mentioning Annalee's and Wendy's credentials, he said simply, "These are the only two chicks at the conference" and barked out a laugh. Now, the dozens of women in the audience who met our eyes with grim looks were worse than outnumbered by the men: They were invisible.

Afterward, Annalee tried to explain to the guy how comments like his were what kept women from coming to tech conferences in the first place. But he shrugged it off. "It was just a joke," he insisted. "It's not a big deal." It's all the more irritating to get this kind of treatment from a fellow nerd, since most male geeks have spent their lives fighting to be something other than the ass end of some dumb jock's "joke." But while the trials—and triumphs—of male geekhood are immortalized in movies like *Spider-Man* and in the career of iPod overlord Steve Jobs, those of female geeks are ignored.

Where are the triumphant female nerds whose stories of outer space battles inspire generations? Whose software has invaded desktop computers across the globe? Whose policy decisions have the power to chart the courses of large financial institutions?

We're everywhere. We're in your company's information technology departments, as well as in laboratories and public policy debates, at comic book conventions and gaming tournaments. But we're still struggling to be seen and heard. Partly it's because women are often ashamed to "come out" as geeks, obsessed with obscure or technical topics. But it's also because the stereotypical nerd is a guy, and the media reinforces that stereotype at every turn.

We didn't realize how sorely needed this book was needed until we emailed a few people asking if they knew any women who might want to write stories about their lives as nerds. Our request got passed from mailbox to mailbox, and soon it was getting blogged—BoingBoing.net posted it, and so did StarWars.com. We were excited to see a blog full of Swedish with the words "submit essays to *She's Such a Geek*" in the middle. Canadian public radio even did a feature on the buzz we'd created. Everyone seemed to share our sense that there were zillions of female geeks out there who just needed to stand up and be counted.

After the blog-storm of attention, we found ourselves with over two hundred essay submissions for this book. We started joking about what we'd call the sequel. *She's Even More of a Geek? The Wrath of She-Geek?*

We heard from programmers at Microsoft and Sun Microsystems, and women who'd worked in nuclear power plants and flew airplanes. We read about what it was like for women to study genetics in graduate school, teach mathematics, write science fiction, and design video games.

What we found as we read these women's stories wasn't just a common love of dorky Star Trek jokes, though there were plenty of those. We began to see a tragic pattern to many women's lives of nerd-dom. Growing up, many of our geeks fell passionately, even orgasmically, in love with math, astronomy, and life science. But as they aged, many of them found that their undergraduate degrees in science didn't lead to jobs in science—or, when they went on to graduate programs, they found themselves isolated and unhappy in male-dominated departments.

In fact, statistics show women flourish in geeky fields—until they hit a wall. The National Science Foundation reported in 2001 that 56 percent of U.S. bachelor's degrees in science and engineering went to women. But women hold only 25 percent of jobs in science and engineering. More women than men are graduating in the sciences, but a hostile job market and chilly graduate programs are keeping them from achieving their goals.

So we were thrilled to see so many success stories. Women had battled stereotypes and their own insecurity to become formidable gamers or leading programmers. Some, like Kory Wells, manage to toggle between their careers and families, and even teach their own daughters not to let anyone tell them what they can do.

The she-geeks in this book are tomboys and girly-girls, cheerleaders and lab rats. Some women dealt with testosterone-heavy environments by suppressing all femininity in themselves, and even realized they were "female misogynists," like computer scientist Ellen Spertus. Others flaunted their femininity, daring men to doubt their competence because of their flowing skirts, like astronomer Diana Husmann.

Many women explore different roles by playing in fantasy worlds. Devin Kalile Grayson, the first woman to launch an ongoing Batman comic, talks about discovering her inner sidekick, and Michelle Villanueva explains why she pretends to be a Harry Potter character on the Internet. And Morgan Romine, who formed the Frag Dolls, an all-woman team of competitive gamers, tells how her hyperfemale character became empress of a mostly male tribe in an online game called Shadowbane.

The women in this book adore genomics, are obsessed with blogging, hack their own sex toys, and aren't afraid to match wits with men or computers. Celebratory, polemical, wistful, angry, and just plain dorky, the women you'll meet in these pages will explain what it means to be passionately engaged with technical or obscure topics—and how to deal when people tell you that your interests are weird for a girl. Every female geek whose voice you hear in this book, and all the ones you meet on the street, are busting stereotypes of what it means to be a nerd, as well as what it means to be female.

More than anything, *She's Such a Geek* is a celebration and call to arms. It's a hopeful book that looks forward to a day when women will pilot spaceships, invent molecular motors, design the next ultratiny supercomputer, write science fiction epics, and run the government.

growing up nerd

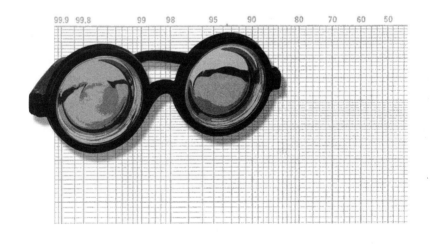

»»»»really good for a girl

Kory Wells

My mother calls me inside our neighbor's house, tells me to scoot all the way back on the sofa, and gives me a bowl of hand-cranked strawberry ice cream that cools this hot July Georgia night. I don't know which is better, eating in the living room, which I'm never allowed to do at home, or being up past my bedtime. But I know I'm still waiting on the very best thing. I'm waiting on Neil Armstrong.

An expectant audience has gathered in the twelve-by-sixty house trailer next door to our own, and I have the best seat in the house. Right in front of me, a small black-and-white TV with a gaping metal V on top commands my attention. Walter Cronkite talks and talks about the lunar module that landed hours ago, burning time like rocket fuel until a man in a space suit appears—a marshmallow man, all roly-poly and white. He takes that first step onto the surface of the moon and says the words that are famous as soon as they leave his lips. The fuzzy images and distorted sounds tunnel deep into some groove of my four-year-old brain, deep into some chamber of my big dreamer heart.

Days later, I'm still taking exaggerated steps like Neil Armstrong. I tell my mother I want to be an astronaut. She tells me I can do it. That I might even be the first woman on the moon.

My mother had no reason to say this. Nothing in her own experience should have made her think it was possible for a woman to reach such a goal. Less than a decade before, she had been the first female in her entire family to graduate from high school. Her hardworking parents, a carpenter and a housewife descended from sharecroppers, didn't understand why she needed "so much education." Mama wanted to go to college.

"All you need to know is how to diaper a baby's bottom and cook a pot of beans," my grandmother told her over and over. So my mother did what was expected, at least for a while, marrying at eighteen and having me at the "old" age of twenty-one. Her own mother had birthed five children by that age.

My mother always encouraged me to dream big. And while my dreams have led to many accomplishments, they don't compare to the marvel, maybe even the miracle, of Mama being so independent minded and determined to break free from low education, stereotypes, and anything else that might keep a girl, her girl, from living a big life. In my prekindergarten years, she did three things to prepare me for such a life: She taught me to read, she sent me to charm school, and she doggedly communicated the message that a girl can do anything. While charm school, a staple of Southern living, might seem at odds with feminism, Mama saw it as a way to instill me with confidence—and good posture—at an early age. Today, I love to read and write. I have a firm handshake and sometimes remember to stand up straight. And I have a career and interests that have been sometimes challenging—but never restricted—because of my gender.

When Mama was little, she thought that people who had books and magazines in their homes must be rich. An avid reader and writer by the time she was a young mother, she used the power of words to bust the traditional gender roles I observed as a little girl. If I said I wanted to be a stewardess when I grew up, Mama would say, "That's nice, but what if you were the pilot? You'd get to fly the plane." If I said I wanted to be a nurse, Mama would say, "That's great you want to help people. You could help even more, and make more money, if you were a doctor."

When we moved to a new town in the middle of first grade, Mama took me to my new school to enroll. The principal looked me up and down in my pantsuit and told Mama that I needed to wear a dress to school. "Why is that?" Mama asked. The principal, a woman, told her that girls behaved better if they were dressed like little ladies. "Do the boys wear ties?" Mama asked. Of course they didn't. Mama informed the principal that I would wear pants to school, and if I was ever a behavior problem, to let her know. Within two weeks, all the little girls were wearing pants.

In second grade, I came home upset because my teacher said only boys could lead fire drills. Mama paid a visit to the school, and I led the next fire drill. A few weeks later, she was back again, talking to the teacher after I complained that girls weren't allowed to listen to *Casey at the Bat* on headphones during our directed free time. I imagine the elementary school staff giving a collective cringe every time Mama rolled up in her '65 Mustang Fastback.

Although my mother worked hard to nurture my general love of learning and can-do attitude, she didn't limit me to her own inclinations and
aptitudes. While I absorbed Mama's enthusiasm for antiques and history, I also developed a fascination with anything related to technology,
especially computers. I was irresistibly attracted to machines that communicated in a code that, with a little effort, I could understand. I was
a Nancy Drew fan, and perhaps this kind of decoding was an extension
of my love for mysteries. My heart raced when I saw a box with flashing
lights, or printed letters and numbers fashioned out of dots. Interacting
with a machine that mimicked human tasks and thinking mesmerized me.
My access to those machines was limited to museums, where my parents
would have to pry me away from the rudimentary computer games and
exhibits so someone else could have a turn.

I'm a native of the Tennessee Valley, not Silicon Valley, but I grew up
in the shadows of two centers of scientific activity: Oak Ridge National
Laboratories (ORNL), the "secret city" of nuclear and atomic development, and Arnold Engineering Development Center (AEDC), a flight-
simulation test facility where I would one day hold a college internship
and the first full-time position of my professional career. In the fourth
grade, I wrote to ORNL and asked about their computers. To my delight,
I soon received a reply in a large manila envelope. A letter encouraged
my studies in math and science, and a booklet described computing at
Oak Ridge. This wasn't a booklet for kids, but I read it cover to cover.
With that inspiration, I did my fourth-grade science project on magnetic core memory, using electrical wire and washers scavenged from
my father's toolbox to build a three-dimensional, if manually operated,
demonstration of binary storage. It was 1973, the same year that future
Microsoft chairman Bill Gates was entering Harvard. The same year that
Mama decided to go to college.

After a decade of mothering, Mama had perfected her "you can do it"
speech, and she spoke often of *when,* not *if,* I was going to college. Now she
was applying all those pep talks to her own life. As an adult, I know it took
a lot of courage for Mama to go back to the classroom, a lot of energy for
her to tackle homework on the kitchen table after supper every night, and a
lot of letting go to allow Dad and me to try to handle the household chores.
But as a child, all I knew was that Mama was excited. I learned alongside
her, posing history questions from index cards, memorizing architectural

terms, watching pictures develop in the low light of the campus darkroom. I saw firsthand that pursuit of a higher education meant late nights and early mornings, hard work and fun times, struggling with frustrating requirements and passionate dedication.

As my own education continued in middle school, I was among the best math students, and yet in high school I signed up for the slower-paced algebra I class. Although I don't recall my conscious reasoning behind this decision, I wonder if it was my one foray into not wanting to compete with boys. But I found myself in the higher-level algebra class on my first day of high school. With a full dose of adolescent indignity, I raised my hand and told the teacher I shouldn't be there. She smiled big, explained that the guidance counselors probably placed me based on my prior grades, and then dangled the carrot that would motivate my entire high school career. "We'll have fun in here. Finish your work, and you'll get to use the computer."

The "computer" was actually a teletype machine with an acoustic link to our local university's Honeywell mainframe (you picked up the phone, dialed the mainframe computer, and then set the phone receiver into a special cradle), on which we played painfully slow games of Asteroids and dreamed of "faster, better, cheaper" years before the Mars Pathfinder project made those words famous. As it applied to computers, though, our vision was close to coming true: It was 1978, and Steve Jobs had just rolled out the Apple II microcomputer a year before. I became active in the computer math club and dreamed aloud of having a lab of Apple computers at our school. By the time I graduated, several candy-sale computers populated our club's windowless storage room. A few years later, I owned my own Apple II, a used model purchased on payments from a mentor.

The dedication of two of my high school math teachers allowed my fascination with computers to bloom into full-fledged competency. Math was integrally associated with computers, they explained, so I took every opportunity to delve into either subject. I drilled for regional math and programming competitions after school, alone and as part of teams. Girls were definitely a minority at these events, especially among the winners. I started to understand that a lot of boys weren't interested in girls smarter than themselves, but for the most part that didn't bother me. I regularly placed in the top ten at these competitions. The thrill of victory trumped the thrill of a kiss—at least some of the time.

As a copy editor and photographer on our high school yearbook staff, I enjoyed writing as much as math and computers. Mama graduated from college as I was finishing my freshman year in high school, and it wasn't long before I started planning my own higher education. I thought I would go away to school and made long lists of universities with good programs in computer science and journalism. (My interest in being an astronaut had been sacrificed to my less-than-perfect vision.) I soon realized that the potential pay was a lot better in computer science than in journalism. A professor from our local university got my attention at a college fair. "Our computer science department is recognized throughout the Southeast," he said. "Other schools have modeled their programs after ours." Then the university played its trump card, granting me both an academic scholarship and a work scholarship. I would actually *make* money if I went to school at home. It was an offer I couldn't refuse.

In a university of ten thousand students, I could have been lost. But I soon declared my major and found a seat in the computer lab, where I spent late nights and most weekends throughout college. Since I got a work scholarship in the computer science department, I got to know many of the professors, graduate assistants, and computer science majors. The program was grueling if you intended to make As, but the camaraderie helped see me through.

I continued to enter programming contests while in college, and I had two defining moments at one of them. One January night, students came to the computer lab to compete for positions on a team that would represent the school regionally. We had to solve six programming problems in ninety minutes. Twenty or so students sat at terminals spaced away from each other. The judges were some of our professors, but their identities (and ours) were kept secret. We had to program as many of the six algorithms as we could, in any order, as quickly as possible. The administrator started the clock. With clammy hands I opened my packet and started in on the first algorithm. I immediately knew the solution. It took a few minutes to program, but I was confident. I double-checked my output, then submitted my work to the judges. I went on to the next problem, and the next, and I seemed to see the solutions more by intuition than by logic. Many scientists would be uncomfortable with that statement and would instead suggest that my math and logic training was ingrained in my thought processes. Either way, to this day I believe that logic blurs into intuition more often than not as I program and troubleshoot various systems.

When the administrator called an end to the contest, I'd solved four out of six problems, and I thought I might make the team. As my friends and I talked in the hall waiting for the judges' results, I realized my chances were better than I'd expected. Most of the others had submitted only one, maybe two, of the algorithms, and weren't even sure they had those correct. Then the judges arrived and matched up our anonymous IDs with our names to deliver the stunning news. I'd placed second out of five winners, bested only by a graduate student I admired and surpassing several other graduate students and upperclassmen. I was a sophomore. I was elated.

On the way out of the building that night, my favorite professor, who'd been one of the judges, called my name. "Congratulations," he said. "We were watching those solutions come in and couldn't imagine who was doing so well." Then he hesitated. "Don't take this the wrong way," he added, "but you are really, really good, for a girl."

The awful thing is, I understood what he meant. I didn't agree with his thinking, but I also didn't take that much offense (unlike Mama, who would've been incensed). The other four winners that night were male, even though quite a few females had entered the contest. My professor was reporting what his own experience had taught him: It was rare for a girl to rise to the top of the computing field.

I believed then, and still do, that it is not a question of capacity of the male versus the female brain for math and logic. I am convinced that children come out of the womb with different personality traits and aptitudes, and certainly some of those differences may be based on gender. But I'm also convinced that we do ourselves and our community a huge disservice when we consciously or subconsciously limit our children's play, academic performance, or dreams by imposing the traditional roles of our culture.

During my freshman year of college, I worked as a part-time shoe sales-clerk. But by the spring of that year, operating a cash register had lost its luster and I had bought all the discounted shoes a girl could want. Besides that, I was eager to use my academic computing skills in a "real" job. I sent my résumé to one of the mission-support companies at the Air Force's nearby Arnold Engineering Development Center and was quickly hired as a summer intern, launching my professional career at the age of eighteen. The summer help, a dozen young people, were processed in through security on the same hot June day. As we talked while waiting for name badges and employment forms, I realized that everyone in the group except me was related to someone who worked there. Without that advantage, I'd have to stand out. I put my best handshake forward and gained challenging work in an instrumentation calibration lab. My first assignment, to make a slight modification to the code of a spreadsheet program called VisiCalc, was easy and took only an afternoon. My supervisor, an engineer who soon took on the role of mentor, later confessed that he thought that task would take me all summer. "You need to go to Systems," he said frequently, peering over his glasses at me. "They've got some sharp people. You'll like it over there." But that was his longer-term plan for me. For two summers he kept me busy working on a variety of computers, programming numerical-analysis problems.

At the beginning of the summer before my senior year, I moved over to "Systems," which was an altogether different discipline than what I'd experienced in the calibration lab or in my college classes. Whereas my previous work was limited to learning how to solve problems and automate processes in FORTRAN and Pascal, I was now faced with learning proprietary IBM job control and assembly language to define, control, and maintain the mainframe computers themselves and their database, communication, and peripheral systems. It was like moving up from being an automobile driver to an automobile mechanic. I loved being "under the hood" of these machines. It is, as I would tell people back then, very close to being God. A few months after my summer stint, I returned to work full-time at AEDC with the systems group. While I had limited system privileges as a junior staff member, to be in a group of people who had that much power over entire computer systems was intoxicating.

At AEDC I learned from intelligent men and women. But after a few years, I felt I was always going to be the low-ranking member of a staff that was stable, or even entrenched. I wanted more responsibility and less dependence on some commander's approval for my projects. I wanted to try the corporate world. A bank was opening an insurance services division in Nashville and seeking people to help build a data center from the ground up. I probably drooled on myself during the interview, but if so, it didn't hurt my evaluation. The bank hired me as an online systems specialist, the primary support person for a number of subsystems. I had the good title. I had the responsibilities. I had the phone calls at 2:00 AM when unusual messages appeared on the operator's console. I had the test time at 4:00 AM, because there was only a brief window each day when we didn't have users in some part of the country accessing the systems. I also had a programmer husband by this time, and we decided to embark on the ultimate interrupt-driven (as we nerds would phrase it) life. That is, we decided to have a baby.

Kelsey was born February 1, 1991. In contrast to my skilled professionalism, the best adjective I could claim as a new mother was "conscientious," certainly not competent. Birthing class hadn't prepared us for this. Diapering was awkward. My C-section hurt. The baby wouldn't sleep unless we held her. She nursed every two hours. The occasional all-nighter I'd pulled at work had never been this demanding. I couldn't catch up on my sleep.

Kelsey was tiny, just five pounds the day we brought her home. Warned by the doctor that she mustn't lose any more weight, we worried that she wasn't getting enough milk. How could we tell? Managing the situation as well as two nerds could, we kept a log of every diaper change for weeks. Most days got a little better, but some days I didn't get a shower. Most days Mama came over, spread a little love and Lysol, and said, "You can do it."

My job had great benefits—twenty weeks of maternity leave. By the ten-week mark, we were getting into the groove as mommy, daddy, and baby. But I realized the only call I wanted to answer at two in the morning was my child's. I couldn't imagine fulfilling duties to a twenty-four-hour, seven-day-a-week shop while also giving my best to my daughter. I talked to my boss about part-time work. He said it wasn't available. I talked to a headhunter about part-time work. She wasn't encouraging. For the next ten weeks I cried almost every day, torn between my job and my vision of the best possible life for my daughter and myself. Just before the end of my leave, I loaded Kelsey into her car seat, drove to the office to show her off to everyone, and submitted my resignation.

The headhunter, a respected woman in the region's information technology industry, said flat-out that I was making a mistake, and I detected some head-shaking from other colleagues. But my husband and I agreed that I'd finish my master's degree (I was "all but thesis"), look for a new position, and possibly start my own computer consulting company if no other opportunity looked better. I started watching the newspaper for a new job: one that would be family friendly. Had part-time or flexible hours. Had a limited need for late nights or travel. Was close to home (I had always commuted seventy or more miles a day). Systems programming work was probably out of the question. I had a few interviews, but nothing felt like a good fit for my skills or ideal family life. Then there was a call. The manager of a mainframe shop, himself the father of young children, needed a project done. If I could do the work in a reasonable amount of time, he didn't care what hours I kept. With the help of technology and a philosophy that was almost unheard of in our region at the time, I could even telecommute.

Not long after that, another mainframe shop needed a systems person temporarily due to an outsourcing project. I had to work on-site, which was a step backward, but my visibility paid off. Another manager who met me asked, "Can you program PCs?" The answer was no. I was candid in answering her—and in seizing the opportunity. "Can you give me a week to look at it?" With my husband at my side, we delved into a database system called Paradox. I went back the next week and told the client I could do the job.

This introduction to PC-based programming was my permanent work-from-home pass. I would develop systems on my computer at home and only visit the client for meetings and to deliver the product. Develop during naptime. Develop at night. Develop on Mother's Day Out. Develop when the grandmothers could baby-sit. Before long I had incorporated my business and was doing small to midsize database projects for companies throughout the region. Before long I had another child, a son named Matthew. Soon after that, I hired a former colleague, herself a new mother, to assist me. I learned to say, "I have an appointment that day," when a client suggested a meeting and I already had plans—with my kids.

Now, more than twenty years into my professional career, I walk into a training seminar as a featured guest and am taken aback that the men still outnumber the women three to one. I am old enough that some of the men in the group call me ma'am, and I am less one of the boys than I have ever been. This is good. I have been with the boys in college electronics lab when they compared the sine waves on the oscilloscope to their girlfriends' breasts. I have been with the boys in computer operations when they gave their assessment of every woman who passed by. I have been with the boys in the aircraft hangar when they whispered about my student pilot ass, the only female ass in the place. As a younger woman, I tried to shrug these things off, but they made me consider many men with a shade of distrust. Now I am blessed to live and work in conditions of mutual respect with men who personify equal opportunity. And my daddy still calls me up just to say he's proud of me, like he always has. These are the men I want my son to emulate.

After seven years of having my own business, I went to work for one of my steady clients, another small business. It was a win-win proposition. The company wouldn't have to compete with other clients for my time, and I'd be freed from administrative hassles. I kept all of my flexibility plus the promise of doing whatever interested me: coding, website development, corporate communications, and more. In a culture that almost forces specialization, I love a small business because you get to do it all, especially if everyone else is out for the afternoon. Sometimes I answer the phone and the customer assumes I'm the receptionist. When I was younger, that would have bugged me; now I don't bother to point out that I'm also the director of product development.

I still work from home often, and this leads me to worry sometimes that my kids won't remember my face, they'll remember the back of my head obscuring a computer screen. They'll remember me shushing them with violent sign language as they scramble in the house, barking basset hound at their side, when I'm on a call with a customer. They'll remember that I had to work during the Christmas holidays, when I said I wouldn't, because my customers needed help. They won't remember that after days of sickness that swept the family, I gave up all pretense of professionalism and answered the phone "Kory's Computer Service and Daycare." They won't remember that a client surprised me with an impromptu conference call at the very moment my toddler son climbed the stairs for the first time. But maybe they will remember that I've tailored my career to be the best mother I can be. Maybe they will remember that I believe in small business, in personal accountability, in making your own way even if that way isn't quite everyone else's.

∞

I'm pushing my two-year-old daughter in her stroller through a gymnasium crowded with children's clothing, toys, books, playpens, rocking horses, and more: a community consignment sale. We round one of the racks and run into the plastic sword of a little boy about three years old. As he widens his stance and tentatively pushes the tip of the sword toward my daughter, his mother says, "Oh, no, Jeremy, she's a little girl. She doesn't want to play with your sword."

I lean over to my daughter and say, "Don't listen to her. You can play with anything you want." I hope the woman hears me. I want to get in that mother's face and say, "Hell yeah, she can play with a sword," but my Southern charm-school experience holds me back. Nevertheless, I've become my own mother, or at least a confounded version of her, dismayed that her message, a message of the '60s and '70s feminist movement, hasn't yet reached everyone a full generation after its birth.

A few years later my daughter is bored in elementary school. I know this because she tells me, because she's mastered language and math skills at home before doing them in the classroom. But my daughter is quiet, compliant, and reluctant to speak in public. She wouldn't begin to complain to her teachers. Two times we have her tested for giftedness. Two times she doesn't quite make the criteria, a teacher's checklist that I challenge. Why must she be disruptive in class in order to convince someone she's bored? Why are so many more boys than girls in the gifted program? We try a third time and she's in. Two years later she must be "recertified." I find myself in yet another meeting, prepared to argue in her defense. The psychologist tells me that IQ scores aren't supposed to change much, but hers have. She's got the highest scores of any student he's tested in nine years. The counselor starts talking about advanced placement, private universities, and scholarships.

"You did the best you ever have," I tell Kelsey after the meeting. "Any idea why?"

"That guy was nice," she says. She is in eighth grade by this time, much more poised than before. She explains that the earlier test administrators made her nervous. "One lady kept trying to give me a Coke," she says. "I didn't want a Coke."

Finally she's shown everyone else what I've been telling her all along. That she's smart and capable. That she can do anything she wants to do.

It's too hot for high school football, but this September night won't succumb to any hint of autumn. A friend and I sit on the bleachers and marvel that the dust suspended in the stadium lights doesn't drift one bit all evening. We fan ourselves and feel sorry for the football players, who must be smothering. We feel even sorrier for the band members, who are wearing more clothes than the football players. Then my daughter walks by on the sidelines. Her shoulders are back and she is looking straight ahead. I elbow my friend.

"Doesn't she look good in a uniform?"

My friend laughs and nods. She has a child in the band. She understands.

I'm already excited because tonight the band director has pulled me aside to say he's so glad Kelsey is in the band. She's "nailing" the music and showing abilities they don't often see in freshmen. He says she's a "quiet leader."

The band takes the field at halftime. Kelsey pushes a marimba bigger than she is onto the forty-five-yard line. Later this year she'll march with a bass drum. "Don't let anyone tell you that girls can't be drummers," her instructor has told her. I like him.

On the drum major's signal, the band starts to play. A big, strong, lean-back-and-give-it-your-all sound. For the next twelve minutes, I watch my daughter navigate the keys of the marimba, vibes, and chimes. My child who will not dance in public keeps obvious rhythm with the movement of her right leg. With her head cocked sideways to hear the drummer's cues, she nods to her fellow section members at the right moment and pounds out a grand finale on mounted cymbals. There is only one word to describe her playing: bold. I know in this moment that my quiet little girl is almost gone, but I am easy with this truth. She carries her mother's legacy of believing in dreams. She's become a young woman who understands firsthand that claiming her passion and intelligence is really good for a girl.

»»»»dial-up desire

Jami Schoenewies

The day a child realizes she's smarter than her parents is the scariest of her young life. No longer can the forces of parental bonding protect her from society. No more will the nerd-child feel reassured by "Everything will be all right," when that child's power of reasoning surpasses that of the speaker of the encouraging words. No longer can the youth trust her parents' decisions, and for the first time, she must learn to direct her own life goals.

Late in May of 1991, my mother and I went dress shopping for my eighth-grade farewell dance. The shopping evening started off pleasantly enough, with light conversation about school. I remember babbling at length about how our student population really should gain some maturity, now that we were all headed for high school. I didn't come right out and say the popular girls were still picking on me, but toward the end of the monologue I think my mother finally got the hint. She froze mid-browse through a rack of gowns and glared at me as if she didn't know me. Partly confused and partly disgusted, my mother wore an expression that could freeze hell. No sign of compassionate understanding, no response like, "I agree, dear, but when you're all out of school none of this childish taunting will mean anything." Just a glare that meant our mother-daughter rift had opened wider.

When she finally did speak, a sickly sweet tone veiled the disappointment in her voice.

"Then it's settled. You will try out for cheerleading. When you finally start acting like a *normal* girl, then they'll be your friends!" Even in the eighth grade, I thought to myself, "She must have a fucked-up sense of logic." The rest of the time in the store I didn't speak, but tried to sort out why Mom was taking so hard the not-so-breaking news that her daughter was a nerd. She began a long and merry memoir about her own cheerleading days and how much fun high school is when you're in the "in" crowd, and how *not* sorry she felt for the girls who chose not to be among them.

"How boring their high school experience must have been! I never saw any of those bookworms at even *one* football game! It's tragic, and I don't want you to have to go through that." After that first verse, I tuned her out completely, mentally reviewing my youthful past. At four years old, I sneaked crayons into dance class so I could draw on the large mirrors while the other girls obediently twirled. In fourth grade, I begged my mother to let me play the violin after being mesmerized by a violinist who came to speak in our class. I couldn't help but be drawn to the softness of the notes, the graceful way the player glided the bow across the strings. It was such a beautiful instrument, one I really wanted to learn. My mother insisted that only nerds played the violin and forced me to take up the clarinet instead. I hated its hollow notes and the spit that flew everywhere when I blew into the mouthpiece. I refused to practice, and I quit nearly as soon as I'd started.

I half-noticed my mother holding a hideous mauve-pink dress with waves of ruffles in the rear, as images of fifth grade came to mind. After watching my stepbrothers play soccer, I too wanted to play soccer, or maybe hockey. Instead, my parents signed me up for softball. "It's the girls' sport," they said. Softball gave me a great opportunity to stand in a humid field for hours on end, watching the ground for crawling insects. Sadly, it seemed whenever I found an interesting caterpillar or butterfly to focus on, some shrill girl's voice would scream at me to go and find some stupid ball that supposedly flew over my head. The image of a bat shaking in the air while adults shouted, "Don't worry about her, this one won't swing if you throw her a beach ball!" vanished at the *ding* of a register, concluding a transaction for the worst dress I'd ever seen.

On the ride home I had to endure more of my mother's selfish "You should be more like so-and-so" lectures, while in my head I continued my self-evaluation. In a bizarre mix of fear and embarrassment, I realized that, up to this point, I had been trying too hard to be the daughter she wanted, agreeing to her worthless schemes to be someone I was not. Listening to her advice had only made it harder for me to fit in. This was the end. I needed to accept who I truly was and maybe, just maybe, find some happiness.

At fourteen, my interests included video games, computers, reading, drawing, comics, college radio, and R.E.M. My female teenage counterparts' interests revolved around shopping, cheerleading, heavy makeup, bulimia, and New Kids on the Block. In class I took notes and got As. Whenever I got all the information I needed for a test in my notebook, I'd draw pictures, filling whole spirals with doodles. The other kids in my class usually slept, drooled on their books, and failed or barely passed their classes, and that made them cool. I was a geek and a disappointment to my mother, and I needed to accept it.

"Are you even listening to me?" my mother would interrupt my reverie randomly.

"Yeah, be a cheerleader, be popular, smile more, life will be better. Got it," I lied, as my head filled with possibilities. From here on out, things needed to change. Regardless of whether my mom accepted it or not, I needed to take my own direction in life if I expected any happiness.

Mom kept talking pleasantly to the windshield until we pulled into the driveway.

"I'm so glad that we had this discussion. I think you'd be better off and a much happier person if you would take my advice and at least try out. Okay?"

"Mom, if I try out for cheerleading, will you buy me a computer?"

My mother thought computers weren't a life necessity, and saw them only as nerd accessory. Besides my promise to try out for cheerleading, I had to convince her I needed a computer for schoolwork (which was true).

It was during that wretched eighth-grade year that friends of mine, Dana and Kathleen, introduced me to the world of computers, and then bulletin board systems, or BBSes. We played games like *Scorched Earth* and *Battle Chess,* and drew pictures in Windows Paint. I was so jealous of my friends for having computers, and being able to play games and do their homework at home rather than having to stay at school to type up an essay. The computer that Dana's family had, however, could do much more than just run games. She could talk to people through the computer. All she had to do was type to them from a prompt, and they'd respond! She sneaked onto multiuser BBSes using her stepdad's computer when her parents weren't home. The main reason we were so interested in this new world of instant chatting? Boys. On the BBS circuit they outnumbered girls fifty to one.

Our little shy-girl group wasn't the worst looking in school. But we were clueless about makeup and had almost no fashion sense, so we never even hoped to win any popularity contests. To make our dateless status even worse, our school had a reputation for its cutthroat cliques. If you weren't at the top of the totem pole, you didn't get dates. Geeks didn't dare to date other geeks because of the fear of taunts from the popular fascists. Any odd movement at all and you became the butt of the week's joke. It was way better for us to try not to exist at all.

Every afternoon in the summer before I got my computer, I'd go over to Dana's house and chat under her handle with boys I never met in real life. There was no intimidation. They couldn't see me, and I couldn't see them. We would type endlessly about Nintendo, music, comics, and other teenage nerdy stuff. Dana and I were demigoddesses, chatting with whichever male our age sounded interesting to us. After listening to U2 for hours one night and chatting endlessly with a few flirtatious guys and feeling, for the first time in my life, really damn good about myself, I created an account and chose the handle "Desire." It was the birth of my own Jekyll and Hyde story.

As a female, I quickly found acceptance in the geek underworld. Desy, short for Desire, was a girl full of confidence and brimming with pride, evident in each of her words glowing purple against the black screen. Every cynical comment or whimsical joke I typed gathered a round of *applause* and *rolling with laughter* from the chat room guys. I quickly learned BRB (be right back), AFK (away from keyboard), J/K (just kidding), and all the other abbreviations people used. I learned who had their own one-phone-line BBSes, and I left posts on every computer in my area. Because I was a girl, the guys would do anything, *anything* to get me to chat with them. And I loved every minute of the attention. Hell, I even had my own smiley that everyone online recognized as my hallmark: ; }

But I still had to live in Dr. Jekyll's world, my *normal* life. Each morning at school, I'd see the same people who'd tormented me over the years. Yet something about those people changed as my freshman year wore on. Their numbers thinned, and their words grew more insignificant. I parroted the same comebacks that my online friends used on their school enemies. Soon, my high school nemeses left me alone altogether. Were they maturing, or had the glory of my abstract world given me the confidence to deal with them?

My first attempt to meet someone from the BBSes didn't go according to plan. Dana and I had plotted to meet two boys our age, at a mall far from our neighborhood. We talked Dana's mom into driving us, and we figured out where to hide so we could scope out our prey without detection. We weren't just nervous because we were meeting two boys when we'd never dated in our lives. It was more that they already knew too much about us, without even knowing what we looked like. Patton, the boy I chatted with the most, knew what I ate, what I dreamed, my favorite bands, what school I went to, my grades, what I wanted to become someday. He told me everything about himself too, so it felt comfortable to share so much from behind a screen. We'd send each other flirtatious messages without knowing or really even caring what the recipient looked like. And now Dana and I were going to put faces to the boys we had confided in.

I started to quietly panic about the dangers of this escapade. Maybe they weren't two young boys who went to a local high school, but murderous older men looking for teenage girls without their parents around. After all, we started BBSing by following the example of Dana's stepdad. And we'd told these boys everything. *Everything.*

The mall was crowded on a Saturday night, and we set up our stakeout on a bench a floor above the spot where our two imaginary boyfriends and/or ax murderers would materialize into real flesh. Ten minutes before the posted meeting time, I spotted two boys, one sporting a green coat and khakis, the other black jeans and a gray jacket. Both boys were wearing the exact clothing they'd described to us in their email. Lots of teenagers came and went, but these two paced anxiously in the same twenty-foot circumference, looking in every direction. Dana kept asking if I thought it was really Patton and Spidey pacing below, and I was pretty sure it was.

I spent the next few minutes desperate to figure out which boy was which from the brief descriptions I'd read on a monitor half an hour before. The boy in black jeans had a disastrously pimpled face, greasy dark brown hair, and a lanky body sporting dumpy rags for clothing. The boy in the green coat, however, I couldn't help but watch with want and awe. He had nicely groomed dark hair, a sweet and blemish-free face, and nice clothes on a well-fit body. Time check—five minutes until we were to show ourselves. Dana and I frantically tried to figure out who was who; all the while she continually waffled on whether they were really our online friends at all. The real question ringing in my head was who would be stuck with the pimpled dork and who got the prince? Two minutes to go, they were walking in circles with a furiously nervous pace. Just when

I was about ready to give up the game and suggest we go introduce our-selves, Dana shouted at me.

"We shouldn't be here! What are we doing, meeting people from the computer? They could be dangerous! Let's go home, please. I'm gonna find a phone and call Mom right now!" Without waiting for my reply, she flew up from the bench and stamped off, leaving me sitting con-fused. Her outburst caught the attention of our two subjects below, and they both looked right up and glared at me for a full minute. For the next few minutes, I sat there waiting for Dana, barely glancing down at the two boys, both whom were glancing up toward me every few moments. Time check—fifteen minutes past posted meeting time. Just before Dana got back, they shouted something that I couldn't under-stand and stormed out of the mall. The whole way home I felt sick, sad-dened, and I desperately needed to get back to my computer to email an apology.

When I got home, however, my little mailbox on the BBS was filled with hate mail from both guys, and I knew then that I deserved all of it. The worst came from Patton, who wrote, "I really wanted it to be you two on that bench, but you guys wouldn't come down! Desy, I knew you were sitting by yourself. But you and your friend were too good to come and actually talk to us. I hope I never do meet you, you shallow bitch!"

Being called a bitch I could handle. I remember thinking that it was a bitchy sort of thing to do, just sitting there on the bench knowing they could tell it was Dana and me all along. But *shallow,* that was hard to deal with. At school I had to deal with shallow people all the time. My world was filled with shallow people, and I'd always hoped I was better than that.

The truth is, it didn't matter who got "stuck" with the ugly duckling that night. Our online friendships were the most important thing, and we blew it. I wouldn't have wanted to date the boy I found unattractive, but if he was my friend Patton, I still had a friendship with him that wasn't based on outward appearance. Yet on that bench I forgot all those nights of chats, emails, and encouraging words and panicked about his looks. Whether or not it was intentional, Patton was right. It was a fucking shal-low thing to do.

The next few times that I met people from the BBS circuit went much better. About a week after the Patton incident, a fellow BBSer's mom drove all over St. Louis picking up underage BBS kids who couldn't drive so we could all meet for an "event," a BBS-sponsored get together. This first event was at a drive-in that was showing some movie I didn't care about. I just wanted to meet the people I'd been chatting with for almost a year. I lied to my parents, telling them that Dana's mom was picking us up, rather than explain that I'd be picked up in a van by someone I'd never met, who was picking up a bunch of kids I'd never met. Dana was going too, and by this time she'd met most of the people who would be in the van. So when the van pulled up to my house, I ran out the door. I heard *"Desy!"* screamed in my front yard. I remember being overwhelmed by strange teenagers hugging me and sharing their pseudonyms and real identities all at once. It was a glorious moment, being wanted and greeted by all these kids my age whom I'd never met but somehow already knew. When we got to the show, we met up with seemingly hundreds of others, mostly teenagers but a few older, swapping stories and hardly paying attention to the movie. I was one of half a dozen girls among a sea of mostly harmless teenage boys.

That night I was completely comfortable, and a little more extroverted than normal. I reveled in conversations about music and books that I could only have had with a few others at my school. And yet, boys flirted with me. Cute boys, older boys, interesting boys, intelligent boys, rich boys, working-class boys, writers, artists, musicians, and mathematicians were willing to speak to me. I'd never even so much as kissed a boy before this day and yet, here they were, lining up, politely shoving forward to tell me their aliases, reliving words and flirtations typed into a computer, vying to impress me as if I were some kind of eligible royalty given the choice of any prince. So I vowed to be friendly to everyone there, even if there was no attraction. We talked about *Red Dwarf, Monty Python's Flying Circus, The Young Ones,* and other British comedies I thought only I was weird enough to like.

Did I stay friends with many of these guys, listen to their own dating woes, and offer advice on how to deal with other girls? Sure. Of course, my dating advice was probably completely useless, coming from a girl who got along with few other girls. Did I use my femininity to gain respect in the online world, and to learn information and new code? No shit I did. I used being a teenage hacker girl to my advantage as I gained free access to pay boards all over the city and higher status in underground BBSes. I became co-sysop (co-system operator) on at least ten other BBSes, and the smartest guys answered all my questions about BBSing and hacking. They even gave me all the info I needed to run my own BBS.

All it took to run a BBS was a PC, modem, and dedicated phone line. BBSes were totally text based, with no graphics except for the pictures people made out of alphanumeric characters. People used BBSes then the way they use web forums now, to post messages for other people to respond to. But most BBSes could only accept one—or a few—users at once. Many BBSes contained any number of conferences (designated areas for main topics), subconferences (breakouts from the main topics), an email section, text games, and a file-sharing section. Users could rename subtopics as they posted, carrying on conversations one post at a time. The sysop would give each user who dialed in a "user level" that determined how much control over the BBS he or she would have. At first you'd be a visitor, only able to read posts without responding. Then the sysop could upgrade you to "user," with your own "handle," which meant you could post messages, email other BBS users, play games, and trade files. Higher-status users could change subconference titles or add and remove games and software in the file-sharing section. The sysop could do anything from change the colors on the message boards to access the BBS's hard drive remotely.

In 1992, I befriended a BBSer called Elfling, who remains one of my best friends today. I ran my BBS on Wildcat software in the early days, but it crawled and sputtered, especially in the face of my ever-rising dial-up traffic. Wildcat kept crashing, and I wanted to try a program called WWIV. Elfling was one of the most brilliant, intense, and raving-mad programmers I'd ever met. His electronic achievements at the young age of fifteen, legal and illegal, were staggering. Together we modified the WWIV program with some new code, and Desire's Little Popsicle Stand was born. I got the name from a local British rock deejay who called St. Louis "our little popsicle stand of the Midwest." I thought it would be ironic for a nice girl to start up a BBS with an implied phallic title in a subculture already saturated with dick. Once I listed the Popsicle Stand on a local BBS directory, the dial-ups were nonstop. My parents couldn't understand why I used their phone line whenever I needed to make calls. They thought, being a teenage girl, I needed my own phone line to talk to my friends. They didn't know I was using my teenage line to operate a computer messaging system with over five-hundred users dialing in.

By May of 1993, at the age of sixteen, I was sysop of one of the most popular BBSes in the St. Louis area. I connected five-hundred-plus high school and college-aged nerds, dweebs, grunge heads, and alternative geeks in our area. All thanks to a computer acquired by leaving cheerleading forms on my desk for one week, and in the trash can the next. I never did try out, and my mom never knew.

It was hard to be a normal geeky teen with an alter ego named Desire. I am still called Desy by those friends from the boards, while family or noncomputer friends know me as just Jami. By day I was just Jami, the little nerdy artsy girl with curly brown hair who sat in the back of class and doodled. At night, Desy arranged for scores of people to meet up at Denny's, Steak n Shake, coffeehouses, concerts, parties, the park, and the mall for mallwide hide-and-seek until the guards kicked us out. I was running into people from the boards everywhere and developing a confidence I'd never known. Each morning I returned to a world full of the same people who'd tormented me at school. But they too were changing as the years wore on. Instead of teasing me, the popular kids started asking me about bands and concerts and trying to impress *me* with their two-years-too-late knowledge of Pearl Jam and other bands I'd picked up from the online scene. I wore what I wanted, even if it seemed silly or not in line with current fashion. I even tried to stand out, wearing brightly colored tights and crazy skirts whenever I could.

I never dated anyone from my high school. Instead I dated fellow BBSers, because I could sneak a glimpse into their souls before I went out with them. I dated guys who went to private schools in the suburbs, lived in the city, had important fathers, or were born in foreign countries. Meeting a boy with the same eclectic interests as me had seemed so hard, but it became so easy with the bulletin boards. As each relationship ended, the whole circuit knew about it, and another guy lined up. Avoiding ex-boyfriends became more and more challenging, because the BBS world was a microverse. Patton was the first guy I had to avoid, especially after I learned that Patton had been the cute boy in the green coat.

The BBS scene gave me self-confidence and saved me from being another faceless girl dressed two seasons behind. My dreams grew bigger as each person I chatted with shared new experiences and concepts for me to take in and translate into my own reality. It doesn't bother me that I stole some extra attention because of being a rare female online, because

I never would have gotten that much self-confidence any other way. The nerdiest skill, programming and mastering computers, helped me survive in the social world. I have my teenage nerdiness to thank for being a stable adult today.

The fall of BBSes came about 1996, when the Internet started to look the way it does today. Full of graphical interfaces and the kind of global networking that no homespun BBS could hope to provide, the World Wide Web dealt a deathblow to BBSes everywhere. Some BBSes remain in survival mode on the Net. Others have evolved into web forums or other message systems, but none have the same classic look as BBSes of yesteryear, pixilated text on a black screen. I took down the Popsicle Stand on December 31, 1996. I had moved homes in '95 and was preparing to live in England in 1997. Many of my former users either couldn't find the relocated BBS's new number or, like the rest of us, had become infatuated with the vast offerings of the Internet.

I also took a different career path than my geek friends, who mostly went into computer science. I chose to pursue a degree in painting. I considered a career in programming after falling deeply in love with computers, but I also have a passion for creativity. I still read nerdy books and got riotously excited when the movie *Hitchhiker's Guide to the Galaxy* came out. All that sketching in school has led me to figure painting, where I paint real people, with their wonderful real wrinkles, dimples, and pimples. Of course, the art world is another area dominated by men and ripe with sexism, but that's a topic for another essay. ; }

»»»»high school politics

Jessica Dickinson Goodman

standard misconception about nerds is that they are solitary, they don't have friends, they just sit in their dark little rooms playing with their computers; they have no lives. This is bullshit. I have geek friends who live the nocturnal lifestyle—but when they're on the computer at 3:00 AM, they're instant-messaging friends, talking to comrades in a computer game, or writing on their blogs. Most of the nerds I know, myself especially, function in communities. From web rings to peer-to-peer (P2P) games to the blogosphere, the Internet is based on human connections. The physical aspects of communication may not be perfectly replicated online, but friendship, caring, and support are everywhere. I guess I could be called a communal nerd. I have always wanted to be around people who love the things I love, and I have more fun when I'm in community with others doing the same thing. This kind of community is not something that is always easy to find, and it takes work to build it.

Through most of my early school years, I struggled to find where I fit in. Most boys disliked me for my ardent feminism. When I was in preschool, one little boy walked up to me and said with total conviction, "Girls can't fight." My teachers told my parents that I knocked him over and, as I rubbed his nose in the dirt, chanted "Yes they can! Yes they can!" While the teachers found this massively entertaining, it didn't win me any friends, let alone popularity.

But sometime around fifth grade, a group of us who didn't fit in with the other kids found each other. The classes were so small that the boys hung out with other boys and the girls only hung out with other girls— except for our group. It wasn't unusual for someone to say, "All the girls are eating in the loft," or "All the boys are playing tag." But nobody in our group would be eating or playing tag. To distinguish between us and them, we called the others the Capital G girls and the Capital B boys. We called ourselves the UNS: the United Nonstereotypic Society. We were all nerds in one way or another: We had a math nerd, a flute nerd, an acting nerd, a politics nerd, a fantasy nerd, and a gender-rights nerd. This was my first group of friends, and I never felt especially nerdy compared to them. What is nerdiness to someone who has never known anything else? Without this group I wouldn't be the gender-rights nerd that I am today.

I continued my search for a geek community when I chose to go to Harker, a technical high school where most everyone's a geek, and laptops and TI-30 scientific calculators are required for all students. But that still doesn't mean I always fit in. It can be difficult to be serious about politics in high school as a woman. We're expected to be more mellow, accommodating, and certainly not strident. Some of my peers avoid me when I get onto a topic that I feel strongly about. They'll either change the subject or ward me off. I like fighting, arguing, and being vocal in most situations. This has caused me to stand out in high school, which is not always a good thing. High school is all about conformity, and standing out doesn't always help you make friends.

I struggle to find the balance between the opinionated statements I want to make and the knowledge that being neutrally inoffensive will allow me to continue doing things I love and making community. When I hear immature statements like, "This homework is so gay," or "Don't be a 'tard," I tear down the offending speaker. It's much easier to not speak up than fight all the time, but I feel if I don't speak up, I'm being complacent. This is a dilemma I think female nerds feel much more strongly than their male counterparts. I'm still proud of my convictions, though.

Ever since the start of freshman year, every single review I've gotten from a teacher has mentioned how many questions I ask in class. I've spent many of my history classes junior year trying to explain to my class that not all Southerners are evil, nor was the Civil War started over slavery. My history teacher is cool with my opinions, but sometimes I feel like the only one who wants to know more than what the textbook is saying.

In my sophomore year, I received one of the best compliments of my life. I was complaining that none of the boys at my school were interested in dating. Among a student body of six-hundred, there are maybe six couples. My friend turned to me and said, "Well, you have this really strong woman power, feminism vibe, and it scares them off." A boy at school described another fabulous feminist friend of mine as making him feel as if his testicles were shriveling up when she walked down the hallway, because it was so clear she didn't need him. I take great pride in my "feminist vibe," but it's definitely led to a lack of casual dating. I keep hearing from people that some boys assume I'm going to jump all over them (in a bad way) if they try to talk to me.

My thirst for more knowledge and a forum where I could discuss issues that matter to me led me to the Electronic Frontier Foundation (EFF), an online rights group where I interned the summer after my sophomore year. I got to hang around with supersavvy tech nerds and learned all about the laws and technology that affect my community. My time at the EFF both expanded my technical know-how and gave me confidence to show it off. The EFF tapped into my emerging love of programming, which I'd had ever since a birthday party in middle school when I watched two of the guys at the party pore over a C++ manual and debate the relative value of learning C++ versus Java.

After my EFF internship, I started hanging out with the programming crowd at school. Even at a geek school like mine, these guys are hardcore geeks. Until that summer, I usually zoned out during programming discussions—not only did I not have the vocabulary to understand, but I lacked the confidence to ask. Now I can even out-techie-talk most of the techies at my school, especially when it comes to online privacy, since I spent that summer learning about Internet privacy laws and technologies.

That year I picked a fight with the administration at my school about their censorship policy. The Harker administration uses Bess filtering software to block websites they deem inappropriate, which I believe violates our school honor code. This software not only affects library computers but also personal laptops and teachers' computers. After my time at EFF, I have developed a strong dislike of censorship, and the school's use of this filtering software is particularly problematic for me. I think it is important that students have the option of deciding what content they will gain knowledge from and what will not be useful to them. At EFF, I learned all about Tor, an open source privacy protection program that uses a process called "onion routing" to hide your Internet traffic inside several layers of data (like the skin of an onion), which makes it difficult for website operators to figure out where their online visitors are coming from. I use Tor to work around my school's filtering programs, which censor some content on our computers using criteria that isn't made public. After a number of meetings with members of the administration about their filtering policy, they have actually implemented standard procedures for reviewing blocked websites. Now the library staff reviews the websites for appropriateness, rather than anonymous administrators.

At my high school, everyone assumes that most boys and girls are computer literate. The biggest gender difference I've found is in computer maintenance. Many of the girls I know use their laptops with brilliance but would be hard-pressed to tell you their processor speed, or sometimes even what operating system they're running. After working at the EFF, this is no longer a problem for me—being surrounded by people who expect you to know these things makes you learn them pretty darn fast.

That's one of the biggest problems for girls just learning about computers: They're not expected to be interested. I still get looks of surprise from my programmer friends when I talk about the pros and cons of the open source software movement, or the latest update issues with my Mac. Hardware-wise also, girls are expected to be ignorant. I've taken apart my laptop several times (the darn Airport card keeps dying, probably because I accidentally threw my computer over a fence one time). I don't think most girls have done that. I love using power tools, and am in a very small group of girls who help construct the sets for our school plays. But, due to concerted efforts on the part of the technical director, I'm not the only girl. Technical Theater (like most power tool/electronics-based vocations) is very male dominated, but at my school girls are encouraged to do it.

Because I grew up around computers, I never really had to separate my geek identity from my identity as a girl. I see no conflicts between loving baking and loving open source programs, or between wearing makeup and wearing out a keyboard. I was a confirmed geek before I ever really got into girly things, so I never differentiated between my geek self and my girly self. Having a well-updated laptop is way more important to me than having the latest fashion in dresses. My peers don't always support this prioritization, but my friends are cool with it.

I hate to label myself a "female geek" because I don't like being labeled as a "female" anything. Because there are so many ways of being a woman or a man, there's really no absolute value of what it means to be either. But I'm proud to be a geek among geeks. To me, a geek is someone who is passionate about something. I love computers, fanfiction, power tools, electronics, and chemistry (especially as relates to baking). I have at one time or another devoted all of my energy to the study of each of these things, and I continue to love all of them. However, I do not really have one life-encompassing, self-defining love, except for my love of people. I'm lucky to have friends and teachers who are as obsessive as I am and who will at least listen politely, if not with rapt attention, as I ramble about my newest love. Without the UNS, my family and teachers, and without living in an area where books like this one get written, life would be much harder. I find that no matter what I do, I love the people who share my passions. That's why I'll always be a communal nerd.

»»»» the dress

Diana Husmann

t first glance, there's nothing unusual about me. Nothing about my petite size gives any hint about the logs I love to drag to various forts scattered around my back yard. Nor do my near-invisible glasses suggest that I spend hours watching my collection of extended Lord of the Rings DVDs, quoting the Elvish in the movie. And certainly my long summer dresses don't tell the tale of the time they spend hiking up several-thousand-foot mountains with the Boy Scouts. Before talking to me, almost no one can tell that I spend my free time pondering the possibility of an infinitely large multiverse.

I enjoy being a "geek in a dress," since I refuse to adhere to the "nerd" stereotype almost as much as I avoid acting like a conventional "girl." What can I say? It was just too much fun to watch the faces of my Driver's Ed instructors as I plopped down on the asphalt in my skirt and proceeded to change a car tire by hand rather than cheat by pushing the lug wrench around with my foot. I love proving that it's okay to get grease all over your dress.

As much fun as breaking conventions is, it stings just as much to come across a stereotype too deeply ingrained to be removed. When I was first admitted to the Massachusetts Institute of Technology in its Early Action program, I thought that my days of being typecast as a "girl" were over—no longer would I have to prove my geekiness to anyone. That was until I heard a rumor in my high school, saying I'd only been accepted because I was a girl. It was so painful to learn that all my natural intelligence and carefully planned study hours could be swept away like dirt under a rug, to be replaced by that single description: female.

One of the first things I noticed at MIT is that no one could make the mistake of assuming that any student had been accepted for any reason other than his or her brain. Everyone—man, woman, black, or white—was absolutely brilliant. Surely no one could ever be sexist in a place where the women were so obviously capable. This was true—to a point. Although no one at MIT doubted my intelligence or my interest in black holes, some people questioned another important aspect of my particular brand of geek. As a child, my most blissful hours were spent in the woods, where I scouted out fort locations, dug up anthills, and built dams in streams. My love for science grew out of my natural curiosity about the grubby, gooey, and sometimes gross things I found in the forest. Part of my identity comes from my willingness to go out, sweat, and get messy. Yet at MIT, I found people treating me rather strangely, as if they were afraid that dirt and manual labor would somehow hurt me. Never did I notice this as much as when I got my first job in a laboratory.

When I started working with Professor Lane at MIT's Plasma Science & Fusion Center, I was impressed that the four youngest members of my eight-person group were women. It was nice to feel like Professor Lane was fair-minded enough to work with the same number of each sex. But that was before I began to notice that whenever he needed work done, he always asked the male students to do it—especially if it involved moving equipment around.

Sure, these guys were older than me and had worked under Professor Lane for much longer. It was only natural that he turn to them for assistance. Yet I prided myself on being stronger than I looked and chafed that I couldn't offer my help to Professor Lane. As the newest member, there was little that I could do to help analyze data or come up with new theories; I could only patiently wait to learn from the older students. I only felt useful when I helped move and set up equipment, but sheer chance always seemed to get in my way—or so I thought.

One reason for my excitement about the new job was the fact that I'd get the chance to do actual field research at Arecibo Observatory in Puerto Rico. I spent hours listening to Professor Lane describe the tiny chirping frogs called *coquis,* the small shack of an optical building where the group stayed up all night long, and the adventures of looking for an open restaurant on Thanksgiving Day. The entire time, I pictured myself standing next to Professor Lane, finally doing what I loved most: hands-on research. I'm not a theorist; I'm an experimentalist. Finally, I'd have the chance to prove my worth to the entire research group. Unfortunately, that chance was long in coming.

When we finally all piled to that aluminum-sided optical building, four big, beat-up boxes awaited us: the large instruments that we'd shipped ahead of time. There were only four more hours until sunset, so we immediately got to work. Since this was my first time in Arecibo, my only goal was simply to do what the others told me. I would take an extension cord or bundle of optical cloth out of the box, then wait until an older student pointed where it should go. Even though I wasn't familiar with the experimental setup, I still really enjoyed myself. Not only was I helping my fellow researchers, but I was learning all about the equipment as I went.

Finally, the seven of us had the computer and dry-nitrogen tank all set up; the only thing left was our prized instrument, AIS. It's a giant camera that takes pictures of the night sky through a hole in the ceiling. But in order for it to peer through the roof, it needed to be mounted eight feet high on supports set in the ceiling—requiring someone to hold AIS up until it was screwed in. It was then that Professor Lane, who had been watching from the sidelines, stepped in and ordered the four youngest members—in other words, all of the women—out of the way.

As Professor Lane bent down to help the other guys take the sixty-pound instrument out of its box, I started to worry about the sixty-something-year-old man. It probably wasn't fair to assume that he needed help, but I still called out, "Wait! Professor Lane, I can help hold up AIS."

"Don't worry, Rob and Jason are strong," he said, indicating the two men to his right.

Bristling slightly at the implication that I was weak, I responded softly, "But I am strong too. I know I can help."

Over his shoulder, Professor Lane called, "Then why don't you climb to the roof and help guide AIS into position."

Relieved to at least be given a job, I headed outside to the metal ladder leading to the roof. Putting one foot over the other, I pulled myself onto the roof and headed straight for AIS's hole. Pulling slightly at my uncomfortably hot pants, I sat down and waited for the *men* to lift AIS up. I looked on as the large instrument slowly rose to its height and offered the occasional "further right" or "turn it counterclockwise" as the machine settled into place.

Hearing the soft gasping of a tired undergraduate, I called down the hole and offered to hold the top of AIS from above.

"No thanks," came the short reply, "We can handle it down here."

Sitting back in frustration, I noticed that Linda had come up to watch the procedure from above also. She looked at AIS knowingly and sat down with a satisfied smile. I remembered how new I was at everything.

"Linda," I asked softly, "does it bother you that Professor Lane only makes the guys hold up AIS? I've been on swim team for years. I think I can be useful."

Linda looked slightly embarrassed, as if she didn't want the topic brought up. Shaking it off, she shrugged, "To be honest, it doesn't really bother me. I like letting the men do the hard work; it saves me the trouble."

Afraid of making too many waves in my first research job, I adopted a neutral response. "Maybe you're right. It's just . . . nothing." Looking back into the dark hole, I wondered if maybe I was overreacting. Maybe Professor Lane just needed to get to know me. Maybe, with a little more time and experience under my belt, I would get the chance to better prove my value as a strong and hard worker.

Back in my hotel room, I sat down at my laptop, writing my daily email to my parents. Going over the events of my first day, I decided not to mention my frustrations. I was obviously tired and probably overreacting. It was time to go to bed.

Just then, Rob knocked on the door. "Professor Lane wants a meeting before bed," he said, then ducked out. I sighed softly and stood up. Remembering that Professor Lane would need more chairs in his room, I grabbed one of my chairs, set it on my head (my favorite way to carry chairs), and carried it down the hall to Professor Lane's room. When he answered my knock, he looked up at the chair in surprise, "You didn't need to carry that, Diana. I could have had Rob bring in one of his chairs."

"Oh, it's no problem," I replied, feeling a bit too pleased about bringing the chair before Professor Lane requested it.

Professor Lane uncomfortably moved out of the way to let me set down my chair. I happily plunked myself down and watched as the others arrived. Feeling much more in control, I settled down for a nice, somewhat boring meeting.

I had no idea that my small display of strength would count for absolutely nothing, until the meeting came to an end. As I stood up to go, Professor Lane turned to Rob and told him to carry my chair back to my room.

Surprised, I turned back to him. "No, thank you, I can take it myself."

Rob, who had already taken hold of the chair, looked questioningly back at our professor. "Don't worry, Diana," Professor Lane said. "Rob is strong—he can take the chair back for you."

"But I carried it in myself—I want to carry it back." My jaw was set and I stood up tall, but I could see that Professor Lane was eyeing the dress that I had changed into after work.

"No, it's very gentlemanly for Rob to carry it back."

After giving me an apologizing look, Rob started taking the chair out of the room. I couldn't resist telling Professor Lane what I was thinking. "But I don't think of myself as a lady."

He looked at me, confused, and I finally realized that there was no way I could make a conservative sexagenarian understand my objection to his opinions. I walked out of the room and followed Rob and my chair back to my room. Rob looked just as embarrassed as I felt, so I tried to make light of the incident.

With a quick "thank you," I grabbed my chair and took it into my room. After closing the door, I paced the room a few times in frustration. I understood that Professor Lane was just trying to be polite—to show some of the courtesy he'd been brought up with. But as much as I knew that he didn't understand the insult, I was still hurt that people thought of me as someone who was weak and needed to be taken care of—and all because I was a girl in a dress.

Well maybe I couldn't outright tell him to stop treating me this way, but I could still show him that I could wear a dress and still be just as smart, strong, and, yes, *geeky*, as I was before. Taking my carefully folded pants, I tucked them in the bottom of my suitcase and grabbed the top-most dress.

The next day, I showed up at the optical building wearing my light and cool summer dress. It was so nice to be back in comfortable clothing, and although Professor Lane looked me over carefully, he didn't say anything about what I was wearing. Instead, he asked who would be willing to put the protective cap over AIS's giant lens. Volunteering as I headed out of the building, I was at the bottom of the ladder before anyone could object. As I climbed up the metal rungs, I reflected on the fact that long dresses really were as good as pants—they let me move as I wished, yet covered my legs completely. Even better, they were cool in the hot and humid Puerto Rican air.

Mounting the last step of the ladder, I noticed Professor Lane standing outside, watching me. He held his hand up to shield his eyes from the morning sunlight and frowned slightly as he looked up at me. Most likely, Professor Lane was there to make sure that I didn't slip—even though a nine-foot-high ladder scarcely seemed like a threat to me. Even so, I couldn't help thinking that he was frowning because he thought I shouldn't be working in a dress.

And so it continued. For twelve consecutive days, I never missed a chance to go up to the roof in my various summer dresses. It was fun to clamber around all of the rooftop instruments and see the rolling Puerto Rican hills from the treetops. Only one thing seemed to dampen the bright, sunny setting—the fact that Professor Lane never seemed to trust me to be able to climb up a simple ladder, even with other students around. He was always on hand to follow my ascent with his frozen, stony frown.

By the end of our observations at Arecibo, I was ready to do anything to get away from Professor Lane. I'd never had a more stubborn and cautious shadow in my life. If I was on the roof, he was on the sidewalk below, making sure that my dress never somehow caught on the edge of the roof—a prospect that was impossible, since AIS was located near the center of the building. If I wanted to go swimming in the nearby pool, I had to ask him for permission beforehand, even though my years of experience on a swim team gave me a better idea of what was and was not safe in a pool. If I stood next to a tree, he waved me away from "dangerous" spiders, regardless of the fact that there were no webs nearby. I later checked with the local scientists—it turned out that the centipede was the most poisonous insect in the forest.

So when I found out that our next research destination, the University of Alaska in Fairbanks, was holding a summer school just for students—professors stayed elsewhere—I was ecstatic. I was tired of having no say in what I could and could not do—and as a result, I was starting to interpret everything that Professor Lane did as a genteel form of sexism.

Luckily for me, although my fellow students noticed that I always wore dresses—even when we were visiting rocket launch pads in the middle of the Alaskan wilderness—all they did was ask me if I really felt that much more comfortable in summer dresses. Back in the world of familiar questions like that, I finally relaxed and bragged about my days spent hiking with the Boy Scouts.

Of course, I knew that for the last five days of summer school, the students and the professors would meet in a research facility so we could do our final experiments. I tried not to think about the eventual meeting, but all too quickly the time came. At first I was a little nervous about being restricted by Professor Lane's worries, but he seemed pacified by the summer school's less stringent, yet always constant, safety demands. I still found myself tiptoeing around him until the day that Roland, a graduate student from Stanford, asked if some people would accompany him to a radio receiver he'd set up in the middle of the woods. He needed company to guard against the Alaskan bears, and it was a perfect opportunity for me to satisfy my curiosity about the woods.

As I agreed to walk out into the forest—and assured Roland that I would be fine in my dress—I looked across the classroom and saw someone else volunteer: Professor Mason, from the University of Utah. I had gotten to know Professor Mason when he elected to stay with the students in order to explore a glacier with us. We became fast friends when we showed each other various rocks that we had collected. Professor Mason also enjoyed hiking through the forest, and I looked forward to seeing the woods with him.

All three of us clambered into the research van and drove to the very end of the dirt road. All around, the short pine trees gnarled by the harsh Alaskan winters crept closer and closer, until the road petered out into a wet, marshy area. As we stepped out, the area technician came by to give us hand radios and waterproof boots. Holding up the supplies, we discovered that there were two pairs of boots for three people. I looked down at all of our feet. I was the only one wearing sandals—the other two men were wearing sneakers and socks. Obviously, I was the only person whose feet would dry in a reasonable amount of time.

I looked up at them. "Don't worry—I can go without boots."

They looked at me incredulously. "But your feet are going to be freezing—and you're wearing a dress."

I was prepared for this argument. "Actually, it's better that I'm in a dress, because I can hold the hem of my skirt above the water, whereas you would never be able to prevent your pants from getting wet."

They looked at each other, agreed that I was right, and pulled on their boots. I was so thrilled about my chance to finally get messy that I couldn't stop beaming. Professor Mason saw my face and grinned right back. He knew how much I enjoyed exploring, and I knew that he liked it just as much. With one last glance back at the van, we headed to the marsh.

As I took my first step off the road, my foot sank into half an inch of water. This was it—there was no way I could turn back now. Picking up my dress slightly above the water, I continued with a loud *Squish, squish, squish!* The other two looked back to see how I was doing, but once they saw my wide smile, they chose not to say anything and continued on. Since they were wearing boots, I let them go slightly ahead at first, but I soon discovered that the squishy Alaskan tundra never sank more than an inch down in the water. I barely needed to hold up my dress. It was fun to watch the brown water swirl around my toes as my feet sank in and slurped out of the moss. The water wasn't very cool, and since we were walking at a fair pace, I felt completely warm.

Soon I was no longer the last in line, as Professor Mason stopped to take more and more photos of the stunted, brown-green flora. He pointed out twisty red vines to me while I showed him the spongy gray mushrooms. Before either of us knew it, we had reached the radio receiver. As we watched Roland work on the small box at the base of the antenna, Professor Mason leaned over toward me. "You know, I never would have thought that you would make it all the way here in your dress and sandals. Now I'm never going to assume that a student can't do something just because of what she wears."

It was such a relief to hear Professor Mason say those words. After all the time I had spent fighting what seemed like a losing battle against a professor whose archaic sense of chivalry was too deep-rooted to be removed, I finally remembered how much fun it was to success-fully show someone that "dress" didn't mean "delicate" just as much as "geek" didn't mean "unpopular." As a way of thanking him, I gave him a wild blueberry.

As we munched our way through a patch of sweet berries, we came upon another discovery—bear scat. Thank goodness we had accompa-nied Roland on his journey into the woods. I was particularly glad no one had suggested that this very real danger was a good reason to prevent me from seeing the woods; instead, I remained vigilant as we looked for more signs of bears. Professor Mason took a photo of the bear scat, and we made a slow, steady patrol of the edge of the puddle-filled space where the antenna stood.

After we concluded that there definitely weren't bears nearby, Professor Mason and I continued looking at the various resilient plants that lived in the tundra moss and among the short pine trees. Just as Professor Mason snapped his last photo, I noticed something fluttering in the top of one of the trees. I motioned to him, and as we crept closer, I realized that it was a wild pheasant. And right behind the plump brown bird was another pheasant! The birds were aware of us and turned their heads from side to side to get a better view. When we got too close, they flew off to another pine one or two dozen feet away. Professor Mason and I crept closer.

I was in my element; this was why I enjoyed science so much. I loved the thrill of the unlooked-for discovery, whether it was an instability in the plasma high above Puerto Rico or these lonely birds in the middle of an Alaskan forest. It was obvious that Professor Mason felt the way I did, and we both continued following the birds as they flew from tree to tree. Finally the birds became completely flustered and flew away. Professor Mason and I smiled at one another, then returned to Roland and his antenna.

A light rain had started, and the mosquitoes were attacking with a vengeance. Since I had spent five years living in Minnesota (the land of ten thousand lakes and the home of ten million mosquitoes), I didn't mind the bugs, but I could see that the rain was harmful to Roland's electrical equipment. Professor Mason and I told him about our pheasant encounter while I held my coat above his equipment. With our help, Roland packed everything up, and we were back on the mushy path to the van. The light rain had stopped, and Professor Mason clearly wished that he still had photos left in his camera. I simply walked slowly along the path, pointing out various discoveries to Professor Mason on the way. We talked a little about the amazing way that animals survived in the harsh Alaskan environment, and before we knew it, we were back at the van.

Roland had radioed ahead, and the technician was waiting for us. He smiled when he saw the lone graduate student forging ahead of us. As Professor Mason and I reached the road and began shaking the moss off of our feet, the technician came up to us.

"You know," he looked at us, "I learn something new every day, when I see two men splashing through puddles in boots and one girl getting along just fine in her sandals and dress."

Hearing that comment, I proudly showed the technician my soaking-wet sandals underneath my still-dry dress. I had made the decision to forge on through the forest, choosing not to care about the wet ground, bumpy path, or possibility of bears. And just as I knew from the outset it would, the trip had turned into an adventure, with the amazing discoveries of mushrooms, wild blueberries, and pheasants—exactly the sort of unexpected surprises that piqued my interest. Finally feeling like myself again, I smiled at the three men around me—three men who now understood that a geek could still wear a dress.

high tech

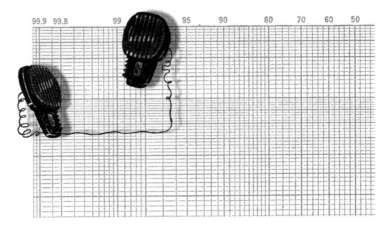

»»»»professor in a circuit-board corset

Ellen Spertus

lthough I've been a geek all my life and am now a computer science professor at a women's college, I wasn't always a feminist. I used to be a male-identified misogynist.

I grew up in an upper-middle-class Jewish family dominated intellectually by my father, an MIT graduate. Next in line was my brother, Michael, a mathematics prodigy; and then there was me, who took to computers like a sponge to water. The best way to retain my status and self-respect in our family was to act like a male and disdain anything feminine. I felt I had little in common with my housewife mother and older sister, Debby, whom I considered not very smart or interesting (after all, they weren't good at math and science). I once asked my little sister, Andrea, if she thought of me more as a brother or a sister, and she responded, "I think of you as a sibling."

My mother, on the other hand, didn't know what to think of me. She had earned her position in life by attracting a wealthy husband, and she considered conspicuous intelligence incompatible with femininity. My brother, who was otherwise encouraging, teaching me math and telling me inspiring stories, told me about the theory that mathematical ability was correlated with testosterone and that the best modern female mathematician was very ugly. I concluded that women in science were necessarily unfeminine.

I also felt that female scientists were lacking, not just as women but as scientists. While I was easily the top girl at math in school (at least until MIT), there were always boys smarter than me. I remember telling my high school friends that I judged the difficulty of a class by how few girls were in it. My brother was a constant example of male superiority, locally famous for mathematical achievements that I was never able to match. I concluded that the best woman would never be as good as the best man, and the best she could hope for was to associate herself with the biggest genius.

When I began dating, I chose men who were brilliant at science, regardless of their other qualities. In high school, I dated the boy with the top score on the National Math Exam (I was the highest-scoring girl). I gushed to him at prom that, of all of the couples there, we had the highest combined National Math Exam score. At MIT, I dated even higher scorers, although fortunately I got over my obsession with intelligence at a young enough age not to become a Nobel Prize–winner sperm bank.

Despite my prejudices, I wanted to meet another girl like myself. I went to one of the first computer camps in 1981, where the male-to-female ratio was about six to one. I was the only girl in the top class, and I told an *InfoWorld* reporter that I was disappointed there weren't more girls. In my first (but not last) media misquote, he wrote that I was disappointed there weren't more *boys*.

When it came time to choose a college, I visited several schools, such as Yale and The University of Chicago, diligently taking notes on the size of their library holdings. Then I visited MIT, where I stopped writing in my notebook because it was immediately obvious that I belonged. Everyone looked like a pointy-eared nerd. I'd grown up listening eagerly to stories about elaborate pranks at MIT from my brother, which made the place all the more appealing. When an admissions officer told me during my tour of the campus that I had been admitted before the early-admissions announcements, I knew I'd found my new home. My father called it one of the happiest days of his life.

After a lifetime of not fitting in, at last I lived at nerd central. Status was determined by achievement, not whether you matched the cultural standards that prevailed in high school. At least that was the theory. But only certain types of intelligence were admired, and there was a kind of anti–dress code. I remember having negative responses to the rare female students who dressed attractively, styled their hair, or behaved in a "feminine" manner—feeling they made it more difficult for women like me who just wanted to be one of the guys.

I still wanted to have female friends but couldn't find them. This was partly because my major, computer science, had the lowest percentage of women on campus. I continued to believe that there were so few women in science and engineering because they were either stupid or lazy. Sometimes this belief extended into mocking self-deprecation. I told my electronics lab partner that if I did poorly on an exam, I would quit and have babies.

I was deeply suspicious of women's colleges, like MIT's "sister" school, Wellesley. Still unsure of my femininity, I viewed Wellesley students as better-equipped romantic rivals. I was not alone. A boyfriend told me his MIT-grad father had advised him to find a Wellesley girl instead of a "vector girl" at MIT. My mother reinforced this sentiment: When I brought home my MIT freshman picture book, she leafed through it and exclaimed in surprise, "Some of these girls are pretty!"

I complained bitterly that we were required to take a "soft" humanities or social science course each semester. Since it didn't seem to matter which one I took, I chose based on which books in the college bookstore I wanted to read. That's how I came to sign up for Women in Literature. Its booklist included *Middlemarch*, which had been recently recommended to me. On the first day, the professor announced that she was teaching the course for the first time because the previous (male) instructor for Women in Literature had only included books written by men about women. She would be teaching only books by women. With my Reagan-era prejudices, I thought these would be lower-quality, "affirmative action" choices, since the selection would be limited to authors of the less talented sex. I was wrong. *Middlemarch* was excellent, as was *Their Eyes Were Watching God*. I had attended a high school renowned for its English program, and I thought I knew good literature. But I realized that because none of the authors we read in high school were female, I had mistakenly concluded (from a biased sample) that no great writers were women. I started to see that women's work wasn't less valuable, just less valued.

The same year, a female graduate student named Sharon Perl gave me an amazing report called "Barriers to Equality." MIT's women in computer science had written it in the early '80s to explain the many ways that women—even after they'd made it to MIT—were treated unequally. For the first time, I realized that the playing field hadn't been level. To paraphrase Ann Richards, the women were dancing backward and in high heels.

I also joined an email list for women in computer science called Systers, and for the first time was part of a community of hundreds (now thousands) of technical women, almost all of them senior to me. While the practical advice I got from the list was helpful, such as what to wear (and, more importantly, what *not* to wear) when presenting a paper at a conference, even more valuable was how it changed my view of other women and of myself. Instead of feeling that these women were beneath me, I was awed and inspired by their achievements. I wasn't the best woman around, and I couldn't blame my limitations on my sex anymore.

Senior year, I took a class called Women and Computers, taught by Sherry Turkle. For my term paper, I wrote over a hundred pages—four times as many as were assigned—on why there were so few female computer scientists. In the report I quoted Dorothy Zinberg, who expresses how I had come to think (and still do):

> As the data from women's career studies and anecdotes from personal experiences of women professionals begin to accrue, one of the questions that arises is not "Why are there so few successful professional women?" but rather, "How have so many been able to survive the vicissitudes on each rung of the career ladder?"

When I released my findings as an MIT Artificial Intelligence Lab technical report during my first semester of graduate school, I expected my status to fall. Clearly, I wasn't conforming to the "one of the guys" model anymore. Instead, my visibility increased. I even received an award for the report from the Department of Electrical Engineering and Computer Science, albeit incorrectly addressed to "*Mr.* Ellen Spertus." When author Katie Hafner visited to write a story about female computer science students at MIT, she kept getting directed to me. I ended up with my photo and profile in *The New York Times* under the headline "Woman, Computer Nerd—and Proud."

The report launched my career as a feminist beyond MIT, leading to invitations to participate in panels, serve on committees, and give presentations, including one at Smith College. Until then, I had the usual MIT goal of being a professor at a research university or a heavy hitter in industry. But my growing respect for women began to extend to their institutions and values, and I questioned whether I wanted the high-status, high-pressure career for which I was tracked. When I told my then adviser I might want to teach at a liberal arts college, his response was, "Oh, Ellen, I'm sure you could get a job at a research university." My adviser had been a father figure to me, but I was becoming less concerned with doing what he (or my father) considered important and more interested in following my own instincts.

∞

Some people have trouble finding research ideas, but I never have. To me, every annoyance is an opportunity. For example, back in the early days of the web, my then-boyfriend ran a controversial political website and got a lot of flame email. Looking at these hostile messages with him, my response was that it should be possible to write a computer program to identify the flames so you don't have to read them. I went on to design "Smokey," the first software system to automatically recognize flames, which not only yielded conference publications but also coverage in *Wired* and *Maledicta: The International Journal of Verbal Aggression*.

Another peeve of mine, back in '95 when I was looking for a thesis topic, was how bad web search engines were. Searches were based entirely on the words on a page, using decades-old technology for searching "flat" text collections, such as collections of newspaper articles or legislative bills. With the web, the world was no longer flat. It was a network, with structure across pages (hyperlinks), within pages (HTML headers and lists), within URLs (e.g., indicating that two URLs were on the same server or in the same folder), and within domains (e.g., "Tom" ~ "Thomas" in the dictionary of first names). Search engines, I argued, needed to make use of that structural information. I went on to develop tools and techniques for structured search. I was not the only one to have this insight: Link analysis is what makes Google one of the best search engines available.

I now had a female adviser, Lynn Andrea Stein, a junior faculty member who was not only a feminist, but—even more scandalously—a mother. Academic women are advised not to have children until receiving tenure (typically six years after becoming an assistant professor, when a university decides either to fire them or to grant them a lifetime contract). Not only did Lynn have three children, she actually spent time with them. In contrast, the grande dame of our department, Mildred Dresselhaus, had taken only four days of maternity leave from MIT in the course of giving birth to four children. Lynn truly valued teaching and advising, and did not follow the common practice of making her advisees work on her research or take credit for her advisees' own research. Unfortunately, those activities are not rewarded, and she was eventually denied tenure by MIT. I didn't think I was any smarter than Lynn, and I certainly didn't want to work even harder than she did, so my opinion of a career at a research university kept dropping.

I still felt the need to dress and act like one of the guys in order to fit in. I'd had a full dance card in high school (thanks to math team) and at MIT, but I was very conscious of being the beneficiary of a skewed male-to-female ratio. When I dated a particularly good-looking graduate student, I rationalized that the uneven ratio was what allowed a mousy woman like me to date a long-haired blond (one of my weaknesses). When I later met the man I would marry, I first thought that he was too handsome to be in my league. When we began dating, I again attributed much of my good fortune to the ratio, which allowed an unexceptional Midwestern girl like me to marry a long-haired blond California man.

Some married academic couples live apart because they can't find desirable jobs near each other. I joked that Keith and I were old-fashioned in that we wanted to live together *after* we married. Consequently, we both applied for many positions: I applied for more than one hundred, at research universities, liberal arts colleges, and industrial labs. Entering the market during the Internet boom (when departments were growing and faculty leaving) with lots of published research and a specialty in web search, I received many invitations. I used the job search process to figure out what type of place I wanted to work, even though it meant asking so-called forbidden questions, about topics like maternity leave. The conventional wisdom was that female applicants shouldn't raise such questions, as if by being silent they could prevent search committees from noticing they were potentially burdensome mothers.

My interview experiences confirmed my impression that research universities were unpleasant places for junior faculty. One question I asked was what hours they worked. One assistant professor replied, "This week I've been getting up at 6:30 [AM] and going home at 2:00 AM, but this is an unusually tough week. Normally, I go home at 1:00 AM." I ruled out that school.

Even though I didn't know if I wanted to have children, I did want to be somewhere where it was allowed. I asked administrators whether any women who became mothers while on the tenure track had gotten tenure. When no data was available on that, I would sometimes ask about the retention of female faculty. Of course, nobody came out and said that I couldn't get tenure if I had a baby. One president said, "I don't see why that would be a problem. That's just three months out of six years." Huh?

In addition to being unpleasant places for junior faculty and their families, it didn't seem that research universities were good for undergraduates, either. While administrators always proclaimed that teaching was "very important" at their institutions, faculty members always laughed when I repeated this to them. The conventional wisdom was that you should spend as little time on your teaching as possible. Publishing and bringing in research grants were far more important for getting tenure. Even with a fat list of publications to your name, though, one might not be granted tenure. Departments "on the rise" often deemed the faculty they'd hired six years earlier not good enough for them, and would dump them like a rising executive's loyal first wife.

I was delighted, then, to receive an invitation and later an offer from Mills College, a women's liberal arts school in Oakland, California, within commuting distance of Silicon Valley, where Keith received an offer from his dream employer, NASA. While Mills was less prestigious than many of the other schools at which I interviewed, I felt I would be happiest there. I was confident that discrimination or tokenization wouldn't be a problem at Mills, where most of the faculty, the provost, and the president were female. My work on advancing women in technology would count as a positive, rather than casting suspicion on my seriousness as a scientist. My primary responsibility would be teaching the students I saw every day. Research would also be required, but at a reasonable rate that I would enjoy.

My MIT peers on the academic job market were all hired by research universities, and some eventually won tenure, others not. I saw one a few years ago, when I gave a talk at his school on the challenges faced by women in academic computing. When I mentioned the difficulty of caring for a child while on the tenure track, he said that as a junior faculty member he didn't have time to care for a hamster, much less a child. Despite his years of hard work, he was soon denied tenure and didn't even have a hamster to comfort him.

Mills turned out to be a great match for me. For the first time, I was a woman among women, and I enjoyed it. Had I been in a computer science department with few if any other female faculty, I would have felt the need to behave like one of the guys, but also to represent all women. I would have dressed professionally and hypermodestly, in an attempt to be taken seriously and be considered as asexual as possible. At Mills, however, a new path was open to me.

I knew Mills would be different from MIT, but I didn't anticipate how the subtle differences would add up. For example, I was surprised during my first semester that students asked questions in class when they didn't understand material. At MIT, you only asked questions to show off. If you didn't understand something, you kept your mouth shut and hoped nobody noticed. There was good reason for circumspection: Many students felt we were divided into "winners" or "losers," with the winners getting the resources (professors' attention, funding, others' respect) and the losers getting nothing. Winners continually feared becoming seen as losers, from which there was no escape.

At Mills, the world wasn't divided into winners and losers. While an MIT professor once openly stated that he lectured to the top 10 percent of the class, at Mills we feel responsible to all the students. My job is to help each student learn as much as she can. In this environment, students can admit ignorance or uncertainty without penalty, giving the teacher an opportunity to dispel confusion. I developed a teaching philosophy of "rigorous *and* nurturing," in marked contrast to MIT, where the two were considered antithetical.

Another difference is Mills's respect for nontechnical disciplines and our students' desire to make the world a better place. This means our students study the so-called "softer" subjects, but it also means that I can openly discuss social issues in computer science classes. On the first day of Operating Systems, I talked about the problems of software patents, the Microsoft antitrust suit, and open source software. I wanted to show that the material they were about to learn wouldn't just be about computers—it would be about passionate people with different ideals who wanted to change the world.

I went on to direct Mills's unique Interdisciplinary Computer Science graduate program, which provides a route for students with bachelor's degrees in another field (typically in the liberal arts) to learn computer science. Students entering the program are usually somewhat apologetic for having an academic background in, say, American Studies, instead of computing. I tell them, with complete sincerity, that straight computer science graduates are a dime a dozen, but their unique skills sets will make them irreplaceable. I had ceased to deify the narrow technical education that had once been my ideal.

In 2001, my fourth year at Mills, I followed a web link that read, "Are you the sexiest geek alive?" Idly, I took a qualifying test for what seemed to be some kind of geek pageant. To my surprise, I was invited to be a semi-finalist. The winner would be decided by online voting. If I had worked at a male-dominated institution I would never have gone any farther. Just being associated with such an event would have undermined my professional credibility. Plus, I'd never get to be "one of the guys" again. But now there was no reason to stop the fun.

I posted a suitably geeky photograph of myself and a profile listing a dozen of my qualifications, including:

>> I'm MIT[3] in Computer Science (bachelor's, master's, and PhD), where I was active in the Nerd Pride movement.
>> The license plate on my electric car is "V EQ IR" (Ohm's law).
>> I was one of three MIT women profiled in *The New York Times* under the headline "Woman, Computer Nerd—and Proud."
>> I've had a lifelong weakness for male geeks. When I was about eleven, I ran electricity through my braces to get the attention of a young he-nerd.

I emailed my friends and told my students, one of whom told me she voted for me many times, and I won a position in the June pageant, to be held in nearby Silicon Valley.

What would I wear? Normal geek attire would be blue jeans and a free T-shirt, but I no longer felt constrained by the antifashion uniform. Instead, I wanted something simultaneously geeky and glamorous, showing that one could be both at the same time. The centerpiece of my outfit was a black corset inscribed with a circuit board pattern, which I wore with a black slit skirt. Through the slit you could see strapped to my leg the slide rule handed down by my father from his days at MIT. The look was inspired by the poster of Sandra Bullock in *Miss Congeniality,* where she's done up in pageant attire with a gun strapped to her leg.

For the five-minute talent round, I considered and quickly dismissed the ideas of reciting pi or playing *Robotron*. I wanted to capture my broad range of geekiness, as well as answering in what way geeks are "sexy," a question already put to me by several reporters. My position was that geeks are passionate, powerful, and playful—all sexy qualities. So I decided to create a video about my life. It began with my early experiences learning to program a mainframe as a small child and attending computer camp; my MIT years, including an endorsement from free-software icon Richard Stallman; and, most importantly, my years as a professor. I argued that I was the sexiest candidate because sex is fundamentally about reproduction, and I had reproduced the most geeks. "I aspire to be a geek fertility goddess," I said. The highlight of the video was a montage of dozens of my students (and their students) proudly displaying electronics and computer projects, accompanied by Cyndi Lauper's "Girls Just Want to Have Fun." Always the teacher, I concluded the video with a quick lesson on how to count in binary on your fingers, which I accompanied live onstage before the dumbstruck judges.

Contest judge and reporter Sue Hutchinson described the outcome in a front-page *San Jose Mercury News* account:

> Ellen Spertus was wearing a strapless computer circuit-board corset and a slide rule strapped to her leg when she was named "Sexiest Geek Alive" in San Jose on Wednesday night. A group of her computer science students from Mills College looked like they might weep over the splendor of it all when she was crowned by the reigning Miss California. . . .
>
> She offers hope for all beleaguered geeks suffering through gym class. . . . They may not be sexy now, but one day they will be dazzling.

Five years later, the only visible remnant of my experience is a *Weekly World News* article taped to my office door. I hope, though, that the spirit of that contest remains in what I try to teach my students: To succeed, we don't need to follow anyone else's model. Stereotypical geeks are commonplace. As for the rest of us—we hold world-class titles that may not be "official," but they still meaningfully define us.

»»»»the overloaded activist

Wendy Seltzer

I've always been a feminist by default. *Of course girls are as capable as boys,* I thought when my junior high advanced math class had two girls and one boy. Women's equality of ability still seemed obvious as I entered college, though the female-to-male ratio in advanced math there skewed sharply in the other direction.

By the time I entered law school, I was seeing plainly that equality of ability didn't always translate into equality of opportunity and achievement. Surveys showed that on average, women were paid less for the same work as men. Women were outnumbered in most of the places I'd spent summer internships. Not absent—I'd worked with smart women in scientific research laboratories, in Congress, and in the federal district court. Those women leaders encouraged my ambition, reminding me that for every statistic about women's lesser opportunities, individuals were breaking the mold. I resolved to join them as an outlier.

I got into technology law in the same spirit. When Harvard Law School's newly formed Berkman Center for Internet & Society advertised for a webmaster, I volunteered on the strength of experience running a web server under my desk. I was soon running the center's growing assortment of technologies, writing class-discussion software, and leading online courses. While there were few women involved in technology, I found that my technical and legal skills—plus a readiness to learn more—could usually dispel any gender-based misgivings. At least, this was true in law school.

From law school and the Berkman Center, I moved to the "real world" of intellectual property litigation with a New York law firm, where despite a gender-balanced entering class, most of the partners were male. This reminder of how recently women had attained full status in the profession was offset with lunches for women attorneys designed to assure us "that was then, this is now." But I still wondered, when helping to prepare for a deposition, whether I was the one to be asked to get coffee because I was female, or merely because I was the most junior.

When I moved west to work with civil liberties group Electronic Frontier Foundation, I encountered the challenges of being a woman in technology even more directly. At EFF I was both a technology lawyer and a technology activist, writing briefs and white papers as well as traveling frequently to tech conferences to enlist others in the fight for freedom online. Though EFF's small staff has several women, we were still clearly outnumbered in the field. At conferences, I was often one of a small number of women in the audience and one of even fewer onstage.

It didn't take any advanced math to see that the unbalanced ratio of women to men was not a statistical anomaly, but a feature as characteristic of tech conferences as the PowerPoints and plastic-encased name badges. Lines at the women's restrooms—a persistent bug at theaters and concert halls—were comically absent even at the most crowded tech conferences. I often had the sense that even though the bathrooms were prepared for women, not all the audience members were.

I don't mean to say that most men in technology are nasty or exclusionary. To the contrary, many are welcoming. When asked why there aren't more women on the stage, many conference organizers respond that they can't find more, or that women haven't applied. But applying and appearing, or failing to do so, becomes self-fulfilling. For if women don't go to the networking events and get up on the stage, they won't be seen as potential speakers for the next round. Those who do, on the other hand, get typecast as "the woman speakers."

Some women respond to this dynamic by ignoring it, expecting that their technical merit and expertise will ultimately shine through. Others respond by consciously engaging with the issues at women-centered events, like the BlogHer conference, first held in 2005. The conference, organized by and for women, cites this as its mission: "to create an opportunity for all kinds of women bloggers to pursue exposure, education, and community." It mixed standard tech-conference fare with discussions about gender equality. One of the goals of the conference was to build lists of women experts so that men could no longer claim that there were "no women available" to speak on a variety of topics at technology conferences.

At first I resented the invitation to speak at the 2005 BlogHer conference. It was scheduled for the same weekend as Defcon, a thirteen-year-old hacker and computer security convention that regularly attracts more than five-thousand people to Las Vegas, where it takes over an entire resort. Serious talks, where new software exploits are revealed and inse-curities dissected, are interspersed with evenings of "Hacker Jeopardy" and drinks around the pool. Defcon attracts few women. One, who wore a "403: Access Forbidden" tank top (which repurposed an error message from Apache web server software to declare her own assets were off-limits), didn't get the technical side of the joke. Sadly, she was the rule rather than the exception. There were smart women hackers at the confer-ence for sure, but the "booth babes" selling T-shirts outnumbered them.

Even though I needed to wear an EFF cap to remind the hackers I could hold my own, I liked the Defcon atmosphere. The Wi-Fi shootouts, core wars, and lockpick contests all contributed to a celebration of technology for its own sake. We didn't need to take ourselves too seriously, but we'd still leave with new insights and connections. And despite the plethora of other attractions, there were people listening when I talked about online civil liberties or the fight to keep reverse-engineering legal.

You'd need to stack up about twenty BlogHers next to a Defcon to get anything like a balanced gender ratio. In its first year, situated in the neatly labeled lobby of a Santa Clara hotel, BlogHer was serious where Defcon was carnivalesque. Instead of Defcon's "wall of shame," where passwords transmitted insecurely over the conference network scrolled by for all to see, BlogHer had a panel of "mommy bloggers." The women who would be headed to Santa Clara were great technologists, writers, and lawyers, but would BlogHer leave any room for geeky fun?

I flew to BlogHer from Las Vegas with a sense more of duty than antici-pation, and quite a few questions. Shouldn't I be able to focus on the tech-nology and politics of copyright law without a heaping plate of gender politics on the side? Would the "women's issues" overwhelm technical discussions?

Yet the atmosphere in Santa Clara pleasantly surprised me. Instead of the earnest but boring event I had feared (my own prejudices echoing those I was trying to fight: Why did I assume that women couldn't have fun with technology?), there were heated debates, interesting discussions, and fun conversations on the side. The panel Lauren Gelman and I gave on blogging and the law could have happened anywhere, while discussions on increasing the visibility of women bloggers needed to happen here because they weren't happening enough elsewhere. For those women who needed a bit of encouragement to start publishing themselves online, events like this give a needed boost. For organizers looking for speakers on a whole range of technology topics, the event offered a roster of exciting participants. For BlogHer to succeed in achieving its goals, however, its message must also be heard outside its Santa Clara site. Women and men participants need to take the ideas generated there to other more general-interest forums.

I don't believe women see technology differently from men. I wouldn't claim that women bring any unique "feminine" perspective to design or tech policy. Our solutions can be as elegant or as clunky as those men find. So when I look at a field that pays less attention to half of its potential innovators than to the other, I see a discipline letting petty prejudices shorten its vision. So long as old boys' networks persist, we women will have to work harder for the same visibility as men, but at least each cohort of us can make things a bit easier for those in the next round.

In many programming languages, functions and operators can be "overloaded," made to perform different actions depending on the types of inputs they are given. Overloading serves as semantic compression, letting the programmer store multiple related contexts in the same names, while the program's mechanical compiler keeps the contexts straight. When you call an overloaded "print," the function knows how to respond appropriately to print whatever you throw at it.

The woman technology lawyer is an "overloaded activist." She is called upon at times to speak about technology, at times to argue about law, at times to lead public action on tech law, and at times to address social and gender issues. This concurrence can often feel like literal overload, when contexts collide or pressure from one area impacts work in another—like when I couldn't clone myself to appear at Defcon and BlogHer for the whole weekend each—but at its best, this overloading can bring a new efficiency of response to each context in turn.

But when I teach technology law to law students, I don't specifically address the role of women in the field. I don't do anything gender oriented beyond giving "Jane Doe" as prominent a spot as "John" in my hypothetical questions. I feel I don't need to be explicit. Just standing in front of an Internet Law class, discussing cases I've litigated and policy battles still to be fought, I'm a role model, encouraging women to think of technology law as a viable option for them too. Women still number fewer than half in my field, but the ratio isn't as heavily skewed as that of Defcon men to BlogHer women. I hope my students will bring the ratio closer to balance.

»»»»gimp geek

Thida Cornes

The Toshiba T1100, the first laptop-size IBM-compatible PC, prevented me from failing college. I have a movement disorder called myoclonic dystonia that causes me to jerk when I write. I also write incredibly slowly. I can't take notes in class writing by hand, and before college I got away with never taking notes at all. But after almost failing my first semester, I knew I needed to find a way. My capacity to absorb the flood of facts and figures in college weeder courses had greatly been exceeded. The dean suggested I record all my lectures on tapes, listen to them later, and then take notes. I could have spent an hour in class and then three hours listening to the taped lecture, painstakingly pausing the tape to write down my own notes. For just four class meetings I would have had to spend twelve hours a week just taking notes.

I petitioned for a better solution—a laptop, which at that time cost over $3000. My dean said, "We don't have the funding." And yet the college had funding for a human to take notes for me in every class, even though this would have cost more money. I'll never forget her words when I pressed her to explain this: "What will we do with a laptop after you're done? No one will have any use for a laptop but you." Even at the time, I knew how wrong she was.

Before my laptop, I rarely claimed the label "disabled" for myself. Like most people, I thought "disabled" meant wheelchairs or blindness. But needing this laptop to take notes forced me to realize that I belonged to an underserved community. At the time, everyone considered laptops to be elite items only for spoiled executives, and on top of that, there was very little computer technology available for disabled people. Apple had developed a few products for the blind, but it seemed that nobody expected disabled people to use computers at all. The maw between the technology haves and have-nots loomed large.

I wish I could write that through my heroic campaigning I scored a victory for disabled people at my small women's liberal arts college by persuading the college to cough up the money to buy the laptop. But when

I summoned up my courage and spoke to the college president, she said, "There's nothing I can do. We don't have any money for capital equipment. And a laptop is capital equipment. I'm sorry."

So I wrote an editorial for the college newspaper. I exposed the short-sightedness of the university's policies and pointed out that the school had very few genuine resources for the disabled. I'd like to think my efforts created a ripple effect, because eventually the college hired a disability resource specialist. But it didn't buy me a laptop. Instead, I appealed to my parents. They had bought an original IBM PC three years earlier, which had improved my high school grades, so they believed a computer could help me. But I still had to convince them a portable computer was more useful and that I wouldn't break it.

I caused a stir as I lugged my laptop around campus. Students in my classes would stop and stare at this new invention. "Wow, is that a computer?" They marveled at its LCD display. "Your computer has a screen and keyboard built in this one little unit?" Before my laptop, personal computers still took up entire desktops. Servers hogged entire rooms. People called me "Miss Computer Geek." When I let my laptop run on battery, people peered at it, asking, "How does it run?" One person even asked, "Does it run on solar power?" When I plugged it into the wall, inevitably someone yelled "Argh!" as she tripped on the cord. Even though the cord was dark black against a lacquered wooden floor, you don't see what you don't expect.

Though the laptop weighed down my backpack, it freed me. For the first time in my life, I took tests in a reasonable amount of time. I studied properly from accurate notes. I participated more in class, because I could refer back to my notes. I wrote better papers. Thanks to that laptop, I developed into a bona fide scholar.

Some professors saw not a technical marvel, but a distraction. They complained about the clicking of my typing. "It's too loud. You'll have to sit in the back." I sat in the back and tried not to bang on the keys. One day my dean called me into her office for a conference. "Your professor says your laptop is disrupting class," she said. I hauled out my trusty laptop, turned it on, and typed a little for her—it wasn't very loud.

"My laptop is a tool to aid my disability," I explained. "I need this laptop as much as a deaf student needs sign language interpretation." I looked up at the dean. The Americans with Disabilities Act had just passed, and the college worried about being sued for all kinds of reasons. The dean sighed. I never heard complaints from professors again, at least not through my dean.

The laptop was just one in a series of computers that rocked my world.

I managed to land a job at the campus computer center, where I discovered Bitnet. The Internet wasn't widely available yet, so instead many colleges used Bitnet, a point-to-point store-and-forward service. What this meant was that we could use Bitnet to move our email, files, and other "sends" directly from one computer node to another. Sometimes the transmission passed through several different nodes to reach its final destination. I "sent" to men all over the world and one lone woman.

"Sends" helped me meet another geek woman online. "Jo" ran a politics email list. Gawky, socially awkward, and extremely thin and tall, Jo was often mistaken for a man—perhaps not just because of her appearance, but because she was a computer geek. Jo eventually decided she was a lesbian. In fact, most of the female computer geeks I knew in the '80s were white, able-bodied lesbians, usually butches with short hair, patched blue jeans, and T-shirts with computer logos that they'd gotten for free at conferences. Some lesbians insisted that my interest in men was "just a phase." But I knew I was mostly attracted to men even if I loved computers. I was confused about a lot of things, but I was secure in my sexuality. I just confused other people. It wasn't until the '90s that I saw other types of female computer geeks.

Female computer geeks were rare in the late '80s, particularly geek women of color. I was usually the only woman of color in any online forum. Most of the students of color at my college used typewriters, not computers, but that all changed when other women of color on campus and I got involved in the student newspaper. Women of color were a small fraction of the student population, but they contributed disproportionately to the paper.

The student newspaper was run primarily by women who tended to espouse radical feminist and liberal views and encouraged women of color to contribute, but its publishing depended on old white males at a typesetting service, which was very expensive. To cut costs, my college told the newspaper staff they had to convert to desktop publishing within a year. In a panic the editors turned to me, Miss Computer Geek. I had written a couple of articles for the paper but knew nothing about the publishing process.

I'm amazed the college trusted me with spending over $10,000 on equipment when I had no track record of any kind. Of course, no one else knew about computer desktop publishing. I was lucky to grow up at a time when people didn't quite understand the magnitude of the tech-related tasks they were giving us, so students like me still performed major undertakings. I'd never before made any choices that would affect people for several years, and I had certainly never managed such a huge budget.

Once I'd chosen our desktop publishing software and whether we should have PCs or Macs, I had to teach a bunch of scared people how to publish a paper using computers. It was no small task. Some had never used a computer before. Students who wrote for the paper had to learn how to use a computer to write their articles and save them to a disk. Most of them didn't have their own computer, so they were using the computers in the computer center. Previously the computer center had been populated by mostly white students, but thanks to the opportunities available through the college newspaper, there was an influx of students of color using the computer center. One editor literally shook with fear at the thought of using a computer, refuting the stereotype that Asians are great with computers. A few months later, I watched that editor, now confident with computers, teach someone else. "It's really quite simple," she said.

I learned a lot about myself when I taught the newspaper staff how to use computers. I'd never considered myself a person of color, even though my mother was Burmese. When I looked in the mirror, I saw my relatively pale skin and mostly white features. I was several shades lighter than my siblings but certainly darker than my English father. My mother called me "the whitest tiger in the jungle." No one else in my life besides my family knew where Burma was, or anything about Burma. Most people assumed I was white. If they ever noticed I wasn't white, they assumed I was Hispanic, or maybe Native American. I felt a mixture of pride and shame about my Burmese heritage and for the most part, I remained quiet about it. For the first time, through computers, I forged a connection with the politically active women of color on our newspaper staff. Computers gave me a sense of authority, but it was these women who taught me to speak up and claim my own identity.

Their lessons served me well as a member of the Academic Computing Committee, where I and others pushed for our college to join the Internet. The summer between my sophomore and junior year, my college finally did it. For the first time, our academic server ran a new protocol just for the Internet: TCP/IP. We also had a shiny new fractional T-1 bridge running alongside our Bitnet modems. My boss took a leave of absence, so I put my college on the Internet with some help from her via email. It's one of my proudest achievements. I even chose our college domain name. By my senior year I had worked my way up to run the academic server as the sysadmin (which is short for system administrator). A sysadmin maintains an entire computer network.

I knew I was a true computer geek when the director of computing called me during break. "The academic server has crashed, and I can't get it back. No one can get anything done." I had him read me the printout of the server logs over the phone and discovered a hard disk had failed. Then I walked him through replacing the disk and restoring from backup. I later discovered I had probably saved his job. A tenured professor was running some incredibly long batch job under a tight deadline, and the crash had come at a bad time. If the server hadn't come back up, the director would have been in a lot of trouble.

After college, I expected my computer life to continue to be as exciting and challenging as it was in college. I took a job performing remote sysadmin work on VAX boxes for credit unions on the West Coast. I was one of two women on a team of twelve. The other woman was ten years older than me and had never been to college. Hard-boiled and tough, she wore silk blouses open to an ample bosom, and brightly colored, tight-fitting suits with A-line skirts. She chain-smoked and had the husky voice and throaty laugh to prove it. She flirted with the customers and told lots of dirty jokes, but she also knew her stuff.

The company had a dress code, so I borrowed dresses from my new roommate Jo, the butch lesbian geek I had met online while I was in college. She was the last person you'd expect to have dresses, but Jo's mother gave her these *Little House on the Prairie*–type dresses in an attempt to make her look more feminine. Jo didn't need to wear dresses in her new job working as a materials engineer with a bunch of men, so she lent them to me. The dresses were not very professional looking, but they at least made me look feminine. I didn't fit in, and I didn't know how to. I knew the dresses were not appropriate really, but it was easier to just wear them than to figure out what to wear myself. I felt awkward at my new job, and I withdrew into the computer instead of trying to reach out to my coworkers.

Eventually I made friends with Anne, a fellow computer geek twenty years my senior who ran the Information Systems group. She told me I should openly discuss and joke about my disability, which I'd never really done. She didn't have a disability, but she was a lesbian, and she saw the similarities, at least in being out. I'm still working on her advice.

After a few months, I started my own computer consulting business working with small companies. I designed and installed PC and Apple systems and networks. At a small marketing company, I taught a sixty-year-old man to type and how to use a computer. The rest of the company had given him up as a lost cause. I made decent money working as a computer geek, which was a dream come true. But I was living in a suburb of Philadelphia, hardly computer geek land, and I hated the cold and snow. I also missed California, where I spent most of my teenage years, so I decided to "leap into the bay" and move to the San Francisco Bay Area.

I trusted the Net to catch me. Usenet hadn't yet been spammed to death, and I found great roommates through ba.housing. The housemates sounded very nice via email and phone. I packed my worldly possessions into my car, shipped the rest to the house, and drove west. My parents worried, aghast that I was moving in with people sight unseen, but the house and housemates proved to be utterly charming. The house was built in 1920, wooden, rambling, slightly disheveled, but not too unkempt. My roommates were two earth-friendly pagans with long fluffy hair and a cat with long fluffy hair.

I had no local friends and no job. However, I did have an email friend: Jed, who had never seen me before in his life. We finally met in person when he sent me an invitation to his New Year's Eve party.

Jed had a friend who was leaving his job as a sysadmin, so I took over his job at a start-up. It was located in a huge warehouse loft in San Francisco, and I spent the first few days of the job literally crawling around on my hands and knees, rearranging the 10Base2 cabling. I was back in holey jeans, and I loved it. I also impressed several people at the company by writing a series of scripts for regular backups and the ability to restore data. It's so easy to save the day sometimes. So began my life working for a series of start-ups that all held the promise of great wealth and changing the world. Of course, they never delivered.

In those halcyon years during the dot-com boom, I rarely applied for a job. Whenever my current company started to run out of money, I'd tell my friends, "I'm looking for a job." Someone would say, "Oh, my company is hiring." I'd go interview there with good references from someone who worked at the company, so it was easy to avoid the awkward question of my physical disability. Folks knew about my disability beforehand. At the interview, they'd take me to lunch—sometimes at five-star restaurants like Chez Panisse—which would always draw attention to my movement disorder. When I jerk, food tends to fly all over the place. But I joke about it, and things turn out okay. Only one person has ever directly asked me, "Can you do this job with your disability?"

It may seem odd that someone who jerks when performing small motor activities chose to become a sysadmin, but I've found ways to cope with it. A lot of "sysadminning" involves typing and gross motor activities anyway. As I moved into jobs that played to my strengths, including management and design, I mostly stopped working with things like jumpers (small switches that change settings on some hardware devices). Jumpers were always a problem since they're incredibly small and fiddly.

Most mornings I woke up and thought, "I get to do work I love, and I get paid!" I even worked for a special effects studio. My name appears in the credits of the movie *Starship Troopers*.

These days people in my industry actually have to look for work and interview. But I believe the time will come again when jobs are plentiful and computer geeks reign. I guess my dream of a computer utopia has never really died.

My utopian dreams are part of what led me to nontraditional hiring choices when I was in a position to do so. Although Asian men are represented everywhere in IT, there are still far too few Asian women. In my last full-time job at a broadband Internet service provider, I was hired by a Chinese American woman whom I'd met online. Then I hired an Indian woman engineer named Anu. Other engineers, particularly men, initially passed her over, because she never bragged about what she did or "geeked out." However, after they saw her code, they came back for more. Folks started asking her for information, and she became known as a guru.

When I was promoted to Director of Engineering and given several teams to manage, I promoted Anu to a management position. My boss questioned my choice. "Anu's so quiet. Folks will walk all over her." I knew he was wrong. I had seen Anu in action. She didn't storm about like the white male engineers when crossed. She just kept arguing and coming back with reasons until she got her way or until she was convinced that she was wrong.

Anu built a team of mostly women engineers, most of them Asian like herself. She didn't set out to do this. Like the teams that mostly consist of white males, the team self-selected. Many white males interviewed, but they didn't answer the technical questions accurately or seem comfortable with the team. My philosophy was to hire people who were smart, understood the fundamentals of coding, and had a hunger for learning engineering. It just so happened that the Asian women felt more comfortable interviewing with Anu and her team, appeared intelligent, and answered the basic coding questions well.

The ten-person team we built was so unusual that it gained a reputation in the three-thousand-person company and became known as "the ladies." Two men, one white and one Asian, joined us, but the group was still called "the ladies" by other people in the company.

I fostered cooperation and information-sharing among all my teams. I encouraged people to get to know each other by spending a little time talking about things outside of work. Formal reviews and raises only happened once a year, but I tried to motivate people with many things other than money. The trick is to find out what works for each person. I made it a point of appealing to the senior engineers' egos to mentor the more junior engineers. Many geeks are happy to share their knowledge with other geeks, but they may need a little prompting to get off the computer and talk to other people. That's what I needed at my first job. When there was a conflict on my team, I'd try to get each side to see the other person's point of view. I have to say I had the most success with Anu's team. They helped each other out a lot, and all ate their lunches together.

We made a lot of jokes. Everybody had a nickname coined by a woman who loved comics and had a wicked sense of humor. Of course we also had meetings. I tended to jerk sometimes and throw things across the room, which would result in general laughter. I had taken Anne's advice and found that joking not only made others feel more comfortable with my disability, but made me feel more comfortable too.

Unfortunately the company started to crater. Rumors flew that cash was running out. The inevitable layoffs always spared my teams, but the company kept making really bad decisions. When I had to explain these decisions to my teams, I felt an overwhelming urge to quit. I had a new boss whom I didn't trust, and at first I tried to transfer out from under him, but at the same time I didn't want to abandon my teams.

I should have trusted my instincts. I was in the evening MBA program at UC Berkeley, and had to leave at 3:00 PM twice a week to attend classes. One evening I was riding in a car with a fellow business student when I got a call on my cell phone from my boss: "Hello, things need to change right now. X [one of my managers] needs to step down immediately because he upset W. I'm going to replace him with Y [one of his favorite engineers]." X had been recently promoted to management, but he had had problems for several months, especially with W, who thought he should have gotten the job instead. I said, "Look, I'm in a car with another person. I can't really talk. And I can't do anything about it now. I'll deal with it when I get back."

"No," replied my boss. "You're not here. W is really upset. I'm doing this right now." He insisted on delving further into detail. My driver, hearing my end of the conversation, kept giving me horrified looks.

It wasn't the first time my boss had tried to take advantage of my absence. He had held important meetings while I was gone, claiming it was the only time available. But this latest move really upset me, a rare thing for me, and spurred me to call his boss. His boss recognized the quality of my work, and he began running interference for me.

But customers were leaving in droves, and my boss's boss, a high-level executive from an outside company, had far bigger problems. So for the first time in my working life, someone tried to use my disability against me. My boss deliberately assigned me complex drawing tasks on the computer that required a lot of fine motor control. I told him I couldn't do them. He wrote me up for my "bad attitude." I considered whether to go over my boss's head again or just quit. I decided to quit.

I made the right decision. A few weeks later, the company started mass layoffs. Some people got paid, but others never received their paychecks or received them late. Either I would have been laid off, or would have had to explain to people in my team why they were laid off and didn't receive their paychecks. I really didn't need the stress. I had just discovered I was pregnant. After I quit, I decided not to interview for another management job and just focus on finishing my business degree. I never stopped working with computers, though. When I was trying to get pregnant with my second child, I started fertility charting online at www.fertilityfriend.com. Through the site and its message boards I found a wealth of information and started sharing it with other women. This led to a job as a "guide," answering questions on a special subscription-only board about fertility charting. If someone signed up for a subscription, I got a small percentage. This site really helped women get pregnant, and I found it to be very rewarding work.

Unfortunately after my son was born with a lot of medical issues, I had to stop working—I now need all my sympathy and patience for my family. I know I can always go back to it, or something else will come along when I have more time.

What matters to me now is that my legacy of engineering management lives on. One of my other managers went onto to become a chief technology officer at a metal distributor. "You managed by inspiring people to do the best they can, and you hired people who had that hunger in their belly," he told me recently. "I always hire geeks, but you expanded my definition of what it means to be a geek. I hire different sorts of folks and work hard to make them into a cohesive team."

It's been almost twenty years since my parents bought me my first laptop. My four-year-old daughter already has her own laptop and takes for granted the technology that I once found so amazing. She already plays video games online. When she can type and communicate online, I hope she'll find many girls like herself. It's too early to say whether she's a computer geek or she's just imitating her parents, but I hope she'll feel free to do whatever she wants and won't be held back by her gender or her color. And for my son with one arm that just doesn't work, I hope that technology continues to close the gap so that he can do whatever he wants to.

When I was a little girl, my mother inspired me with stories about her struggles to make it as a corporate lawyer, as well as how she grew up in Burma and hid in a cave during World War II. I wrote this essay for my children, so they'll know their mother's story of being a woman gimp geek of color. Along the way, I learned new phrases like "person of color," and most recently "gimp." Like "queer," gimp is a defiant word, a formerly pejorative word, that some disabled people use to describe themselves. I like it a lot, because ironically the people who discriminated against me for my disability often helped me to find myself. When I rallied against them, I found some pride.

Technology has shown me that what I do has a ripple effect. The exchange of knowledge and information through computers can create real change—in ourselves, and in the world.

»»»»the hacker's guide to what's in her own panties

Violet Blue

I joined the online role-playing game *Second Life* on a whim. Someone told me people were having all kinds of sex there, and you could watch or participate—or both. An hour after signing up and downloading the program to my hard drive, I was still fussing with my hair, makeup, and outfit. But I wasn't *just* doing my eyeliner; I was changing the shape of my eyes, my eye color, and the shape of my face and body. Once I looked as much like a seriously fuckable computer-generated Angelina Jolie as possible, I was ready. As I moved forward, I didn't hit the arrow keys on my computer fast enough, and I accidentally walked my avatar into a tree and stumbled sideways down a ravine. And all I could think was, *As soon as I can walk in a straight line, I'm going to one of the* Second Life *shopping districts to buy myself a really nice pussy.*

It's always been like this. I see new tech and immediately try to figure out how I can use it for sex. When I got my first iMac and joined the Internet world in 1998, I knew the possibility for sex was out there somewhere, but at the time I was more interested in getting a sex education that I could use in a professional capacity as a writer. My iMac Strawberry was little more than a sexy word processor, a means of communicating with my other web-savvy friends. But I knew some people were figuring out all kinds of ways to get off with the new tech, and it nagged at me every time I made a disappointing trip to the porn section of the video store.

At last I found myself on the verge of exploiting the similarities between the Mac's operating system and my own. While I poked, prodded, rubbed, and massaged the Apple OS, I was in the midst of an intense sex-ed training program for my new job at a local sex toy retailer, one that considered education of their clientele a key component of getting their product into the hands of more horny customers. All of us in the training programs were learning more about sex and sexuality (and by default our own sexual pleasure) than we'd expected when we got hired for the

$9-an-hour job of slinging dildos and making vibrator sales. Naturally, we were all inclined to take our work home with us, so like those old commercials where chocolate collided with peanut butter and became a tasty treat, my vibrator met my mouse, and it was the beginning of a beautiful relationship.

Like all relationships, this one had technical difficulties. As any hacker will tell you, the limitations of technology are all in your mind—the misfires should only challenge you to engineer a better situation. At least that's what it seemed like when I vowed to do everything I could to make technology bend to the will of my libido. The computer and its online world whispered a million possibilities: I could get off in impossible positions, have sex in another body, attach arousal machines to myself that were attuned to movement and sounds, and find an endless supply of the greatest pornography ever written in an infinite number of permutations. I just knew I could really get off the way I wanted to if only the tech worked the way it was supposed to. Unfortunately, it mostly worked like the cheap Chinese vibrators my employer insisted on buying, despite the fact that they conked out under their own stress.

At least, that's what I thought at the time. The promises aroused by the mixture of technology and sex were this girl's first lesson in fantasy versus reality, a lesson equally valid for the realms of both sex and tech.

For instance, I've long had a fantasy about having a threesome with two men, and have devoted many valuable minutes imagining the action in vivid masturbatory detail. At the same time, I'd always worried about trying the fantasy in real life; too many things can go wrong and ruin the fantasy. What if the guys I picked up at the bar were smelly and (worse) protested about condom use, or paid no attention to what I wanted during the encounter, or were too homophobic to enjoy having the kind of threesome I envision, where we're all a tangle of limbs and hungry mouths? And it's not just an in-the-flesh fantasy that could fail me. Technology can fail the same way. More than once I've bought a big, juicy new vibrator, barely waiting to get home to rip the packaging off and get busy—to find that only part of the toy is functioning, plus it's made of a smelly rubbery material and stops working completely at the most crucial moment of all.

I went through the same range of sexual promise, hope, and near-comic disappointments with the sexual Pandora's box of my computer. At the time I was fantasizing about threesomes, buying crappy vibrators, and eyeing my computer in a lascivious way that would make anyone nervous, the rest of the wannabe cyber world was adorably naive. That was the era of "virtual reality" (VR) sex fantasies, and unrealizable ideas for cyber-suits whose all-over sensory interfaces would blur the difference between a real sex partner and the virtual world. It would be like those scenes in *The Lawnmower Man* where the computer-generated world meshed with the real world in moments of sexual pathos and violence. It was laughable even at the time, but companies actually were trying to create full-body sex suits and VR sex—and they blasted the marketing hype into the stratosphere, trying to make us think *The Lawnmower Man* could happen in real life.

Vivid Entertainment's Cyber Sex Suit was a classic example. Porn companies have always been the quickest to adopt new technologies and the worst at making them functional. Their ventures into VR cybersex became a cautionary tale for anyone hoping to hump anything in cyber-space. In 1999 Vivid's David James created a neoprene bodysuit equipped with thirty-six pads that delivered sensations to the wearer (supposedly) at the click of a mouse from a remote user over the Internet. The sensors used electricity controlled by software to produce five sensations—tickle, pinprick, vibration, hot, or cold—to specific sensors within the suit.

James predicted that the suit would change the online porn biz dramatically. He said it "will . . . virtually revolutionize the 900- and 800-number-type business." He also planned to market DVDs (then practically unheard of by consumers) with interactive programs specifically for suit owners' satisfaction. But before issuing a permit to sell the suit as a consumer electronic product, the Federal Trade Commission required that it be safe enough for pacemaker wearers and free from potentially dangerous electrical surges—not to mention that it would need to withstand moisture, since a successful encounter in the suit would likely result in a certain amount of wetness.

No girl wants a shock from her wet panties—it would be aversion therapy at its worst. This didn't seem like anything I wanted to beta test. I envisioned playing out my threesome fantasies with anonymous guys in chat rooms in the safety of my own home, but electrocution and hospitalization didn't figure into my plans for post-sex activities. And I had to wonder, are wetsuits lined with suction cups a turn-on for anyone but rubber fetishists? The seriously ugly, unitardlike suit was never released commercially. But that didn't stop more porn entrepreneurs from trying to create dozens more bad cybersex devices (that ultimately failed). It also meant that nobody was making hot sex possible with the tools that were already available: namely, the web and everything on it.

That meant it was up to me (and everyone like me) to use existing tech and online services to get off, without risk of electrocution.

Somewhere, I knew, there were anonymous sex partners, possibly in a chat room, who wouldn't blanch as my real-life lovers did when I asked them to do something really extreme to me. Plus, the "me" in question wasn't even a body that could be hurt or catch an STD—it was just me at my computer, safe and sound and wanking away by myself. So I visited my first chat room, stumbling clumsily around the different sections and looking like a total idiot until I figured out what a PM (private message window) was. Eventually I could type out a private conversation with one of the twenty guys who had been trying to talk dirty with me since I entered the room. The first person I did this with seemed ready to talk really nasty, but was slightly put off at my request that he tell me how he'd force anal sex on me.

We overcame that stumbling block within about a minute. I have no idea what the process or realizations must have been like for my shocked but still game sex partner somewhere out in cyberspace. It became increasingly difficult to type as I angled my vibrator pleasurably in my office chair and hit Return to keep the chat going. My typing got worse as I neared orgasm, which as a writer *really* bothered me, and his typing became unintelligible. There were also time lags in sending and receiving the chat. It made me wonder if my sex partner wasn't just rolling his knuckles over the keyboard and hitting return because he was too polite to end the session. I shoved that thought aside long enough to have my orgasm and close the window. Satisfied, mostly.

It was absolutely clear to me that this was a fantasy. I'd never, ever want to meet or chat with this guy again, and that was perfect. He could imagine I was a big-titted blond college student all he wanted, as long as he forcibly fucked me up the ass so I could come and go on with the rest of my day. Thanks to the web, I had the world's most perfect glory hole right on my desk.

That is, if you like your glory holes on dial-up. It was obvious after my first chat sex experience that the guys at Vivid had probably never even visited a chat room, let alone tried to jack off and chat at the same time. But here they were, selling everyone the idea of shared remote control sex toys like the suit, while much of the online world still didn't even have access to fast broadband connections.

I wasn't a computer geek yet, but even I could see that online sex was still just a fistful of promises. Our fantasies outstripped the bandwidth, software, and hardware available to us. We wanted VR cybersex, but no one knew how to make a good cybersuit.

I quickly discovered that the state of online porn was no better. Some of the same guys who tried to sell us on the cybersuit were selling us online videos that had major technological bugs, flaws, and problems. I'd visit a free video link, get turned on, and the video would stop and shudder, or the controls on the site's built-in interface would stop working. The wetware's just fine, thanks, but do you think you can keep the video from buffering when I'm about to come? Worse, the porn I was finding was yawnworthy: antiquated panoplies of plastic Barbie blonds and sexist caricatures that no respectable geek girl would waste a single stroke of the clit over.

When the porn sucked, I went back to the chat rooms. But like many chat users, I wanted something more from the interface, something I just knew could be possible with the right amount of geekery and lust. I wanted teledildonics. "Teledildonics" refers to sexual encounters that include some sort of sex toy controlled by an online partner via a web interface. The term has become a catchall for anything from VR suits like Vivid's to remote-controlled vibrators. But what teledildonics boils down to is the ability to control a vibrator (or other toys, like a penis sleeve) over the web. It seems like a really simple idea, and yet no one has been able to get it right yet.

In the late 1990s and early 2000s there were many fly-by-night companies vying for the teledildonics dollar, making all kinds of bizarre claims and weird contraptions with "secret black boxes." Now there are only two companies—Sinulate Entertainment and HighJoy Products—that sell USB-powered sex toys that can be used over the Internet. These companies are so greedy that they've patented all their wares and force users to join their services or register on private websites to use their products.

Both Sinulate and HighJoy have a selection of USB sex toys with proprietary software that allows for remote web control. Sinulate sells its toys with software that the user installs on her computer. It works with a free network interface where users can register their toys for use with a remote partner. Unfortunately, Sinulate's clunky Flash interface resembles an adolescent boy's idea of an airline cockpit. It operates a Rabbit Habit (dual-action) vibrator in a variety of ways, with a throttle (rotate), slider (vibrate), and three buttons that execute combined rotation and vibration programs.

Sinulate and HighJoy also offer registered users a network of singles, pay-for-play camgirl shows, and "interactive 3D sex fantasy games." They also have very sketchy privacy policies. Neither company offers options for Macintosh users: We Mac girls are still stuck having cybersex the old-fashioned way—that is, until we start hacking software and toys ourselves, and open-sourcing the programs that run USB sex toys.

All the ingredients for cybersex exist today: We have ubiquitous wireless devices, Macromedia's Flash animation format has revolutionized browser interfaces, and anyone can send live video through a cell phone onto a website. So why hasn't anyone made teledildonics a reality? The answer is, quite simply, money. Companies use their half-baked teledildonics products to make money on promises, and put no thought into actually pleasing their end users.

That's why even the most notorious hucksters in the sex tech field can't get the masses to jack in and jack off. Even when their tools actually work, they ruin the product or ruin the user experience with nightmarish Flash interfaces. Greed blinds them, and they make products and services that are so exclusive and proprietary that girls like me may never get their hoped-for versions of *Second Life* or Friendster with glory holes. Unless we reverse-engineer them.

Any girl knows that when the up-and-down strokes don't work the way they usually do, you try the left-to-right ones. Maybe you experiment with circles, or even a few light slaps.

From my work as a sex educator, I had learned how to hack my own sexuality to make it do what I wanted. So, I thought, why not take that approach into the realm of technology? Why not hack the web itself, remixing the porn I found there to make something that worked for me? When I started thinking like this, every lame-ass idea about sex on the web became a doorway to finding good porn and workable video-delivery systems. One mission became to find the video system that could be hacked, tweaked, and forced to get me off, on my terms. Seeking links to truly hot sites turned into a private sex game and an art; learning how to find the good porn became my version of foreplay. Large collections of hotlinks known as "link dumps" were like seedy porn stores with jack shacks in the back for the guys; RSS, tags used in blogging or podcasts to identify the content of a post or item, and networking with teledildonics hobbyists became the "clean, well-lighted place" to shop for my sex toys.

What I can't find, I must remix using various sources—it is the only true sexual compulsion I have, and nurture. And once I learn how to walk, I am *so* getting laid in *Second Life.*

in the lab

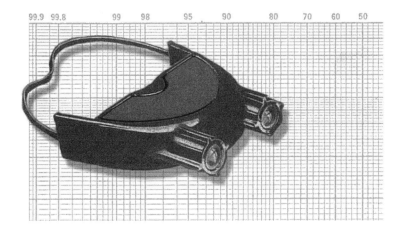

»»»» the making of a synchrotron geek

Corie Ralston

My official job title is a mouthful: "staff scientist at the Advanced Light Source Synchrotron at Lawrence Berkeley National Laboratory." My unofficial title is "beamline scientist." How cool is that? It reminds people vaguely of *Star Trek,* or at least something futuristic and science fiction–like. I am one of only three female beamline scientists working at the synchrotron, among a staff of nearly two hundred.

When I was first hired, my even-less-official job title was "beam boy," since all the other scientists in my group were male. I lobbied to be called "super-duper synchrotron chick," but it never quite caught on. And "beam girl" just didn't have a ring to it, so we all became simply beamline scientists.

The synchrotron is a circular metal structure enclosed in a huge round building. Electrons zip around its two-hundred-meter-diameter ring at close to the speed of light, and in the process emit X-ray radiation, also termed "synchrotron radiation." The synchrotron at Berkeley Lab is at the site of the original cyclotron used in the famous 1940s atom-smashing experiments conducted by Oppenheimer et al. The building still has the original redwood-plank dome roof, although the inside is completely different now, and the research is all unclassified.

At intervals along the electron ring are "beamlines," which collect the emitted X-rays. There are thirty-six beamlines where I work, and although they are all under the same domed roof, each is used for its own kind of experiments. The beamlines are separated from each other not by walls, but by banks of computers, X-ray optical components, and various other intimidating pieces of metallic equipment. A lot of the most expensive machines are covered in aluminum foil (for heating purposes) and many of the high-vacuum apparatuses look like things from a '50s sci-fi flick: steel tanks with glass portholes and labyrinths of burbling pumps and hoses. The lack of women on the floor fits right into the '50s feel of the place.

Several years ago, I arrived at work to discover the name of the synchrotron had changed. Its usual name is the "Advanced Light Source." But that day a placard in the lobby declared us the "Berkeley Nuclear Biotechnology Institute." It turned out that several scenes from the movie *Hulk* were to be filmed on location at the synchrotron, and its name had to change for a few days. They might as well have called us the "Evil Government Radiation Facility to Mutate Innocent People."

The idea behind the famous comic book story is that gamma radiation changes Bruce Banner's DNA so much that he morphs into the Hulk when angry. The synchrotron does not produce gamma radiation, but if it did, and if we accidentally irradiated someone (which is of course extremely unlikely given all our safety interlock systems), the result would be very simple: They would die. They would not mutate into an Angry Green Giant. *Hulk* had to mutate real facts in order to make a good story.

But it was further confirmation that the synchrotron building and its labs are fascinating to nonscientists. When Ang Lee wanted a high-tech yet comic-bookish location, he thought of the Advanced Light Source. I love the fact that I can work every day in a place that reminds people of comic books.

Here are some of the real experiments we do at the synchrotron: studying the composition of space dust, increasing the efficiency of solar cells, building nanogears out of polymers, examining the electronic and magnetic properties of superconductors, detecting contaminants in soil samples, imaging live cells. My particular niche is protein crystallography, which is the science of determining protein structure.

How did I get to be a girl-geek scientist at the synchrotron? It certainly wasn't anything like becoming the mutant hero of a comic book.

When I turned fifteen, one of my birthday presents was a three-volume set of essays about famous mathematicians. There was exactly one essay on a female mathematician. I had always loved math and done well at it, but it wasn't until late in college that I started paying attention to the fact that I belonged to a minority: "girls who love math."

I didn't take physics in high school because it was well-known that every year the physics teacher started out his class by telling all the students that girls were simply not as good at physics as boys. He presented it as a statement of fact. In retrospect, it's strange that no one called him on that. His reputation convinced me not to take his class, but I didn't dwell on why.

I was busy enough with the calculus course that I was taking at the university, taught by a female graduate student who always looked tired. (Many years later I would understand why graduate students always looked tired.) I also had to study for my SAT and Advanced Placement tests. I was fortunate to have the complete support of my mother, a professor of microbiology at the university, who commiserated with me about hating high school culture and shared my love for science. It's great having a geek for a mother. Possibly I wouldn't be a super-duper synchrotron chick (oops, I mean beamline scientist) today if not for her.

I spent my spare time reading science fiction: Heinlein, Asimov, Bradbury. The fact that most of Heinlein's female characters become hysterical at some point in his novels and require a little slapping around by the male characters didn't bother me at the time. The female characters in pre '70s science fiction exist only to serve the male characters. In *2001: A Space Odyssey* all the flight attendants on the spacecraft are women and wear those short little '60s miniskirts as they serve beverages to the male astronauts. I mean, really. If you can imagine interstellar civilizations with galactic wormhole superhighways, why can't you imagine female astronauts?

But none of that bothered me back then. I did what I think most female science fiction fans of my generation did when they were young: I related to the male characters.

This mind-set helped me through high school. It made me impervious to what other people thought I "should" do or "should" like based on my gender. When I fell in love, I got my first rude awakening.

I never came out as a geek; I just was one. But I did come out as a lesbian, almost accidentally, when I was a teenager. I was so overwhelmed by being in love for the first time that it never occurred to me other people might not be as thrilled as I was. Conversations went like this:

> Me: "I'm in love!"
> Them: "Great! Who is he?"
> Me: "Her name is Kim."

Them: *"Oh. Funny name for a guy."*
Me: *"She's not a guy."*
Them: *(Shocked expression)*
Me: *"I'm in love!"*

Finally I began to understand that being in love with another girl was unacceptable. So much of what I did was unacceptable in high school—loving math, enjoying studying and science fiction, being an all-around nerd—that I had just lumped being a lesbian into that category. What I found out was that it was different. Really different. People tolerate girl geeks. But not very many tolerate gay people.

That was probably the first time that I realized I had to pay at least a little attention to the world out there, that I was different and couldn't assume that I would always have the safety of being ignored.

Physics and I met in college, and it was love at first sight. Being a fickle but curious girlfriend, I had dated and discarded many other majors before encountering Physics. I was with Engineering at the time, but cast it callously aside after my first physics class. Physics drew me in with its mystery and philosophical sophistication. It wasn't just about problem solving and puzzles, which I loved, but also about the strangeness of the universe. I mean, how much weirder can you get than relativity? If you travel really fast, your mass increases, you get shorter in one dimension, and time runs slower for you. Just try to wrap your head around that. Physics explores the ultimate mysteries of the universe, and uses math to do it. Geek heaven.

In general, lower-division classes at UC Berkeley were so large that the professors never knew the names of their students. As a result, they couldn't practice gender bias even if they wanted to. As I approached upper division, however, the classes got smaller and I began to stand out.

In my third year I took an upper-division math-for-physicists class. It was a great class—I loved the application of math, a fun subject already, to physics, my new true love.

I was one of two women in the class. Not surprisingly, we studied together. In point of fact, I helped her with her homework. She didn't actually study that much. On the first midterm, I got the best grade in the class, and she got the worst. She went to see the professor and then related to me her conversation:

> Him: *"Oh, you're in my class, aren't you?"*
> Her: *"Yes, I'm the one who failed the midterm."*
> Him: *"You are? That's strange. I thought the other girl was the one*
>   *who failed. She looks stupid."*

That was quite a blow. What makes a person look stupid, anyway? I paid rapt attention in class, and possibly my mouth had been open at points. I noticed that some of the male students did that, but I bet the professor didn't think they looked stupid. To this day, I couldn't tell you what made him think and say that. All I know is that I suddenly could not do well on the exams. Math had always been my easiest subject. The homework was still easy, but during exams I could no longer concentrate. It didn't matter that I knew what he said was simply cruel and had no basis in fact. I became entirely self-conscious, and I started to actually believe that maybe I was not smart enough to do math. That was the very first math class in which I did not excel, and math classes were never fun again.

Around that same time I took my very first women's studies course. I learned that there were in fact famous female mathematicians, and that their lives had been extraordinarily difficult. I finally began to notice that the female characters in Heinlein's novels had no purpose except to be sounding boards to the suave, smart, male scientists. Heinlein was no fun anymore, either.

College was an eye-opener in many ways. I stepped outside my encapsulated world of geekdom and began to see how other people view, or refuse to view, girl geeks.

Graduate students are mulch for the university gardens of research. Aside from their expected constant presence in the lab, graduate students in science are given impossible course loads, endless written and oral exams, and overwhelming teaching and grading responsibilities. I now believe that graduate school was designed by someone from est: The plan is to break down the ego through sheer exhaustion until it is a barely visible puddle on the floor, then build it up again in the image of the professor. In graduate school they also teach you how to perpetuate the system in which graduate slaves (oops, I mean graduate students) are subjugated.

Ironically, graduate school was where I began to gain my self-confidence back. Perhaps it was seeing other successful female graduate students and postdocs. Perhaps it was because the world had changed a lot in the intervening years, and people were more conscious of gender bias. If they were still thinking that women were less intelligent than men, at least they weren't saying it. Or maybe it was because I began to teach undergraduate physics and discovered I was quite good at it. It was great to get positive feedback from my students, to show them the love I still felt for physics, despite how the world had tried to pry us apart.

Graduate school is where I met my first geek girlfriend, KT, who painted her furniture with large purple polka dots and played pranks like freezing her friend's underwear in a block of ice from the Cold Room. She was in biology and studied those strange worms that live near deep-sea thermal vents and look vaguely like giant penises. I don't need to repeat the kind of jokes that circulated in her lab.

I met KT at a party where we sat in the corner, drank ourselves silly, and yelled "Geek pride!" obnoxiously all evening. We were not very subtly telling each other that we were both lesbians. I think everyone in the vicinity caught on before we did.

Unfortunately, KT was in a graduate program at a university two thousand miles away. We tried the long-distance thing for a while, but the breakup was mutual: Neither of us knew where we would land a postdoc, and after that, trying to solve the "two-body problem" of finding academic positions in the same city, let alone the same state, seemed an impossible challenge. I sometimes miss her crazy antics—she taught me not to be ashamed of being a lesbian geek, and also how to freeze underwear in a giant block of ice.

I started working at the synchrotron as a graduate student. Much to the dismay of my cohorts, the synchrotron operates on a 24-7 basis. In a group of grad students and postdocs, guess who always gets the night shifts? I was never very good at staying up all night, but I did learn an awful lot about conducting experiments at a beamline, and I was sold on the cool science of synchrotron radiation.

A postdoctorate in science has proved herself to the world by surviving graduate school. She is rewarded with being allowed to do research without having to worry about exams, teaching, or even grant writing. It is a good time in the life of a scientist. During my postdoc, I made many trips to Brookhaven National Lab, where I designed and built my own experiments for one of the beamlines at the synchrotron there. It was like having my very own Tinkertoy shop. And I made the grad students do the night shifts.

During the last few months of my postdoc, I discovered that my adviser had already planned the rest of my life. He had arranged for a junior faculty position at Albert Einstein College of Medicine, had started looking into which grants I should apply for, and tracked down the best grad students for me.

The only problem was that I had realized by then that I didn't want to go into academia.

I could see very clearly what it would be like for me: ninety-hour work weeks, constant worry about funding, no time for a meaningful relationship or hobbies, and never-ending conferences where I would be expected to be a one-person PR firm for my research (it is the irony of modern academia that geeks with no time for a social life are suddenly expected to be good at schmoozing when they become professors). By the time I got tenure, I wouldn't know how to do anything except work all day and night.

No thanks.

Industry seemed a better choice, at least in terms of work hours (as long as I didn't work for a start-up), but the job security wasn't attractive. This was when the biotech bubble was bursting back in 2000, and firms were going bankrupt left and right.

In a serendipitous moment, as I was pondering my life choices after my postdoc ended, I happened to run into someone I had worked with at the synchrotron in Berkeley when I was a graduate student. He told me that the protein crystallography group was looking to hire a scientist. My timing was perfect. I was interviewed and hired, and I became a national laboratory scientist before anyone else could try to plan my life.

Working as a beamline scientist at a government facility has turned out to be an excellent compromise between being a scientist and having a life. In this job I get to stay in the world of science, operate cool equipment, and set up interesting experiments. I even get to teach the students and postdocs who come to the beamline to collect their data. I don't have to write grants, and I don't have to travel the world selling my work as a scientist. Instead, scientists from around the world come to me, and I have a manageable number of work hours.

I also get asked to do tours, which I enjoy despite myself. All sorts of people show up for tours of the Berkeley synchrotron: scientists from other countries, high school teachers, classes of third-graders. Sometimes I feel like a zoo guide.

After my last tour with a group of second-grade teachers, when everyone was shrugging on their coats and emitting their last *oohs* and *ahhs* over the jumble of equipment and gadgets at the beamlines, a woman from the tour approached me. She wanted to find out how to make the girls in her class more interested in science, and what specifically had led me to a life in science.

I wasn't sure how to answer that question. I've always loved math and science. I'm lucky to have parents who love science, especially a mother who was a scientist herself and a strong, supportive role model for me.

But why should luck have anything to do with it? And why should you have to be as oblivious as I was in order to succeed as a girl geek? Maybe the key is not to specifically encourage girls to go into science, but to stop discouraging them from going into science. No one these days tells girls outright they can't be good at physics because of their gender, but girls do grow up knowing that they are valued more for their physical desirability than for their mathematical ability.

Here's what I will tell teachers and parents when I get asked that question again: Stop placing undue importance on things like physical beauty and motherhood. Show your kids that you value female scientists as much as you value male scientists. Let them read science fiction. (But maybe hold off on giving them that bound set of Heinlein's novels.) Let girl geeks be who they are from day one, and don't be afraid to celebrate their geekiness. And bring them to the synchrotron zoo for a visit. I'll be here waiting for them.

»»»»suzy the computer versus dr. sexy

Suzanne E. Franks

My First Calculator

Calculators first arrived at my high school in 1979, in my trigonometry class. Mine was a TI-30, and if memory serves, it cost my parents $30. It had trig functions, which excited me no end. It also had an eight-digit, red LED display and ran on a nine-volt battery. In college, my boyfriend Ward borrowed my TI-30 and returned it in time for my physics test. During the exam, the back popped off the battery compartment, and a note fell onto my desk. The note commanded, "Stop whatever you're doing right now and come give me a kiss! Love, Ward." I was thrilled and aroused, but also frightened—had the professor seen? Would he think I had a cheat sheet? Perhaps worse still was the prospect of being exposed as a sexual being. In physics, I was supposed to be a disembodied creature of intellect. Nevertheless, test stress melted into irritation that physics remained to be done before serious kissing could commence. My body had most definitely accompanied my brain into the classroom.

I still have my TI-30, as well as the calculator that followed it, a Sharp EL-512. The Sharp had many more functions, including a ten-digit LCD display, and you could program it with up to 128 steps. However, it used 357-type watch batteries, so the battery compartment would never accommodate a love note. Despite the EL-512's sleek body, the clunkier TI-30 will always be a more romantic calculator in my book.

The TI-30, a conduit for lust in college, hadn't served me so well in high school. In trig class my male classmates dubbed me "Suzy the Computer" for my mathematical skills and easy way with the TI-30. The boys weren't comparing me to a cozy little laptop—it was two years before the launch of the IBM PC and the first Microsoft operating system. No, the "computer" nickname invoked a hazy notion of a large, impersonal, and unfeeling calculating machine. "Suzy the Computer" was not someone you asked to homecoming or the prom. You went to her for help with your homework, but you didn't flirt with her. "Suzy the Computer" was most definitely not sexual, even in the raging hormonal ferment that is high school.

I was proud of my sharp mind and hurt that boys didn't find it appealing. I began a lifelong love-hate relationship with my own geekiness. I put on an attitude of "Who cares?" and "You're all beneath me anyway." Though it hurt like hell when no one asked me to the prom, I told myself it didn't matter if smart girls weren't sexy in high school. Things would surely be different in college. And I'd have lots of dates once I had my career and my independent-girl apartment.

I had an older friend, Cindy, who was much more worldly and informed than I was. She sat me down before I left for college to give me a birth control talk, since she knew this information would not be forthcoming in my very Catholic family. The subject dismayed me, because of my Catholic squeamishness coupled with my defensive posture on the whole "boy" issue. I proclaimed, "I won't need birth control! I'm not having sex until I get married, and I'm not getting married till I'm thirty." I'm grateful that she didn't let my fantasy life deter her and insisted I should know the details of available birth control methods.

Engineers Do It with Precision!

High school was a profoundly anti-intellectual environment, and I was glad to leave it behind. In college, I was sure smart girls would be hot, and I could start over with a fresh set of boys who didn't know me as Suzy the Computer.

But when I got to college, I found frat parties dominated the social life, and I suspected that smarts might not be a high-value attribute in that scene. Nevertheless, I trotted off to the parties with all my dorm mates. At my very first frat party, a handsome boy chatted me up, until he got around to the question I learned to loathe: "What's your major?" "Engineering!" I offered up brightly in response. He literally took a step back from me as his expression shifted from "prowl" to "backpedal" and said,

"Oh, I guess you're too smart for me to talk to." With that he turned and walked away, leaving me stunned and forlorn. Shit. College: smart girls still not sexy.

In retrospect, I wonder if there weren't at least a few high school boys who found me physically attractive but intellectually daunting. There were others like Frat Boy in college, who showed initial interest and then shied away. I ended up interacting exclusively with other science and engineering students—both male and female. The geek boys were the only ones not scared off by the E word. Plus, they understood my need to spend long hours on problem sets.

Geek boys also understood that they could use homework to hit on geek girls. I didn't recognize this form of courtship at first. A junior electrical engineer offered to help me with my freshman graphics course—how nice of him! One of my nongeek girlfriends had to tell me he had a crush on me. With my meteorologist friend, I thought we were studying for physics, but he thought we were dating. The friendly guy who told me what the forestry major was all about and who gave me a symbolic snake plant was not just being friendly.

Eventually, I did realize that discussions of stress, strain, trusses, and friction could easily turn into experiments with elastic bodies. (In fact, that's how I met my first husband.) I had to overcome my prejudice that in Engineering Land, the crop of boys included fewer exquisite specimens than in Frat Land. Nevertheless, Engineering Land yielded boys who appreciated a girl's classroom statics mastery as well as her dorm room dynamics.

Engineering boys were often socially inept; engineering girls understood, and shared in, some of their geekiness. Since we were a tiny minority of any class, we rarely lacked for the attention of engineering boys. Finally, smart girls were hot! But there was a price. If you were too attractive, too flirtatious, in any way too obviously female, then it was understood that you were Not Serious. You were certainly not as tough an engineer as the boys, even if you outscored them on exams. Conversely, if you took your studies too seriously, you ceased to be truly female. The head of the nuclear engineering department had been a mentor and supporter of my engineering career. But when I told him senior year that I'd gotten engaged, he said, "Oh, I thought you were going to amount to something, but you're just like all the other girls."

I was quite popular with the guys in my small, close-knit engineering class. One of them was my husband-to-be, nicknamed Einstein (he had the smarts *and* the hair). In turn, I became Mrs. Einstein. Einstein was considered by all to be a top candidate for the department's award for best senior thesis. We were all stunned when Mrs. Einstein took the prize instead.

The most quiet, most studious, least flirtatious girl of the four in our department was nicknamed (not to her face) "Ugga-Bugga Balls," derived from the uncool ponytail ties with large plastic balls that she wore every day. So totally not hot.

A male classmate, applying to graduate school and planning his wedding just as I was, said to me in a sincerely puzzled tone, "I don't understand why you are going to graduate school if you're going to get married."

Years later, I discovered that 19th-century doctors had issued dire warnings about the terrible fate awaiting women if they attended college. The development of a woman's mind would come at the expense of her uterus, which would shrivel up as all that mental exertion sapped her energy. What a riot! But this idea lingers today. Nobody suggested to me that calculus would kill off my uterus, but I definitely got the message that a woman's bodily contours would get in the way of solving contour integrals. If we were too attractive, if we were sexy, we could not be good engineers. If we were really good at engineering, we were defeminized. You could be a nerd, or you could be a Playmate, but you couldn't be both. Call it the Nerdonna/Whore complex.

So I tried to find a balance, just the right amount of female and geek. It was wonderful to have dates, and wonderful to trade nerd jokes with the boys. As a member of the American Nuclear Society, I thought it was hilarious when someone suggested that our new T-shirts should read NUCLEAR ENGINEERS MAKE BETTER BREEDERS! Still, I knew I'd never wear such a shirt. For boys, it would mark them as sexually skilled. We girls knew, however, that on us the shirt would speak to childbearing. ENGINEERS DO IT WITH PRECISION! was more to our taste.

And speaking of doing it with precision . . . there was a senior nuclear engineer who was absolutely gorgeous; we all had crushes on him. I could hardly believe my good fortune when he asked me out. Gorgeous he was, but romantic he was not. The date started with him stating the case as to why I should lose my virginity with him. (I was incredibly embarrassed that my virginal state seemed to be common knowledge.) One of his reasons was that he was an excellent lover and I could be guaranteed that my first time would be pleasurable if I did it with him. While this may have been true, his very direct approach was not a huge turn-on. He was nice enough, however, to take me out to dinner even after I declined his generous offer.

I did yearn to get laid, but I wanted it to be romantic and to evolve out of mutual feeling. Well, except for that one night after a dorm party, when I'd been dancing with the electrical engineer who helped me with my graphics homework. He was a really decent guy, so decent that he refused to do me because he thought I shouldn't be so drunk for my first time. He was right, and I was fortunate. If ultrarationality wasn't the right approach, neither was getting extremely drunk. I've always been grateful to my gentleman EE.

When I finally did have sex for the first time, it was in a relationship with an engineering guy who nicknamed me "The Lustful Virgin" and who said he was willing to wait till I knew for sure I wanted to do it. Wow! This whole sex thing could really cut into a girl's homework time. We tried going to the library to study together, but it was no use. After thirty minutes or so of teasing each other in silence, we'd close the books and head to my apartment. It didn't take long to conclude that we needed to study alone.

Still lustful, but no longer a virgin, I was in a panic about the risk of pregnancy. Thanks to my friend Cindy, I at least knew that birth control was a possibility. I don't remember how I found out about the clinic in the neighboring town where you could get hooked up with the necessary technology. I do remember that I had to take a long bus ride to get there, and my engineering boy, who had a car, did not go with me or volunteer to drive me there. I was terrified, and the sour woman who angrily detailed the choices for naive girls didn't help. The IUD was out of the question, I couldn't imagine inserting something as unwieldy as a diaphragm into my vagina, and condoms seemed too risky (ha! the pre-AIDS era). Therefore, the Pill it was.

The Orgasmic Mind

The pleasures of the flesh were much more compelling than anything my books could offer, until spring term of my freshman year. Calculus suddenly started making exquisite sense to me. My stern female professor clearly loathed teaching us, as we were undeserving of, and too hormonal for, the beauties of calculus. But under her tutelage I began to sense the joy in the equations, because she so clearly experienced it even as she condescended to us.

The final exam was scheduled for three hours and consisted of one hundred questions covering the entire semester's material. I was nervous beforehand, but once I received the test and began working, all the nerves went away and I entered a mental zone that I've never again completely attained. Every problem was easy, and I was sure of every answer. I finished the exam in an hour. I reworked every problem, and this took me only half an hour. I *knew* that every answer was correct. I was the first to turn in my exam, and I walked out of the classroom still tingling from the exhilaration of my performance. That math high was as powerful as my first orgasm, and lasted longer, too.

Just like sex, once I'd had a taste of that intense mental pleasure, I wanted more. I wanted more calculus, I wanted physics, I wanted statics and dynamics and strength of materials. I was ecstatic about the chance to run the TRIGA nuclear reactor on campus in one of my classes. You could walk right up to the edge of the reactor pool and see the beautiful blue Cerenkov radiation below. How close I was to the uranium fuel rods! And when the control rods came down in the reactor and shut down the self-sustaining reaction, my mind knew what was happening mathematically and at the atomic level. It was enough to make a girl melt.

Besides calculus, statics and strength of materials were two of my most pleasurable courses as an undergraduate. I liked the way my mind felt when it worked on problems in those subjects. It's a wonder I didn't become a mechanical engineer. There are two reasons I did not: I thought of ME as an exclusively boy's major. And my mind was dancing on fire over the entire curriculum that was available to me. I wanted to take organic chemistry and biology; I wanted to take radiochemistry and solid-state physics. I did manage to take everything I wanted, except biology, by crafting what I and my friends called the patchwork quilt

major. Most students in engineering science concentrated their electives in one of the traditional engineering fields, but not me. I wanted a taste of it all. And that turned out to be the perfect preparation for my graduate career and research in nuclear magnetic resonance applications to living systems.

Sex and Graduate School

My MIT acceptance felt like hitting the jackpot. It was a validation of my desire to do research, and I felt I was on the verge of great things. At first, I reveled in that temple of geekdom, rubbing shoulders with the high priests. I admired the two professors running my program. My classmates were interesting and fun. And I was finally going to work on biomedical imaging, not just read about it.

I should have had a wonderful time at MIT. But I didn't. It took MIT only a few months to kill my sex life.

We'd gone to MIT under difficult circumstances for a couple. My husband was not admitted to his department of choice, but my department offered to take him in order to get me. He was not where he wanted to be, and I was no longer a smart sexy girl, but an object of his resentment. He began spending incredibly long hours on class work and in the lab. When he did come home late at night, he was too exhausted and demoralized for anything as demanding as sex. And it soon became clear that all the hard work in the world would not open the doors for a transfer to another department.

The loss of my sex life was followed by the death of my father at the end of my first year. All the joy, all the promise vanished, and research became an unpleasant chore. In addition, I was in a lab with a competitive, undermining postdoctoral student. My oblivious adviser was having an affair with the lab tech, who got way more attention than I did. His advice for coping with depression and grief was "when you think you can't work anymore, you should just work harder."

My husband was miserable, I was lost, so why not leave?

We got our MS degrees and got out. But now I became resentful, feeling as if he had made me leave MIT, or at least made it impossible to stay. It didn't help that transferring to new graduate schools failed to revive our sex life. The sense of myself as an intelligent, creative, and competent researcher that I had initially had at MIT was nearly gone. I began to view myself as unattractive and research as something beyond my capabilities. I remember one particularly low point when it took me an entire day to make a liter of 150 mM NaCl. Yes, saltwater was more than I could cope with.

Nevertheless, somehow I completed a PhD at Duke through a haze of severe and chronic depression. I was doing interdisciplinary research on nuclear magnetic resonance (NMR) spectroscopy of living cells, and my committee hated it. My "interdisciplinary" was their "undisciplined"— which was ironic, since biomedical engineering is an inherently interdisciplinary pursuit. They told my adviser, "We don't know what she is, but we know she's not an engineer." A second, more bitter, irony is that ten years after I completed my PhD, the department became heavily invested in biomedical engineering at the cellular level. Note to geek girls: If you insist on being ten years ahead of your time, don't expect the professors to be pleased, unless you can acquire a penis.

Even in the worst of my depression, I still found NMR to be a fascinating phenomenon. I dug into the research literature to find original papers by Solomon, Bloembergen, and Morgan on paramagnetism and relaxation theory. Ah, NMR! All the pleasure of physics without being in a physics department and thus subject to its virulent strain of discrimination. (Engineering was bad enough.) All those fun equations, too!

But for the most part, it was difficult for me to find joy in my work. My adviser's main energy went into academic politics, and I was left to make my way as best I could. Without the encouragement of women I met through women's studies, I would never have finished the PhD. The combination of hostility and negligence dished out by my department nearly finished me. As it was, I was mentally exhausted and loathed my research by the time I was done. Only in recent years have I been able to look at my dissertation and feel a small measure of pride in what I accomplished.

Rediscovering the Joy of Sex and Work

The postdoc years brought major change to my life. During the two years I spent in Germany as a postdoc, my withered marriage finally gave up the ghost. However, I had a wonderful boss, a good project, and interesting colleagues. Three things happened at more or less the same time:

1. My work became interesting again and then a real source of pleasure.
2. I became unwilling to remain in a relationship that lacked intimacy, Catholicism be damned.
3. Pent-up desire exploded within me.

I worked closely and constantly with three men in my lab: another postdoc, a graduate student, and a medical student. They were each attractive in their own ways, physically and intellectually. And it seemed that all three were flirting with me. Although I believe I was at least of average attractiveness in my late twenties, I think it was the intensity of the pheromones my sex-deprived body was emitting that served as a siren song for them. Even one of my female colleagues felt the pull. I would kiss all of them by the time my days in that lab were over, and would become more deeply involved with one of them.

My German lover was definitely a geek—by day. At night he became a different person. He had two different wardrobes, one for work and one for evenings and weekends. He had two different pairs of glasses—a traditional, geeky pair and a funky, arty pair. He even carried his body differently outside the workplace. For him, everything he thought of as his "real" life had to be hidden and suppressed in the research lab. At work he was reserved, cautious, and hardworking. In the evenings I spent with him at cafés and nightclubs, he was passionate, witty, articulate, and adventurous. It was his "evening personality" that I loved, and that helped open previously closed-off aspects of my own existence.

Unlike my lover, I couldn't see how to squelch my emerging erotic self during lab hours, nor did I want to. Nerdonna by day, Whore by night was not for me. Eroticism fueled my creativity at work and vice versa, as I was beginning to realize just how powerful a woman I could be. I was less tentative about shimming the 500-MHz spectrometer, and I achieved narrower linewidths and flatter baselines in my 31P spectra of human cancer cells. The cancer cells ceased to be mere research tools; they came to have a terrible beauty to me, and I loved them. Each cell line had its own personality. The colon carcinoma cells I worked with the most were delicately sensitive to their nutrient environment. The cells told me what they liked and didn't like, and together we discovered a nutrient combination that resulted in a metabolism much more like that seen in vivo, which was thus a better model for drug resistance. In nearly every experiment, I was able to tease interesting results from the cancer cells, and I finally achieved what every girl geek most desires—multiple robust data sets. I made beautiful, beautiful science with my cells.

When I returned to the United States for a second postdoc position, I knew that such beauty was possible, but there was no research climax for me in the new lab. I was going through a painful divorce (is there any other kind?) without my German lover or any prospect of reuniting with him. You will not be surprised to learn that depression descended, and my research progress screeched to a halt. I was almost back to the days of trouble with saltwater. It seemed that my brief flowering of powerful, fulfilling sexuality was over, and who knew when or if it would return?

So I determined to succeed at being single. No sitting home alone. I took myself out for Sunday brunch; I explored Philadelphia and had lunch at nice restaurants. I never got courageous enough to try dinner alone, but I was pleased with my lunch victory. One day, because no one would go with me, I took myself to a jazz festival at Penn's Landing. And wouldn't you know it, in the midst of my triumphant Single Girl moment, I met a boy.

Though I do not recommend this as a means to find a partner, I was a smoker at the time, and he approached me to bum a cigarette. We stood together, enjoying the music and commenting on it to each other. Oh, there was such a lovely tingle in the air between us! We spent the whole day together . . . and then the night.

Tom was not a geek boy; he was in the financial industry. Amazingly, the *E* word didn't turn him off! He thought what I did for a living was fascinating and admirable. And, he thought I was *hot!* The explosion of my sexuality was even more intense this time. It was difficult for a while to focus on research because I just wanted to have sex, or think about having sex, or think about the sex I'd had. But soon I was able to return some focus to my work, and I had more confidence about my choices and ideas in the lab. Despite being in a very dysfunctional lab group, work became a little easier, and then pleasurable once again.

∞

Beauty and the Geek

If I were to graph the intensity of pleasure I have taken in my work and in my body, the peaks and valleys of the two would track closely. Yet the prevailing myth of geekhood would predict the opposite. It is widely understood, if not always articulated, that "true engineers" have learned to suppress and control the emotional and erotic aspects of life. (Witness my adviser's recommended "just work harder" coping strategy.) Many men are drawn to engineering because it offers the promise of control, abstraction, rationality, and known outcomes. Social relationships, by contrast, are extremely messy and unpredictable. A relationship with one's computer is much easier to manage.

We're led to believe that the erotic and technologic are in opposition. My German lover's fractured disciplining of his passions resulted from his acceptance of this lie. The hypermathematical weed-out curriculum, with its emphasis on discipline and control, facilitates the divorce of the erotic from the technologic. It makes men out of the boys, and nerdhood then becomes a way of doing masculinity.

When Nerds are only men, then women can only be Whores. Consider the TV reality show *Beauty and the Geek,* where all the geeks are men, and all the women are "beauties." Visit its website and click on the link for "How Geeky Are You?" You'll find the image of a woman clad only in underpants, lips parted, and her breasts replaced with a set of black plastic eyeglass frames, out of which stare two male eyes. The sexualized female body is the object of the disembodied, cerebral male gaze. The producers say they recruited "eight women who are academically impaired and eight men who are brilliant but socially challenged." The contestant profiles reveal that one of the women is actually a dental assistant. Nevertheless, on the message boards, her professional training and skills are ignored, except as vehicles for male sexual gratification: "She could do oral work on me all day," "I would drool . . . she would have to wipe it off as I look down her shirt," and so on. In this theorem, sexual attractiveness in women negates their competence and proves that they are, in reality, dumb.

The producers of *Beauty and the Geek* say that a future season will reverse the genders, with female geeks and male beauties. Would this help any? In a word, no. The idea of the female geek *seems* to be a stereotype buster. But in fact, the figure of the female geek reproduces and reinforces all the negative stereotypes about individuals with an affinity for technology. And because she needs a modifier (female geek) while he does not (geek), she also reinforces the primary notion that technologically competent people are male. She's just a Nerdonna to his Nerd, and neither of them is getting laid.

In addition, the reversal is not truly equal. A man ogling beautiful women is a commonplace of our society, and it is a hierarchical activity—the ogler is an active agent, more powerful than the object that is ogled. A woman ogling a man seems amusing, and possibly whorish, but her gaze does not confer power. Think again about that website photo. What shape would a reversed-gender image take? Female eyes gazing out of geeky glass frames don't have the same cultural cachet as the male gaze. Where would you put the eyes—superimposed over his balls?

Nerdonna, Whore, or Dr. Sexy?

Are there any alternatives? Not long after I met Tom, the lab I worked in recruited another postdoc, who became one of my very best friends. Afsaneh was a physical chemist who had built hardware and developed pulse sequences. She was also beautiful, funny, and kind, and she had the best fashion sense of any scientist I'd ever known. I studied her, watching her exude poise and competence in the laboratory while perfectly coiffed and made up, holding her own with the arrogant males, and wearing just the right scarf to accent her dress. She did not have separate selves for the lab and elsewhere. She was not Nerdonna, and she was not a Whore. She wasn't even a Whorish Nerdonna. She was everything she was, all the time.

Some time before Afsaneh had joined the lab, Tom had bestowed upon me the nickname "Dr. Sexy." To him, my sexiness didn't make me dumb, and my intelligence didn't make me unattractive. Having that nickname to carry in secret was delicious, and I began to understand more consciously the flow between the erotic and technologic in myself. It was Dr. Sexy who'd made beautiful science in the German lab. Afsaneh's example encouraged me to think of myself this way. Together, Tom and Afsaneh helped me to say goodbye to Suzy the Computer and claim Dr. Sexy.

Though I had much joy in my work, the machinations of individuals in my dysfunctional lab group often eclipsed it. Eventually, Afsaneh and I, plus another friend named Annette, concluded the research life wasn't for us. We saw a future of political wrangling and backstabbing, and could foresee the day when we might have to exploit graduate students and postdocs the same way we were exploited. One by one, we left for industry. Annette was the first out. When Afsaneh and I saw her, just a few weeks after she'd left the lab, she looked completely different. Her facial muscles had been so chronically tensed that neither she nor we had realized it. Afsaneh left a few months later, and within weeks her face had undergone the same transformation. We dubbed it "Ex-Scientist Face," and I was delighted when, months later, I got my own chance to develop it.

It would take me years to realize that leaving the research track did not revoke my credentials as a scientist and engineer. Academia had indoctrinated me that a research professorship at a top university was the only destination for success. But in industry, our colleagues valued us—and we had colleagues, not competitors. We found pleasure in teamwork, interacting with a broad range of clinical, experimental, and mathematical scientists. In contrast to the one linear pathway in academic research, industry offered a myriad of choices and possibilities. Plus, it paid really well!

In an environment where my expertise was respected, with a lover who saw me as Dr. Sexy, I blossomed. It was no coincidence that I started gardening around that time. Cultivating my garden was an expression of the joy I felt. Gardening is a sensual pleasure—the smell of the earth and flowers, the astonishing blue of a delicate delphinium, the dappled shade of a river birch on a hot summer day, the sweet taste of tomatoes and spice of basil mixed in soup in September. My life was sumptuously full.

Then, as Tom had come into my life when I was content without a lover, so academe came knocking at my door when I was content without it. A friend on the faculty at Kansas State University recruited me to apply for a new position, director of the Women in Engineering and Science Program (WESP). The program had to serve seventeen science and engineering departments, and the director's charge was, basically, to change the face of the male-dominated tech world. Not a problem for Dr. Sexy—I felt invigorated by the challenge.

When I first went to K-State, WESP consisted of me, a faculty office in an obscure building, a budget of $20,000, and some part-time secretarial assistance. When I left three and a half years later, the program had colonized an office suite in a building next to the student center; we had a full-time assistant, a full-time coordinator of a thriving middle-school outreach program, and graduate and undergraduate assistants, and we had raised nearly $5 million from government, industry, and private sources.

A key factor in WESP's success was extraordinary support from a KSU Foundation development officer and three women in faculty and administration. Together, we were midwives to the birth of WESP. Working with that community of women toward a common goal was the peak experience of my professional life. We were passionately committed to our work, and we fed off each other's energy. There is a powerful satisfaction in managing institutional structures to create change within them, as powerful as anything I ever felt in the research lab. Every fiber of my being was intensely alive in that job. And even though the job meant a commuter relationship with Tom, our passionate commitment to each other was strengthened during this time.

Not long after I left K-State, I suffered a stroke that halted my career, leaving me with impaired vision and chronic migraines. Losing my job was traumatic, but when a woman has achieved a certain level of satisfaction in work and love, there is little that can keep her down for long. In time, I came to realize that one of the consolations for my health issues and lost career was that I no longer had to be polite. At K-State I had to choose my battles carefully, negotiate with the powers-that-be, and keep a neutral face at times when I encountered outright opposition to the mere presence of women and minorities in science and engineering. Now, not having a boss means I don't have to censor myself anymore. I can take on battles for those who can't afford to wage them. I can emphasize that it is not young girls who need fixing; it is science and engineering that need help. I can give voice to angry women who are tired of being polite, making nice, and waiting for the patriarchy to give them a few crumbs from science's banquet table.

Dr. Sexy is now blogging at a website near you.

»»»»all our boys go to the IT industry in america

Roopa Ramamoorthi

As a little girl in India, I loved the *pattu pavadais* my grandmother, my *patti*, gave me each year. They were rich *Kanjeevaram* silk, full-length, umbrella-shaped skirts. As my grandmother watched, I would spin around to see the skirt swell, then stand still to watch it cling to me again. I was demonstrating the elementary principles of moment and torque. These might have been my first physics experiments, even though I did not call them that.

When I was three my father left Bombay and went to Princeton for a year. I could barely spell "cat," "rat," "bat," and "mat," but I decided I would go to Princeton when I grew up.

That same year I went to nursery school at Casa Montessori. When I missed my mother and started to cry, the teacher gave me toys to play with, but I would continue sobbing. That's when Miss Pervin discovered that if she gave me math sums, I would sit quietly and do them. So mathematics comforted me and made me forget about tugging on my mother's *sari pallu*. Was I destined for geekdom even then?

That same year my grandfather gave me two gifts. One gift was a lovely pair of silver *golusu* (belled anklets) that tinkled beautifully when I twirled my *pavadai*. The other, on the recommendation of the nursery school, was an encyclopedia. I still remember the hardbound *Hamlyn Children's Encyclopedia* with orange covers. It became my favorite book. I read and reread every page until it was almost in tatters. Some pictures still come vividly to my mind—the blue whale, the biggest mammal; pictures of airport runways. I don't think there was anything about computers. This was 1971 in India, and we had no TV at home, let alone a PC.

I was born in Tirupattur, a small town in South India. Upon my birth my father distributed sweets to everyone. All the laborers said, "Why are you celebrating? It is a girl child after all." They were thinking of dowry problems, the father having to get the girl married. However, my whole family welcomed me—even the conservative, nine-yard-sari-wearing grandaunt who raised my father. She and my granduncle did not have any children of their own, while my father's parents had ten children. And so, at two years of age, my father was left with his aunt and uncle and became the child they never had. My mother told me that when I was a newborn, my grandaunt put around my neck the gold medal my father received for standing first in twelfth grade. She blessed me by saying, "Study like your father."

Maybe she had unfulfilled dreams of completing her schooling and going to college like her lawyer husband. She did not give me the traditional blessing for girls, which is to have sons or get a good husband. Her words resonate in me though I hardly knew her. She died when I was only seven, and I can't remember how she looked from memory, only from a faded black-and-white photograph.

By middle school, with my father guiding me, I graduated from *Hamlyn Children's Encyclopedia* to *Hamlyn Junior Encyclopedia*. It was more expensive than my parents could afford, so at school during the lunch hour, I would go to the library and read it—mostly the science sections about Galileo looking through a telescope and Copernican theory. This was my refuge. Most of the other children played "lock and key," running around in the school dining room making loud noises. Being a very slow runner, I always ended up being the "den" and getting frustrated at not being able to catch anyone. Planetary motion was easier than the Brownian motion of children. In seventh grade I preferred to go with friends to view the skeleton we had at the school laboratory. If the cupboard was accidentally left open, we would admire the bones and shake hands. "How do you do, Skeleton Sir?"

One day on my way home from school, my mother plucked a blood-red hibiscus flower. "I will dissect this and show you the inside," she said. She had been a botany major at college. When we got home she took my father's razor blade, cut, and explained: "This is the ovary with all the little eggs. The pollen from the stamen lands on the stigma, goes in, fertilizes the egg, and a seed is produced, covered by the fruit."

At that point my mother passed the responsibility of guiding me in my studies to my father. I can still remember sitting at the small, brown Sunmica table specifically made for my studies, and my father sitting on the chair next to me. If I got stuck on a problem, my father would grind his teeth and say, "Roopa, math is not tennis. You don't get a second serve." He stood second in statistics honors in college, and the first ranker is now a full professor in UCLA's Mathematics Department. So even though I always got over 90 in math, I did not meet my father's expectations. Before going to bed, I would lie on the one-and-a-half-inch foam mattress on the floor and ask God to make me better at math so my father would love me. My father pushed me so hard I sometimes cried, but in hindsight I realize how important it was that he cared how I did in math, rather than not caring because I was just a girl with nothing but marriage in her future.

From my all-girls' school I went to St. Xavier's for junior college, which is equivalent to eleventh and twelfth grade in the United States. In the science track the classes were about 65 percent male, while in the arts section there were only a handful of guys. All the arts girls—with their miniskirts, flowing hair, and perfectly polished nails—hung out with the "smartest" of the science guys. Those girls' skirts were twelve inches shorter than my skirt. The guys came to borrow my math notes but gave up once they realized my handwriting was a "cockroach crawl," as one of them informed me. I got secret satisfaction when I defeated those "smart" guys in math. One of the most horrifying days for me in school was Rose Day, when guys and girls spend a rupee to get a rose sent to someone they admire. By the end of the day the prettier arts girls were always carrying bouquets of roses while I did not get even a single one. I was not ugly, but I was still hidden behind my glasses. My legs were slim and shapely enough, but I covered them to midcalf in the conservative skirts my mother and I chose. Few of the guys noticed me, except for my hand always popping up in physics or chemistry class when the lecturer asked questions. As my mother teased me, "The only guy who calls you is the blind boy." But I was the top student in my twelfth-grade class—and eventually I switched to contact lenses.

I went from there to the Indian Institute of Technology for my engineering studies. There the numbers could not have been more skewed. There were 285 boys and 15 girls, making the boy to girl ratio 19:1. The IITs are the most difficult engineering colleges to get into: Only the crème de la crème get in, after taking the Joint Entrance Exam—which consists of writing papers in physics, math, and chemistry. Of a hundred thousand applicants, only two thousand succeed. So I was thrilled to get in but felt intimidated at being part of such a conspicuous minority. In my chemical engineering class, of the forty-two students only three were women. Of course with the ratio being so lopsided, on Chocolate Day—at IIT there were chocolates instead of roses—I actually tied with another girl for getting the most candies, more than I could possibly eat and still maintain my twenty-four-inch waistline. (Yes, I had a twenty-four-inch waistline once, before I started expanding like the universe!)

There was teasing, but even that was in equations. The boys would pun on my initials, writing the equation "$R^2 + X^2 = ?$" on the blackboard—R was for me, not the radius of a circle, and X was for one of them. I got flustered, but with a gender ratio of nineteen to one, what was I to expect? I had to accept it. One time our thermodynamics professor entered the classroom and the joke hadn't been erased from the board, so he joined in the sport and talked about dipole moments and attraction and repulsion for two minutes before switching to entropy and Gibbs free energy.

One weekend when I had come home from IIT, my father threw a big party for his staff. At that time he was chairman of Bombay Port Trust, and the official residence he was given had a beautiful garden with jackfruit trees, a sky-blue wooden swing, a rock garden, and a nonfiring cannon that my kid brother used as a jungle gym. My father introduced me to one of his colleagues at the party and said she was a police officer.

There she was, wearing a beautiful pink sari, slim and attractive, and I blurted out, "You don't look like a police officer."

She replied, "And you don't look like an engineer."

I blushed. I realized I had stereotypes of women too.

$$\infty$$

After ITT I went to Caltech, which was a dream come true. I would get to work with some of the greatest minds in the field. I wanted to get into biotechnology and do cutting-edge research. I had been second in my undergraduate class and felt confident about taking classes in thermodynamics and fluid mechanics, but I was uncertain about fitting into American culture. I had been accepted as a student in chemical engineering at one of the world's best engineering schools, but I did not know how to use a washing machine or microwave. After moving into the graduate dorms at Caltech, I waited for a week to see who looked kind enough to show me how to use these contraptions. Then I could focus on complex numbers, which I studied from my cheaper, Indian-edition textbooks that had no glossy layouts.

∞

At Caltech I chose to do my PhD in biochemical engineering. I had had an introductory course on the topic in India that had jazzed me, and the lab at Caltech was run by the author of the textbook from my earlier class. I chose biotech because genetic engineering was fascinating. It involves manipulating bacteria, treating them as little chemical plants. Plus, my other options—fluid mechanics or process control, in which I could have gotten a theoretical PhD—intimidated me. It wasn't that I was bad at math: I got an A in the only math class I took at Caltech, on complex numbers. But growing up with a father and brother who were both ultrabrilliant in math had given me a secret inferiority complex. (My brother is now an assistant professor at Columbia in computer science.) So I chose an experimental thesis project, though I didn't really think of myself as a great experimentalist either.

During the third year of my PhD, my thesis adviser unexpectedly moved to Switzerland. Another group was ahead of me with the project I was working on, and they published their work, rendering mine irrelevant. So at the end of my third year, I had to start on a new thesis project with an original topic with a new adviser. She was one of the few female full professors at Caltech at that time. I noticed that hers was one of the few groups in Caltech's Engineering Department where most of the group members were women. Was it a mere coincidence? There was a cartoon taped up in the lab about the evolution of authority: It started with sneakers' flat footprints and ended with high heel prints, and that amused me.

Sometimes I felt isolated. The American women in the group were always going for lunch together. I joined them sometimes, but they just seemed so much closer to each other. It is natural, I guess; they grew up in the same culture, or probably they had been in the same lab together longer. One of the women was warm, however, and always tried to include me, and the more experienced European postdocs were helpful too. I still keep in occasional touch with those women postdocs. It was also valuable for me to observe my professor's poise and grace as she balanced a family with two small children as well as a faculty position at a top school. My PhD was enough of a roller coaster ride. At times I felt like giving up, but then I would feel elated when the experiments worked and I got some good results. I was glad when I finally defended my thesis. It was my twenty-sixth birthday present to myself.

After Caltech I did two postdocs, including one at MIT. The postdoctoral period was easier than grad school for two reasons. One was that I already had a PhD, so people thought I knew something, and I had more self-confidence. The other was that I had five years' experience living in America under my belt and was better assimilated. Still, an incident would occasionally throw me off balance.

During one of my postdocs, a lab mate brushed against me inappropriately. I was outraged and wanted to complain to the professor, but I did not because I was the only woman postdoc and new in the lab. Besides, the guy was married, and I knew he would deny it. I, the honest one, would end up being ridiculed, so I just avoided working closely with him on any project. Mostly, however, all my male colleagues have been helpful and knowledgeable, and one odd person does not take away from all the wonderful people I have met. MIT was like the Boston winters: cold at first, but it grew on me like the snowy landscape.

Initially I had wanted to be a professor, but when I did not get a tenure-track position after a few interviews, I decided to work in industry instead. Then, after a relationship that did not work out, I had a semi-arranged marriage.

I was approaching thirty by then, and my father felt I had better settle down. He gently reminded me I was not one of the Sultan of Brunei's daughters, with infinite choices. I too realized that I was getting older, and there were so few Indian men around that if I wanted to marry one, an arranged introduction was the best way.

Of course there were adjustment problems. When cards from his extended family arrived in the mail, they were always addressed to "Dr. and Mrs." First, I had kept my maiden name, and second, I too had my PhD. But that is the way their letters were always addressed. Now I just smile with resignation. He does the cooking half the time, as well as the grocery shopping, but sometimes I know he wishes he had a nice quiet wife who never answered back and who cooked, cleaned, and attended to his every need—the way his housewife mother waited on his father. When he says he has given me freedom to attend whatever events I want, I feel my freedom is not his to give.

But we both share an intellectual curiosity, and he can discuss a *NOVA* program or explain his research to me, which is something I don't think his parents could share. And there is a common cultural heritage we enjoy, though I feel women in my family had a stronger position—probably because on my mother's side, the women had an inheritance and so were not abjectly dependent on their husbands. Or perhaps it's just that my grandfather and father were progressive.

Sometimes when I can't visit India because I don't have vacation time, or I want to go to a writing workshop instead, his parents don't understand why. They think I should just come to India with my husband. They are nice people, but they belong to a different generation. A lot of men in my generation feel they are doing much more around the house than their fathers did, while the women feel they deserve real equality. I guess my situation is no different.

My husband was in Berkeley so I moved there, and after a bit of struggle, I found a job in the biotech industry as a scientist. It was exciting to see medicines being developed to cure people, but sometimes I felt conflicted, knowing many of the latest medicines are not available or affordable to most people in India. I sometimes questioned what I was doing. Was this job right for me? I had always thought I could do what a man can do. I am as intelligent as a man, but when I have to wheel around two-hundred-liter drums to do large-scale purifications, I don't feel strong enough. I always have to ask for help, while the guy scientists can push these drums with ease or kick them up inclines.

Also, while I am very good at designing an experiment, when an instrument breaks down, I am not good at tinkering and fixing it. Partly this is because when I was a child in India, although I gained a lot of theoretical knowledge in math and science, we lived in an apartment and neither my mother nor my father really fixed anything around the house. While I read a lot, the extent of my hands-on work was replacing a light-bulb. There was no working with car parts on the weekend with my father growing up—we did not own a car!

A lot changed for me years later, when I suddenly found myself lying in a hospital gown with electrocardiogram probes attached to my chest and the IV pumping heparin into my right arm. The CAT scan showed I had suffered a stroke. A stroke at thirty-six. A neurologist came and explained to my husband and me that it was in the occipital pole, so only a small region of my vision was affected—the peripheral right lower quadrant. It was a shock. I had taken my health for granted and now, *wham!* Suddenly I had switched roles—instead of being the scientist, I was the experiment.

The stroke was originally misdiagnosed as a migraine. I was prescribed medicine for the migraine symptoms, but ended up having an adverse reaction to the medicine that resulted in vasoconstriction. T inversions showed up in my EKG, which is comparable to a heart attack. However when they did an angiography, my arteries were clear. I did not have a heart attack due to the arteries being blocked.

For two weeks I was subjected to innumerable needle pricks to draw blood for various studies. First my troponin levels were rising. I remembered troponin. When I was a graduate student, I had done a side project where I cloned the troponin gene behind a methylotrophic promoter, but had been unsuccessful in expressing the protein. Now I was meeting it again! I learned troponin was the last enzyme whose levels decreased after a heart attack. As long as it is rising, the doctor and patient do not know if there will be another attack. I was scared to see the levels rising. What if I had a major heart attack? Despite my fear, I was fascinated to see the technology I'd studied really being applied—the doctors were actually measuring enzyme levels as we do in the lab. Then they sent my blood out to do further enzyme assays and found that my activated protein C levels were higher than normal. I too had done enzyme assays as part of my doctoral studies. Now the doctor was wondering if my Factor V gene was mutated. Factor V, I learned, was one of the enzymes in the blood-clotting cascade. So another test was ordered—a polymerase chain reaction, or PCR, to see if the gene was mutated. I had done a lot of PCRs to amplify DNA and introduce mutations during my PhD work and postdoc. All this was interesting as long as I would be healthy again. It was different when I was working in the lab, and the results of experiments were abstract. Then, negative results might mean the boss wouldn't be happy or no paper would be written. But this time it was my health, my life. I prayed. I needed God's help.

As the doctor was piecing the puzzle of my genetics together, my husband was doing Medline searches, and I was doing online research and reading articles right along with the resident on my case. One journal article was about how the combination of the Factor V Leiden gene mutation and birth control pills increase the probability of deep vein thrombosis significantly. I also studied the blood-clotting cascade on the Urbana-Champaign Hematology website. Eventually it was confirmed—I had a heterozygous mutation Factor V Leiden, a single-base-pair mutation in my genome. That caused a slight tendency toward thrombosis or blood clotting, which had been further aggravated by the estrogen in my birth control pills. It could have been worse—blood clots in the brain often kill or cause severe brain damage. All I'd lost was some of my peripheral vision. But there would be no more birth control pills for me.

After getting out of the hospital, I entered visual rehab. The physiotherapist showed me how to use colored pencils to activate the cones on the margins of my vision loss, and then to wriggle my fingers while looking straight ahead to activate the rods in my eyes. Sometimes I cheated. I would look sideways a bit to make myself feel like the blind areas had decreased. Then I looked ahead again. Things gradually improved: My visual therapist showed me my gradually improving field-of-vision tests at different times during my recovery. We even discussed writing a journal article about it, because the jury is still out on whether rehab can help stroke victims recover their vision. Now I am proof that it can be done, though one patient is not enough to be a valid statistical sample set. I ended up recovering around 25 percent of my lost vision.

Although my vision loss affected my ability to drive, I did return to full-time work two months after my stroke. Initially it was harder to read journal articles, and I was afraid of bumping into people, but now I have learned to accept the vision loss and let it interfere with my work as little as possible.

Sometimes I still get upset about gender stereotyping, even though I expect it. Recently I helped an old Indian couple with directions on the subway, and they asked, "What does your husband do? Do you have children?" They believe the myth that "Our boys all go to the IT industry in America." No one asks me what I do for a career. I guess they assume I must be a traditional bride who followed my husband to America because of his career. As for their question about having children, doctors advised me against getting pregnant after my stroke. I could adopt or use in vitro fertilization and a surrogate, but am I going to lay my whole life out for analysis by some strangers on BART? OK, they're Indian strangers, but still. Their answers would be pat: "Don't believe doctors, *yaar,* just get pregnant and have a child. Woman has to have a child." Sometimes I wonder whether I will end up childless like my father's aunt. And I think, *At least I have my education.*

I still have links with many of the other women from IIT, and now there is even an IIT women's Yahoo! group. It has now been half a lifetime since I first joined IIT as one of the few women engineering undergrads, and sadly the ratios are still almost the same.

The other day at work, I was in my white lab coat and safety glasses when the carpenter came in with a question about what needed to be drilled for one of the instruments. Naturally, he was looking for a man to give him instructions. Another woman took out a measuring tape, and we explained what needed to be done.

"We're scientists," we told him.

"No, really, you are not scientists," he replied, shaking his head in disbelief. I guess he assumed we were technicians working for a "real scientist," a male one.

»»»»sex and the single (woman) biologist

Nina Simone Dudnik

On my thirtieth birthday I visited some family friends, and during a drive to the beach they asked me what I was working on. "Well, I'm working on my PhD," I began, leaving out the part about being at Harvard, since it tends to distract people. Then I tried my best to explain: I study nucleosomal proteins that interact with DNA, using fruit flies as a model organism. I'm pretty sure they didn't understand that, nor did it speak to their real interest in me. Because their very next question was "Do you have a boyfriend?"

"No," I answered.

"It's because you're too smart," they said. I tried to laugh it off, making some joke about how "all the guys I meet bore me too quickly." But honestly—too smart? For what?

I've been interested in science for as long as I can remember. When I was nine, I took a science course at the local university every Saturday morning. My crowning achievement was an experiment charting the growth of radish seeds placed in windows facing the four cardinal directions, as well as in the dark under a lamp. In junior high school I did a science fair project on topology—a pretty obscure branch of mathematics most people never encounter even in college. At that time I was the only girl in "Special Math," the pathetic option my very small school invented to allow some of us to move ahead of the other kids. What a great way to make junior high, that stronghold of snotty girls picking on each other for being different, even more enjoyable. No, I wasn't interested in teasing my hair to epic proportions (hey, this *was* the late '80s), I was too busy teaching myself what a plasmid was and deciding that I wanted to be a geneticist. But the fact that most of my female classmates ignored me when I was twelve couldn't have made it clearer that being unusually smart wasn't a valued social skill.

Yet I always assumed I could, and should, study science. In high school I was no longer the only girl in the classroom, and it made a huge difference to have friends who looked and thought like me. Females have made up nearly half of the science classes I've taken ever since, right up through graduate school. And yet I wonder if all these girls heard that same message in elementary and junior high school, that we were weird and different. Because I've often had a subtle feeling that we were out of place, that the male teachers and students were humoring us in our odd insistence on being there.

There was the high school physics teacher who made a big show of encouraging the girls in our Advanced Placement class. If he really believed we were just as good as the boys, would he have made such grandiose gestures of praise? And would those gestures have been directed so disproportionately toward the girls who wore the short skirts? We all knew we had to work harder than the boys. One by one, girls dropped out of that physics class. I couldn't help noticing that many of them stuck around for AP Chemistry, where the teacher made no mention of anyone's gender in the lab.

In college, I majored in biochemistry. Again, about equal numbers of women and men took those classes, but something strange was going on. There were always a few superstar students—the ones who everyone knew were geniuses, who you assumed aced the exam even though you never asked, who asked questions that implied they were already thinking on another plane. These were always guys. The ones who worked the hardest, the ones who actually *did* ace the exams, were always women. Yet these women didn't walk around with that natural arrogance, the knowledge that they were talented. They believed it was just a result of extreme hard work. Hard work that they had to do to compensate for their lack of the effortless brilliance of those guys.

I lived in a microcosm of that ethos during my sophomore year. I lived with five other women: one computer scientist, two chemists, one biologist, and another biochemist like me. Five of us took the same organic chemistry class, which caused us eight months of anxiety. We pitted ourselves against each other to see who studied the hardest, who stayed the latest in the library, who got up the earliest on Sunday morning to review organic synthesis pathways. We bought a giant whiteboard that we carted to the library, and we sat around it and "pushed electrons," trying to figure out how to derive one compound from another. I loved that course, because I learned so much and it was so beautifully logical. But I never lived with those girls again; they stressed me out too much. Why did we drive ourselves so crazy? Did the guys in that class feel the way we did? Ten years later, three of us are in graduate school in science, one works for a pharmaceutical company, one is a business consultant, and one is a museum science curator. What I want to know is, have we come this far exactly because of our self-deprecating work ethic, or in spite of our incredible anxiety? I would love to be compensated for those sleepless nights in the library with the whiteboard.

Yeah, all that anxiety, that feeling that we needed to be ready to defend our intellectual reputations at any moment. I am the last person in the world who wants to admit to gender-correlated differences in behavior, but I'm pretty much convinced by now that a certain competitive aggressiveness is overwhelmingly a masculine trait. Unfortunately, it's what gets you ahead. As girls, we walked the line between competition and collegiality. In high school, we formed study groups for that damnable physics class, pushing and pulling each other through the problem sets every week. In college, we quizzed each other on biosynthetic pathways. But in the upper echelons of academic research you have to get by on your own, and above all, you have to convince everyone, all the time, that your ideas are right. At its worst, this manifests itself in what I can only describe as the intellectual equivalent of boys' locker room comparisons—my brain's bigger than yours. I don't think most women are able or willing to sink to that level, but it's so insidious. I've noticed myself getting more and more argumentative over the last four years. It's gotten to the point where I can't have a conversation about anything intellectual without making it into a heated debate. And I hate this. I want to be confident, not pushy.

I didn't realize that only two of the speakers for my department's seminars had been female until after I gave a talk about my own research. The only other female speaker was another graduate student. Not a single woman postdoc had given a seminar, from September through June. I'm told that 40 percent of the postdocs in the department are women, and I guess it's about the same proportion for graduate students. It's hard to believe none of these women has any data to present. I can't imagine that absolutely all of them are so afraid to give a talk that they wouldn't do it if asked. So I can only conclude they're not being asked by the professors for whom they work. After all, nearly all those professors are men.

I'm concerned that this neglect has convinced many of my female peers to live the stereotype of the shrinking violet. When I mentioned the seminar discrepancy to two fellow female grad students, they thought my anger was completely off base. Volunteering for speaking opportunities was a reflection of personal will and ambition, they said. Women don't choose not to give talks because they feel they're not supposed to, but just because they don't want to. They kept insisting that it was a personal choice for which you couldn't fault the women, and you couldn't force them to speak. One friend said she'd feel worse if someone gave her the opportunity to speak just because she was a woman.

Here's what really made me feel awful: I didn't notice this lack of women speakers for over a year. When I finally did, I could have kicked myself. Has it become so normal for me to see men as the public face of science that I don't even notice the absence of women anymore? I refuse to believe that. My bosses have included three women and two men in the ten years since I started working in labs. I took part in a training course on molecular genetics in Syria, with a group of scientists from around the Arab world. Of the eleven other trainees, two were women: one from Tunisia and one from Algeria. I worked for an agriculture institute in West Africa—under a Cameroonian woman with a PhD in molecular biology. At last year's International Drosophila Research Conference, women speakers were everywhere, and the Nobel laureate who gave the keynote address was a woman developmental biologist. If I've interacted with women working in science across the world, across cultures and religions, how could I fail to notice their absence right here at home? And why did I then have to argue that their public presence should be normal?

And yet, it seems, I do. The former president of my illustrious university found it necessary to raise the possibility that women are just less capable of excelling in the sciences. He offered four explanations for the dearth of women faculty in science and engineering: a societal bias that teaches girls not to enter these fields, discrimination in hiring, unwillingness on the part of women to put in the incredible number of hours required to get tenure, and fewer women in the elite intellectual strata that would qualify them for these jobs. The first two he downplayed, opting to focus on the third and fourth. After all, he argued, the faculty search process would find women if there were an equal number of women to recruit, so there must be fewer capable of reaching that point. I found myself reeling at this logic, at the fact that in this day and age someone trained in a quantitative field, as this man is, could *still* spend any time treating this line of thought as legitimate.

The only thing more remarkable than the president saying these things was what happened next. I'd been at Harvard for nearly four years by then, and issues of women in science hadn't come up in the greater university community. Right after that speech, there were at least two public panel discussions on the issue within a month, as well as a series of open forums for women graduate students and postdocs. The head of my biology graduate program and two representatives from a university task force on women spent over three hours listening to everything we wanted to rant about. And rant we did, about issues across the spectrum: feeling unsafe walking home from the lab at night, negotiating with a thesis committee composed entirely of men, worries about whether organizations like the National Institutes of Health would fund women at the same levels as men, whether it was possible to promise graduate students better maternity leave. I almost thought we owed the president a thank-you card for bringing this situation about. I found myself wondering whether he'd said it all on purpose.

One year later, however, not much had changed. Of the thirty-three principal faculty members in my department, just two are women; one doesn't have tenure, and the other was hired this year. The department is a known stronghold of old white men with wacky hair. The departmental committee on women is run by a man—who else is there for the job? From day one of graduate school I have heard my fellow women students worry out loud about "balancing career and family." Every year this topic is suggested for the obligatory discussion panels at the departmental retreats—again, brought up for consideration by the women. This year, a graduate student five months pregnant with her second child stood up and wondered aloud how she was expected to pay for childcare so she could attend professional meetings.

The professor down the hall from my lab illustrates another reason we all worry. He and his wife went to graduate school together; now he runs the lab, and she's a sort of part-time lab manager for him. So much for having greater career advancement with a PhD. And it seems to be rather common. I know of one professor who runs the lab while her husband works for *her*. The downside: She has no kids and never stops working. When all public transportation in the city shut down due to a blizzard several years ago, she walked the five miles to her lab. The implication seems to be, if you have the misfortune of not being a man in this field, you'd better give up your hopes of having a personal life. Or at least, plan it all out very carefully in advance, and count on being a consummate juggler.

That last message is coming through loud and clear. At the open forum held for female students last spring, it came out that many women feel an obligation to plan their entire careers from the first moment of graduate school. They have to choose the research field they'll specialize in for the trajectory of their careers right at the start. Why? They assume they'll hit a period in which family concerns will overshadow their careers, so they'll need to be much further along in establishing themselves than their male counterparts of the same age. The men always have the luxury of putting off having a family until their careers allow them more leeway. The men don't seem to fear that they will never have a personal life.

This brings me back to the wonderful world of dating when you're a woman scientist.

Exhibit A: During my first year of graduate school, three female classmates who frequented the clubs of Boston hit a serious snag in their search for boyfriends. Time after time, guys approached them—only to walk away the minute the women mentioned their occupation. So my friends started lying. They claimed to be flight attendants, yoga instructors, or kindergarten teachers. And the dating pool magically widened.

Exhibit B: I found myself at a dinner party last month with seven Harvard women PhD students—five economists, one social anthropologist, and me. We argued about politics, jobs in and out of academia, the relative merits of fieldwork and lab work. One economist and the anthropologist went at each other about the utility function. It was an evening of conversations that made me bless the forces that allowed me to live in a time and place where women are so well educated. And then the talk turned to dating, and suddenly I found myself in 1953. Or at least that's how it felt. Here were these amazing women, conversant in everything from higher math to development econ, talking about *The Rules*. That book that tells women never to engage a man in an intellectual argument on a date, call him first, or even stay on the phone longer than ten minutes, a book whose focus is catching and keeping a man. It turns out that all these brilliant women spend a great deal of intellectual and emotional energy lamenting their single state, pining for a relationship, and wondering why the guy they went out with didn't call back. So concerned are they that they're willing to consider following a book that tells them to be sweet, flirty doormats.

These incidents scare me. They suggest the women of my generation are becoming increasingly confident in our professional lives but increasingly at sea in our personal lives. We're willing to consider sweeping under the rug our ambitions, opinions, and scientific careers to "get a man." I don't think any of us really want to, not after everything else we've had to contend with and everything that we've earned. But the pervasive fear is that if we don't, all the men our age will pass us over for adoring, unopinionated Stepford girlfriends: yoga teachers and flight attendants.

There's another fear, though, the exact flip side: that we'll end up selling ourselves short. That we won't find someone who can keep up with us. I've only dated another scientist once, and it was a disaster. We competed constantly—who was doing better in classes, whose research was moving faster. The most adoring boyfriend I've had was a dancer who hadn't gone past high school. We were in no way competing for jobs, and he wasn't threatened. In fact I think he was proud of my academic achievements. Unfortunately, it was hard to find a lot of topics on which to debate him, and by this point, intellectual sparring is what I've been trained to love.

The Economist ran a series of articles on human evolution recently. It mentioned some studies that showed women value higher status in a mate while men do not. This doesn't mean that men de facto prefer a woman of *lower* status, but it sure begs the question. And it led me to wonder if this is the reason women opt out of quantitative fields, if this is why their presence, even in such numbers, is always viewed as a little bit wrong. For if women match or exceed the men in education and achievement, there will be no way for them to find equal, let alone higher-status, mates. Is this all we get from millennia of evolution? I don't consider myself some kind of relationship-averse, unfeeling automaton. But I have ambitions that, if left unfulfilled, will make me feel much more of a failure than never getting married.

I was brought up to believe I could be anything I wanted and raised to measure my success academically. I've been lucky enough to have parents and teachers who have encouraged me to be a scientist all along the way.

For every hint that I was an oddity, there was at least one other female student or teacher there to contradict it. I don't believe I'm "too smart" for my own good or "too smart" for a full and balanced life. I believe I'm exactly where I should be. And I'm sure I'm not alone in this.

»»»»i am wonk, hear me analyze

Charlie Anders

I became a wonk about the same time I became a woman, so the two transitions have always been inseparable for me.

Before I became a woman, I once worked as a reporter, covering medicine for a weekly business newspaper. In that job, I fell in love with the jargon and minutiae of health policy. Broken, messy, and dysfunctional, our nation's medical field held the promise that I would never run out of things to learn. I was getting paid to have lunch with consultants and executives and learn the ins and outs of capitation and other ways health plans were trying to pass financial risk on to doctors. I loved uncovering intricate structures that actually *mattered* to everyone. This was the heyday of managed care, and I spent days and days delving into the intricacies of the Employee Income Retirement Security Act and how it affected self-insured companies, or the differences between "messenger model" physician associations and "specialty carve-outs."

This particular newspaper, however, like a lot of business weeklies in the late 1990s, was a macho stronghold. Not many women ever got to be reporters there. It was all about hard-charging guys chasing hard news. The typical story in this paper read, "So-and-so bought so-and-so for $X million. They're hiring a hundred people and building a new building."

At the time, I was living in the Bible Belt and trying my best to be, if not a manly man, at least not a sprig of parsley. My newfound wonkery, the pursuit of arcane policy issues, helped distract me from a nagging pain I couldn't put my finger on. I began to feel less and less comfortable in my own skin and chafe more and more against my socially defined gender role as a male reporter. At the same time, I was acutely aware from my painstaking research that ill-defined symptoms and psychosomatic illnesses cost the U.S. healthcare system millions of dollars every year.

My gender discomfort finally spiked on the same day my inner palace of wonkdom came crashing down.

One day, my editor came over to my cubicle, where I was poring over a rich stack of documents. He bent over my shoulder. "Look," he said, putting one hand on my mouse to brake its furious dragging and clicking. "You're wasting our time." He pointed to my analysis of PPO/HMO growth trends and said, "We don't want any of this what-does-it-mean shit." Right then, a bomb went off in my head like the cartoon mad-bomber icon my ancient Macintosh displayed on an hourly basis when it quit on me. I tried to defend my arcana, but he just breathed Marlboro-scented condemnation at me until I gave in and promised to stop trying to address larger issues in my writing.

That editor worshipped the "inverted pyramid," an inductive structure that forms the basis for most news writing. You start out with a very general statement, like "I became a wonk at the same time I became a woman." Then you zoom in and provide much the same information, but with more detail. Each paragraph after that gives a more detailed account, until eventually you end up having all the facts at the end of the piece. In the newspaper business, articles that delve into trends or wider context are known as "thumbsuckers," and they're as bad a sin as plagiarism.

After six months at the paper, I was as much of a dick as my colleagues. I had given up on trying to sneak in stories about the bigger picture. And I did get pretty good at the macho reporter thing. I reported some big mergers and layoffs before anyone else and made more than a few PR flacks cry on the phone. One time this guy bad-mouthed his employer to me without going off the record, and I printed his remarks with his name on them. I'm sure he got another job eventually.

But I felt like I was missing out. There was a world of beautiful intricacy that I wasn't allowed to write about, and I had a garden of gentleness and empathy trapped inside me waiting to be expressed. I wanted to emote and prognosticate! I wanted nuance! I wanted to be an Athena of mortality and morbidity rates!

After less than a year, I left the rugged business paper and went to work for a trade publisher covering various health industries. In the job interview, I wowed my new boss with my almost bottomless curiosity about postacute care and "quicker sicker" hospital discharges. He was so impressed that he agreed to let me work from home half-time. Because I was able to telecommute, this job also gave me the freedom to explore my femaleness.

My new boss not only encouraged wonkiness, he required it. Every article I wrote had to start with a long-winded subordinate clause about the theory and practice of postacute care, before it ever told the readers what had actually happened. My coworkers got used to me hopping around the office shouting with excitement about something I'd just discovered on page 900 of the latest *Federal Register*. Every day was like Christmas!

At this time, I also started cross-dressing and fantasizing about being a beautiful, sophisticated woman who understood all about health outcomes and benchmarking. Telecommuting two days a week meant time to shave my legs and torso, put on a lacy bra, panties, and velvety frock from the big Marshalls off I-40, and spend the day gossiping with sources about different interpretations of the Stark physician self-referral laws. Even when I was in the office, my coworkers were tolerant oddballs who didn't hold me to any particular gender standards.

Several years later, I came out to my coworkers as trans/gender queer. There was a flurry of questions, a Southern Seasons food basket, and one of my bosses bought the home office a copy of my radical how-to book for cross-dressers. Since then, though, I haven't brought up my gender with my coworkers again, and I'm still officially male at work. My coworkers are on the East Coast, and I'm on the West Coast, and we hardly ever interact, even over the phone. I asked the most militant trans activist I know whether I should transition at work, and she advised me not to. "You should only transition at work if it's driving you nuts to work as a guy, or if you don't care whether you keep the job," she said. So I decided to stay loosely a boy at work.

Is there any connection between wonkhood and femaleness? I still don't know. I know plenty of male wonks as well as female ones. I do know, however, that wonkitude is a revolutionary stance these days. Our political culture rejects complexity as a sign of wimpiness. Problems should be clear-cut, and a sledgehammer is the only tool you'll ever need.

During the Clinton administration, pundits slammed the president as "feminine," partly because of his empathy, but also partly because of his habit of considering twenty sides to every issue. You could feel the relief among the Washington commentators when a "real man" became president—a "straight shooter" who would never let multiple sources of facts pollute his ideas.

Until the Clinton era, the word "wonk" was an insult—one usually directed at women or girls, according to Nadine Strossen, the current president of the American Civil Liberties Union. Nadine told me that when she was a student, guys would call her and other women "wonks" if they wanted to study instead of going out on dates.

She went to Radcliffe back when Harvard was still all male. Because Radcliffe was tiny compared with Harvard, the women who went there tended to be high-powered. The Harvard guys would complain that "those wonky 'cliffies would rather be wonking out and studying than drinking beer with me," Nadine recalls.

Maybe because of that, "I've always had the association of wonkery being a female-dominated field," Nadine says. In civil liberties and human rights circles, she adds, women predominate except at the top. The leaders of most organizations are still men, but "if you look at the level below that, they're all women."

Nadine believes that women are well suited to be wonks because of their grasp of nuance, but also their meticulous attention to detail. Men are more likely to "wing it" than to stay up all night collecting facts.

In mainstream American culture, taking the long view, looking at the bigger picture, or delving into the details is considered "womanly" behavior when it comes to policy. A "real man" is not supposed to be overly concerned with facts or subtleties. If one is interested in analyzing the wider ramifications of an issue, that person is either a woman or a "girly" man. Small wonder that I associated white-paper mania with femaleness. Yet it still seems that many of the most visible wonks are male. And reams of statistics carry more weight in a baritone. So it's hard to generalize about the gender of wonkery. Perhaps it requires several decades' worth of study.

Fast-forward half a dozen years. I'm legally a woman, with a prescription for female hormones and a driver's license that says F. I've written about nitpicky health policy topics and clinical issues for half a dozen magazines and a bunch of trade publications. I've delved deeply into the research on the pros and cons of inflating a balloon inside your spine. I know the intricate details of HIPAA and BIPA, and the difference between the "doughnut hole" and a cafeteria plan.

These days, I feel as though I have two skills that are worth something: I can figure shit out, and make shit up. I still spend most of my "figuring" time on healthcare stuff, partly because I get paid to do that, but also partly because it's an area where the problems are so complex and there are no right answers. Healthcare is full of trade-offs between cutting costs and improving outcomes, as well as between competing interests.

I'm not sure I could ever be one of the exalted savants of the Medicare Payment Advisory Commission, the elite government commission that chews over statistics and tries to figure out issues such as why an appendectomy costs three times as much in Atlanta as in Nashua, with no difference in outcomes. While I'd love to be among those exalted brains, in reality it's not my scene: Not just because I'm a tranny, but because I'm not a power-suit kind of gal. Big medicine plays with crazy barrels of money, so the real policy fiends tend to be conservative and businesslike. I suspect I'll always be better at interacting with those people over the phone.

I've become much more comfortable with myself as I've developed into a woman with all the bells and whistles. I'm still curious about how the intricate healthcare system works (sometimes), but I don't share my hoards of knowledge in the same "show-offy" way. Instead, I'm working on becoming a serene guardian of this secret language—who can still kick ass when the circumstance requires it.

The new frontier for my wonksploration is blogging and independent publishing. As the publisher of *other* magazine, I've tried to contribute some pieces about big social and political issues facing our society, as well as a ton of essays on queer issues. I blog at othermag.org/blog pretty often, and most of my posts are about some particularly gnarly dilemma facing our society, such as the nature of public space, free expression, and sexual harassment.

The biggest question for me now though is whether I'll be taken seriously as a transgendered wonk in the long term. *What would Nadine do?* I ask myself often as I try to put together a look and attitude that combines both estrogen and encyclopedic knowledge. Already, I'm all woman in 99 percent of my professional interactions. When I go to journalistic networking events and writer soirees, I wear a long dress or a formal blouse with one of my mom's old ankle-length skirts. Nobody in my writer circles ever questions my womanificence for long. I write about clinical issues fairly often for a glossy healthcare magazine, and I always go to lunch with its editors as a woman.

At this point, I doubt I could find another job as a guy. Sometimes I freak out about the U.S. tranny unemployment rate. I'll either have to go all-the-way freelance as a health policy nerd, or find a new day job as a woman.

I'm lucky, in one sense, because the ability to explain the tangled merkin that is the American healthcare system remains pretty rare, and my expertise may be in increasing demand as Baby Boomers age and enroll in Medicare. I'm sometimes shocked by how few people really love immersing themselves in the latest thousand-page federal regulation or Center for Studying Health System Change opus.

My ambition, though, isn't just to keep working as an interpreter of other people's wonkery. One day, I want to make a serious wonkish contribution to the world. In my sweetest dreams, I use my wonky superpowers to advance the causes of feminism and nobody-supremacy. Maybe I can help untangle the mess of childcare problems, inadequate health coverage, and faulty gender assumptions that keep so many women trapped in no-win situations. I have a feeling if anybody solves conundrums like those, it'll be a wonk.

geek,
interrupted

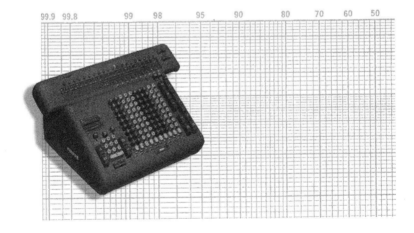

»»»»job security

Kristin Abkemeier

Major in math or science. That way you'll always have a job," my mother told me. I was nine years old, and we were driving back to our suburban Chicago home after a shopping trip to the mall. "English majors are a dime a dozen. You'll have less competition for good jobs if you can handle math."

I was a sensitive, skinny girl with cropped mousy blond hair and plastic granny glasses. As a girl of the 1970s, I was told repeatedly about how wonderful it was that I could do anything I wanted for a career and not be limited to the options of nurse, secretary, or teacher. My mother underscored this message by telling me how her parents hadn't encouraged her in math and science. She wanted me to have the confidence that she lacked in those areas.

I was sorry to hear that English wasn't worth considering, though. Although I was very good at math, I also loved reading stories, everything from *Are You There God? It's Me, Margaret* to The Great Brain series, with its clever boy pranks. I also drew constantly and took countless arts and crafts classes, but my mother made it clear that art was no way to make a living.

Despite all this pressure, I might never have traveled quite so far down the geek road if it had not been for my classmate Jon Frisch, whose mother was friends with mine. My mom and Mrs. Frisch had found each other a few years earlier when Jon was the only kindergartener besides me who could already read. Together they made sure that we got to take reading classes with the first-graders.

Our mothers tried to pass their friendship along to us, but on the only playdate we had, I ended up soaked in water and tears after he invited me to look at a bright ring—and then used it to squirt water right into my eye. My mom made me invite Jon to my sixth birthday party anyway, and he continued to be a tangential part of my life. After my parents moved my brothers and me to local Catholic schools, my mom still kept in touch with Mrs. Frisch. It seemed like each time they talked, I would hear afterward about what clever, advanced project wonder-boy Jon was doing that month.

Then, in the spring of sixth grade, I got sucked into their little competition. It all started when mom and I were in the car, driving the Saturday-morning suburban errand circuit.

"I was talking to Mrs. Frisch, and she said that Jon took the SAT," she said casually. "It's a test normally given to high school seniors, but he took it because there's a special math program that's using the SAT as an entrance exam. Jon scored well enough that he will be taking high-school-level math in the seventh grade next year. I got the information from Mrs. Frisch, and I want you to take the test." My mom's tone implied that this was a settled matter.

My gut tightened like it always did when Jon's name came up. "But why? Is this something I have to study for? You wouldn't make *me* take that class, right?"

My mother reassured me, "No, it's nothing to study for. I just want to see how you do, that's all. You probably won't even qualify, anyway."

I was torn between feeling hurt that she just assumed that Jon was smarter and worried that I might end up in this weird class with extra homework. I sighed and slouched in my seat, knowing that I had no choice. Whatever happened, I did not want to take any extra math class. And especially not with Jon Frisch.

My school gave the test to several of the strongest math students in my class. I was the only one from that group to qualify—just like Jon—scoring just a little better than an average twelfth-grader on the math portion of the SAT. Of course the test wasn't the end of the story. My parents frog-marched me to an information session about the math course a couple of weeks later. On our way in, we spied the Frisches, and I waved a polite hello even though it was their fault I was even at the stupid session.

Mr. Field and Mr. Geiss, the instructors for the program, explained how there would be a two-hour class every Monday and Wednesday evening, and extensive problem sets due each week. If we enrolled, that is. Which, of course, I was not going to do.

"So, how many of you think you'll be joining us?" Mr. Field asked for a show of hands. Mine remained tucked under my armpits. Extra homework? No way.

But my parents picked up the enrollment forms. "We're signing you up. You're not being challenged enough in your math class at school," my mother said. "And I've already talked to Mrs. Frisch about carpooling."

Stuck with more homework and more Jon Frisch, I resorted to denial. On Sunday nights I halfheartedly struggled through the algebra problem sets that I didn't want to do but didn't have the will to refuse to do outright. I was barely treading water, regularly getting one-third of the questions wrong on the problem sets despite my last-minute attempts at siphoning answers out of my dad. On Mondays and Wednesdays I was cooped up in a car with Jon on the drives to and from class. I sat in the back and stared out the window as I heard him guffaw to my father about how a wrong note at band practice was "as flat as a seventh-grade girl's chest." I might have been offended if I'd been able to take Jon seriously.

To my relief, the other kids in the class weren't obnoxious like Jon. The male contingent, numbering twenty or so, was composed of skinny-rubber-band boys wearing aviator glasses with tinted lenses and calculators on their belts, serious Jewish boys in yarmulkes and khaki pants, and shy Asian boys. A geek rainbow, as it were. With my bowl haircut, granny glasses, and, yes, seventh-grade girl's flat chest, I could have fit in as one of the guys myself. I'd already been mistaken for a boy on several occasions when I dressed in slacks and shirts.

I might not have been a beauty, but I did have fashion sense. I scrutinized the half-dozen other girls in the class to see how their outfits stacked up against my nascent preppy style. The girl I envied most wore ornate sweaters with fair-isle yokes, in delicious sherbet colors. I wanted one of her cute tops over all the calculators, Rubik's cubes, and Atari game cartridges in the room put together.

Even though I'd rather have spent my evenings doing just about anything besides studying algebra, I had to admit that it was way cool being inside a high school after hours, racing the other kids down to the cafeteria to buy junk food from the vending machines during lesson breaks. I devoured the candy and took in the algebra via reluctant osmosis while doodling in my notebook and daydreaming. In fact, the math class was becoming my main social outlet. I could talk easily with kids who came from other schools. My regular school had a rigid social hierarchy, and that winter, my clique had dropped me as a friend. We had been far from the popular crowd to begin with, but at least we were still a step above the untouchables, like the girl with the scaly skin or the class goody-goody. And now I was totally uncool, too. I cried and begged them to take me back, but they just didn't want me to hang around them any more. After a couple of recesses hiding at the edge of the playground watching the other boys and girls laughing and flirting, I begged a nun to let me stay inside and help her by counting the Campbell's soup labels she collected to earn discounts on gym equipment.

One Monday night, Mr. Field read the math class an article about the achievement gap between boys and girls in math.

"Society seems to think it's okay if girls don't do as well in math, but that's not what we think," said Mr. Field. "We believe that you can excel equally." Addressing the handful of girls in the class directly, he continued, "So don't let anyone discourage you from pursuing math or science. You can do it!"

I was both shocked and flattered. Though I knew my mother lacked confidence in her capabilities, and that you needed math skills to get a good job, neither of those reasons for studying math had inspired me to give it more attention than any other subject. I had had no idea that girls generally weren't supposed to be as good at math as boys. But if that was society's perception, then by golly, I would carry the torch for feminism on the math front! Forget about my former clique: I had a far more important mission now!

As a modern girl of the '70s, I'd been looking for ways to make my statement for equality. I had fumed inside when my mother admonished me that it wasn't ladylike to sing the hilarious "throw 'im in the toilet till October" verse to "What Do You Do with a Drunken Sailor?" I didn't want to be ladylike; that would set me apart from my brothers, who, like me, understood which gender held the bulk of power in the world. I'd even thought of playing Little League baseball just like my older brother, but that ran aground when I had to admit to myself that I was terrified of a ball being thrown or hit toward me, and I didn't care who won or lost anyway.

I'd been able to keep my head above water when I was putting very little effort into the math class, so I figured I would outright excel if I welcomed the algebra in. I began my problem sets several nights before they were due. Soon I was getting one or two red check marks on my graded homework, rather than twenty or thirty. Once I started paying attention, I also discovered that math had a beauty to it that went far beyond the mundane applications of arithmetic. There were patterns in everything, from Fibonacci numbers appearing in binomial coefficients to the hyperbola of light projected on the wall by a lampshade. I finished the year with one of the top scores on the final exam. I was on my way to scientific and feminist glory.

I felt safe and smug with my girl-geek identity, finally at the top of a hierarchy rather than the bottom. I fit in because I could do the math; my looks and awkwardness didn't matter. I now found a deeper beauty in parabolas, ellipses, and hyperbolas anyway. Even better, a conic section wouldn't change its mind and decide that you weren't cool enough to hang around with the next day—it just was, and wouldn't ever change. Maybe I couldn't get myself voted onto the junior high yearbook staff, despite being the best artist in the class. But I knew how to do a two-column geometry proof.

Now that I completely bought into my mother's idea that math was the key to success, she made it clear that things weren't so simple after all. Like many people outside my math class, my mother had a confused whirl of attitudes about femininity, intelligence, and math. Did Jon's mother ever tell him that it threw off the family dynamic for him to be more mathematically gifted than his older brother? That's what my mother told me: A girl shouldn't best her brother.

Then she would turn around and make the old affirmative action argument that since I was female, I wouldn't have to reach as high a standard to enter male-dominated fields. I also heard, "I thought the women I knew in college who studied computers were kind of weird." Or, "I worry that it's going to be hard for you to date or get married. Men are threatened by very bright women." I had to iron my brothers' shirts because I would need to know how to do my husband's laundry someday—the husband I would probably never have, of course. At least ironing shirts was easier than sorting through the mixed messages.

To avoid conflict I played by the rules and followed directions. For the first three years of high school I loaded up on the academics, focusing on my scientific future with tunnel vision. It wasn't like there was anything else in our sedate suburb to distract me from my studies. I had my escape plan all figured out: If I put in the work, I would get the good grades, and if I got the good grades, I would get into a good college. If I excelled there, I would become a scientist. It was a safe formula—predictable and logical.

But my artistic side started to reassert itself. During the precalculus class I took during freshman year at my all-girls' high school, we had no assigned problem sets; we were supposed to be mature enough to do problems on our own to master the concepts. While Sister Marie lectured about the analysis of polynomial functions, I filled my notebook with sketches of dress designs and overblown hair styles. I read the textbook and aced the quizzes and tests anyway.

One day, without warning, Sister Marie came around to check all of our notebooks. My heart began racing—my notebook was really a sketchbook! I was in trouble for sure. She paged through, looking in vain for evidence of work among my fashion plates. Flashing me a look that conveyed a mix of exasperation and disappointment, she slowly shook her head and with a cluck of the tongue moved on to the next student. As the relief washed over me, I knew I'd escaped the scolding I deserved because I had the highest average in the class. (I felt bad enough for Sister Marie that I did try to pay attention a little more after that.)

My math prowess allowed me to feel exceptional and unique. It was good that I liked being different, because my school didn't expect girls to be as fiercely ambitious in the hard sciences as I was. Until my junior year, girls who wanted to study physics or Advanced Placement chemistry had to carpool over to the boys' high school for first period each day. And we didn't have an actively practicing math team, as my older brother's high school did.

So I kept my geek torch alive under cover of being a well-rounded student. Rather than the math team, the speech and debate team became my blue-chip extracurricular activity. I began high school refusing to wear makeup—I had read how my idol Sally Ride, the first American woman in space, didn't bother with it—but progressed to putting on gobs of blue mascara that flaked into my eyes. It helped me fit in with the other students, plus it made me look more polished in my speech competitions. I also fancied that the eye makeup enhanced a resemblance to Princess Diana. Finally allowed to ditch my glasses for contact lenses after freshman year, I had suddenly discovered that I had blue eyes.

My family's move to Tokyo for my last year of high school broke the patterns I had come to expect. I wouldn't be a senior member of the speech team, sweeping up trophies, nor would I be editor of the school newspaper. Since there were no math classes for me to take—I'd had AP calculus sophomore year, and then statistics, multivariable calculus, and differential equations at a junior college—I went for breadth instead. I signed up for an advanced studio art class at my new international school.

I had been sketching in the margins of my notebooks all along, and had done well in the introductory art class that I'd slotted into my academically intensive schedule the previous year. So I figured I'd both validate my talent and get an easy A. It was just art, after all. And art certainly wasn't rocket science.

Mrs. Imadegawa, the art teacher, was a British woman who had married a local man and settled in Japan. From the start I was fascinated by her spontaneity and dramatic flair and flummoxed by her pedagogical approach. The very first exercise she gave me was to draw something without even looking at the page as the pencil moved on it. I wondered, how the hell was that exercise going to produce anything worth looking at? My blind contour drawings looked gnarly—lines missing each other where they were supposed to intersect, distortions galore—and yet Mrs. Imadegawa praised them for how well observed they were. I thanked her and scratched my head.

About a month into the class, she checked up on how I was settling in so far. I'd been working on my sketchbook, doing the homework assignments, and trying out the airbrush at her suggestion.

"Well, I've been practicing modeling cubes and spheres with the airbrush, but I'm getting kind of tired of that," I said.

"Why not do a painting, then?" she said.

"But what of? I've been waiting for you to tell me what I should work on," I said, annoyance creeping into my voice. I didn't know what I should be doing, or even what I wanted to do, really. That kind of carte blanche was new to me—in all my previous art classes, everyone had worked on the same project. In Mrs. Imadegawa's class, the other girls seemed to be finishing up projects continued from the previous year, and I'd been wondering when I'd be getting my assignment.

"Oh, no," Mrs. Imadegawa shook her head slowly. "This is an advanced studio class, so at this level students are expected to be self-directed. I've been worried about you, because you've been doing a bit of this and then a bit of that. Hmm." She thought a moment. "Would it be possible for you to switch your schedule to come in with the eleventh-graders?"

Was I, the brainy girl, flunking art already? "No, I can't do that, because it would conflict with AP biology," I said in deliberate syllables. Anger flared inside me even as I teared up in my frustration. I finally protested, "I guess I just don't get it. What we've been doing for homework doesn't even look like art. How am I supposed to know what to paint?" I said, my voice growing unsteady.

Mrs. Imadegawa listened to my protests, nodding gently, and then put her hand on my elbow. "Yes, I hear your frustration. How about we do this, then. Let's start you gridding off a piece of paper and painting value scales going from white to black and color complements in acrylic. All the other girls did this in my earlier class. This will be a good foundation, and then we'll find an appropriate project." And she handed me a copy of a color theory book to guide me.

It felt like being sent back to kindergarten, and in a subject that didn't even rate in the math and science hierarchy. But during the field trips to galleries that we took on Friday afternoons, I was also beginning to learn that art was more than just decoration, which had been its sole purpose in my former suburb. Art was also about ideas. I did my color theory regimen because I wanted to show Mrs. Imadegawa that I could master her way of thinking. Also, I wanted to have the kind of fun she was having by seeing creative possibilities in what looked like mistakes to me.

I began a painting based on a photograph from the senior class trip to western Japan. I rendered my landscape of a wall, trees, and sky reflecting into a river with an observant eye, but of course Mrs. Imadegawa's favorite part was the dirt on the riverbank. That was the one place where I had winged it, dabbing on the colors impressionistically like a dirty Monet, no obvious shapes to guide me to a predictable outcome. Mrs. Imadegawa seemed to like seeing me pushed outside my comfort zone. My visual talent began to reveal itself once I learned to take these chances.

But the next year I went to college and got back to my other life, the real one where I did math and science. My first week at Princeton, I discovered that I hadn't known what being a mathematician was really about. When I paged through the textbook for the theoretical linear algebra class, my heart began racing in dread. The text was terse and dense, filled with intimidating Greek letters. Even the very first exercises scared me. They were all proofs that I hadn't the foggiest idea how to begin. How was I going to jump in and do math at this level after my year away from thinking about numbers? I hadn't particularly missed math among the sights, flavors, and experiences I'd explored abroad. For the first week of the term, I tried in vain to understand the lecturer. Then I dropped down to a more applications-oriented version of the class, where I could polish off the problem sets with the minimum of effort to which I had been accustomed. Maybe that was what I had really liked best about math all along?

I flirted briefly with majoring in architecture as a logical blend of art and science. (I also flirted, not so briefly, with the math major who lived next door.) But the subjective aspects of architecture frightened me. Analyzing things felt more natural, and I liked the certainty of knowing I'd nailed it when I turned in a problem set. Also I'd heard that architecture was a difficult career path. But ultimately, I think I still believed in the geek hierarchy that placed math at the top and physics just below it. Why would I want to do anything less than the most challenging thing I believed I could do? Plus, I genuinely did want to understand how the world worked at the fundamental physical level. So I studied math as applied to real-world phenomena through engineering physics.

I labored through countless problem sets and exams, earning As in my physics and engineering courses through sheer determination, working summer jobs at IBM's research laboratories, and winning fellowships for graduate school. I took the occasional art history or studio art elective along the way, but though these gave me pleasure, I knew that expressing myself artistically was just a self-indulgence. Nobody was asking for my drawings or writings, but my laboratory research could make a difference in the world.

After graduation I worked in a lab at the University of Cambridge for a year, where I learned some physics in between falling for various practical jokes as the clueless American and honing a dry wit (my lab felt like a Noel Coward play with physics thrown in). It was a delightful break from the rigors of college. Intense people were described as "keen" there, and flattery wasn't always intended. In my group it was frowned upon to insist on talking shop over lunch or to regularly skip afternoon tea in favor of getting data at the lab bench. We went to see the group's postdoc perform in a Shakespeare play—my lab mates even reread the play before going—and I sketched in my free time once again. And on my long spring break I traveled all over Europe, making pilgrimages to museums, palaces, and cathedrals that I had learned about in those electives. Maybe I wasn't doing the most cutting-edge research, and my boyfriend was back in Chicago, but my life felt satisfyingly full.

Then, just like five years before, I was back in America and my "real" life of going to graduate school to become a physicist. I was the only woman in my entering class, but as in my undergraduate classes, I joined a study group of friendly guys with whom I'd tip back beers after finishing work on the quantum mechanics problem set each week. Buoyed by passing the notorious three-day-long candidacy exam on my first try, I promptly got to work on a new professor's ambitious project to build a magnetic force microscope (MFM) to study the motion of magnetic flux vortices on the surface of high-temperature superconductors. The phenomenon of super-conductivity excited physicists in the late '80s and early '90s and seemed a lot sexier to me than the semiconductors I'd been studying. Hot results about vortex dynamics could be the basis for a real science career.

Scanning tunneling microscopes (STMs) were all the rage, whether for detecting magnetism, probing quantum dots, or studying the surface properties of materials. The plan was to adapt an STM into an MFM because no such thing as an MFM existed yet. Since an MFM also had to perform at low temperatures and under magnetic fields, no commercial STM would work for our purposes. So my adviser bought the driver software for an STM, planning for me to build the other key part of the MFM, the actual coarse approach mechanism that brought the atomic-scale probe near the surface of the specimen. Supremely self-confident and dreaming big, I began researching different mechanisms and building them. When the first one didn't work immediately, that was fine—I tweaked it and tested it until I definitively established that it didn't work. Then I researched and went on to the next promising design.

When I needed to, I'd ask for advice from my adviser or from Ben, the emerging star student in the lab a year ahead of me. Ben had been a lifelong tinkerer. Jury-rigging a quick fix was an afterthought to a guy who spent his weekends grinding his own telescope lenses for the astronomy club. He was only too eager to offer advice on my experiment, and it was a balancing act to decide when to keep him out and muddle through myself so I could learn. I was scrupulously trying to avoid being perceived as the helpless woman, even though many male graduate students were as new to whipping up electronics as I was.

In the meantime, another student from my class named Rich had joined the project. Rich hadn't been part of the boisterous group I'd done problem sets with over the previous year; I didn't have much of a read on him. He seemed all right though, quiet and serious. Our adviser assigned him the job of adapting the software to control the custom-built mechanism that

I was building. Since the code was more under control, Rich finished his task while I was still trying to build a coarse approach mechanism that would actually move. That's when I found out he was building a coarse approach too, to test a different design. I was quite surprised—we'd never discussed this with our adviser.

Parallel testing may have been a good thing for the project, but I didn't like being the last one to find out it was happening. Then, burned-out after a spring and summer of machining, testing, tweaking, lather, rinse, repeat, I took a driving vacation with my husband (that same math major I'd flirted with years before) out west for three weeks.

When I came back, I dropped by my adviser's office. "Hey, I'm back! How have things been?" I said.

"It's been great, actually. Rich, Ben, and I managed to put a few tweaks onto a new idea for a mechanism that looks like it's going to work. It's a good, creative design—we all need to talk about what to do next," he said with his usual enthusiasm.

On one hand, I was glad for any promising development on the coarse approach front. I knew that I shouldn't be territorial, and that work shouldn't be put on hold just because I was away. But I also felt left out.

I had been asking for advice all along, taking care to have exhausted all the good ideas I had first, trying not to bother my adviser more than necessary, since I'd seen him buried under grant proposals. And there had been that time I'd asked him one simple question about a test I was setting up, and he'd come down and completely taken over, much to my distress. I was trying to be considerate of his time as a good team player—but was that the wrong tack? The guys seemed to have had a lot more fun together than I had been having alone.

The small success that my adviser, Rich, and Ben enjoyed in my absence brought to the surface the fear that what I was doing wasn't good enough, that I wasn't working hard enough. And maybe I wasn't. I had a husband, and I wanted to be able to read books and create art in my spare time. For my own sanity I had begun to pace myself on this project that had been just one frustration after another, even as Rich dropped hints about how a friend of his working on a similar quest in another lab was building and testing designs much faster. "Keen" was a put-down in Cambridge; at Chicago, keen was what you had to be just to survive. I began to ask whether perhaps I had liked the identity of being that impressive oddity, a female physicist, more than I enjoyed the laboratory grind. And just as quickly I put that out of mind.

After another few months of meager progress and growing animosity, Rich bailed out of the project. I only heard about it through the grapevine afterward. My adviser encouraged me to go it alone for a couple more months until I, too, decided that I wanted to stop banging my head against the wall for a change. And then I proceeded to beat myself up for being a quitter, even though I'd been the person who had stuck it out longer.

I turned to a more expedient project on semiconductors that had the practical advantage of generating enough data for a dissertation. I compared my pair of nonearthshaking published papers against the teeming masses published by people in postdoc limbo, and I calculated that I would have to make a Major Discovery pretty darn quick if I was to have any chance of making it to assistant professor someday. And that probably wasn't going to happen, since just finishing my PhD had used up every bit of my capacity for stubborn perseverance and deferred gratification. I decided to leave physics on my own terms sooner rather than later.

I moved to San Francisco and did a stint as an information technology software developer during the dot-com boom. Programming got me through the initial phase of my deprogramming from the cult of physics. Now that I'd abandoned a career that had been a core part of my identity for fifteen years, I began to question other notions I'd long held. Just because I'd shown an aptitude for math once upon a time, was I doomed to be manipulating computer code forever? I had internalized my mother's message: "Major in math, major in science, that way you'll always have a job." But what job did I want? What life did I want?

On my thirtieth birthday I started my first class at a local art academy. It wasn't as prestigious as the other universities I'd been at, and studying art pretty much went against everything I'd believed in for most of the previous twenty years. Just a few months before, my mother had told me, "You can paint all you want when you retire." I could do another thirty-five years of secure work I had no passion for, or I could develop the creative talents that I'd relegated to the sidelines. I knew that if I didn't try something new, I would regret it.

In the classroom, our instructor set up for the first drawing demonstration by placing white geometric forms on the stand—a cube, a cylinder, a sphere—and positioning the light to create dramatic shadows around them. We gathered around her as she sat at a drawing bench with her large pad of paper and charcoal, demonstrating how to depict form by rendering the different shades of gray on the facets of the cube.

As I sat down and began my own drawing, I smiled. I'd seen these shapes before in many physics problems I'd solved, their symmetries representing repeating cells or wires or atomic nuclei. But that day, those shapes were the building blocks of my new life as an artist.

»»»» {women} ∩ {mathematics} = {me, at least}

Elisabeth Severson

It happened the spring of my freshman year in high school. I was focused on the final for my geometry class—and when I say focused, I really mean it. I wasn't aware of anything around me: the beautiful spring day outside, the approach of summer, the other students sighing or writing or tapping pencils. I wasn't even aware of my own sighing or writing or pencil tapping. To me, there was nothing but the math. I dove in and didn't surface until I came, with a jolt, to the end of the test. I put down my pencil, breathing hard. My heart beat like I'd been running, or rushing to the end of a really exciting book. As we left the classroom, I turned to my friend, a sophomore in the same class, and held out my hand for her to see. It was shaking.

"Are you okay?" she asked, a bit worried.

"I'm great! What did you think about problem four? It was . . . oh my god, I think I have an adrenaline rush!"

Her expression shifted to confusion and distaste. "You what?"

I was confused too. "I think . . . it was fun."

Until that moment, I'd hated math. It's pretty hard to believe now, and I tend to present my path to math geekiness as clear and predictable. But it wasn't. It came out of nowhere and hit me upside the head. I resisted it for quite a while. I mean, no one likes math. And it's only gotten clearer to me over the years just how true that is. It's acceptable to say you hate math. The people who say, "Actually, I always thought it was rather neat. Challenging and all," are the ones who get the funny looks. I'd always been good at math, but until ninth grade it was just this thing that I could do in spite of having no interest in it.

Every time I talked about how much I didn't like math, my mother sighed and tried to explain that what I was doing wasn't math. "It's arithmetic. And yes, arithmetic is boring. I would never argue with that; I had to learn long division twice because I changed schools in fourth grade, and if you think it was bad once, the second time is even worse. But mathematics, that's different. Mathematics is logic and puzzles and . . ." Usually by then I'd stopped listening to her. Math was that boring stuff that we did in school, solving the same problems over and over, and I wanted nothing to do with it.

I tried to fight the love of math for a couple years, but the teachers at my school were too good, and the subject was too intriguing. Scheduling vagaries meant I wound up taking three math courses my junior year instead of the required two. One of them was an incredible course titled Infinity. It was like a taste of all the really cool stuff you learn in college, leading up to learning about infinities. The day we learned that there was more than one was a revelation to me. I came home and spent dinnertime telling my parents how amazing mathematics was. My father was puzzled but happy for me. My mother—the computer programmer—was quietly thrilled.

I spent the rest of the year sitting at a table of boys, my nerdy friends, in a mostly male class. I was too caught up in the excitement of what I was learning to think much about that fact. I'd found myself in a similar situation when I was younger: As a middle-school nerd, I'd signed up for a science fiction and fantasy elective. Not long before class schedules were given out, my teacher came up to me (in math class) and said, "Elisabeth, I just wanted to let you know, you're the only girl who signed up for the science fiction class. If you want to switch, we understand." I was startled and a little nervous, but before I could say a knee-jerk "okay," everything my parents had ever said about gender inequity flashed through my mind. I looked her in the eye and firmly, like the feminist I was raised to be, said, "No, thank you. I'd still like to take the class." When I got home that night, my mother told me the same thing had happened to her when she was younger. Her teachers had encouraged her to drop senior calculus, and she'd refused too.

I encountered calculus myself the next year. The first half of the two-part course was derivatives, which involved learning a bunch of rules and applying them. This reminded me uncomfortably of arithmetic, so I didn't enjoy the class much. I do remember learning how to differentiate exponential functions: I walked up to the teacher afterward, and said, "So, if the graph of 2x and its derivative looks like that," and pointed to the graph he'd drawn on the board, where 2x lay above its derivative, "and the graph of 3x and its derivative look like that," pointing to a second graph, of 3x below its derivative, "then . . ." I looked at him for a hint that I was on the right track and wasn't making a fool of myself. He didn't say anything, but his expression seemed encouraging. "Then that means that somewhere in the middle, between two and three, there must be an exponential function whose derivative is itself." I paused again and looked at the board. It came to me in a rush, and I wondered how I could have been so slow. "It's e! Of course, because the derivative of an exponential ax is ln(a) times ax, and ln(e) is one. So the derivative of ex is itself."

My teacher had lost interest. "That's right." He turned to erase the board. I stood there a moment longer, then left. That was the high point of differentiation, and I was pretty sure it would be the high point of calculus—until I discovered integration.

The cool thing about integration is that it's intuitive. I remember vividly the first time I integrated. We'd been slogging through summations, maybe on the theory that if we did enough of them, we'd come to appreciate integration as the simplifying marvel that it is. Or maybe writers of calculus textbooks just like to torture people. Either way, I could see what was coming for weeks before we actually got there, and I wanted it now. At last, our teacher wrote an integral up on the board. He explained that the sign for integration looked like a smoothed-out summation symbol and gave us a simple example, the integral of x2.

"Integration is sometimes called antidifferentiation, because to find an integral you figure out what you would differentiate to give you that expression. Now, does anyone want to try this one?"

I looked at it and raised my hand. The teacher looked a little surprised, as if he hadn't thought anyone would volunteer. I shifted in my seat and looked around nervously.

"Well, it would be x^3, except that then you'd need to get rid of the three out in front, so it would be $\frac{1}{3}x^3$."

Everyone stared at me, including the teacher. Then he recovered, and said, "Well, some people can do integrals just by looking at them, like Elisabeth. For everyone else, there are techniques you can learn to see what might work best for a problem like this." He went on to explain some of the simplest rules of integration. I leaned back in my seat, heart beating fast and hands trembling slightly, the adrenaline from speaking up and the exhilaration of understanding racing through my body.

For the rest of the course, I skated ahead of the class pretty much all the time. I did the homework quickly and with the same excitement I felt the first time I integrated. But the class itself frustrated me. It split into two groups of people: the ones who understood everything but didn't bother to do any of the work, and the ones who did all the work but had a hard time understanding the material. You could also label those groups another way, for the most part: the boys and the girls.

We were supposed to spend the first part of class going over homework from the night before, but no one ever finished the homework. Except me. So the beginning of class stretched into the middle of class, then into the end of class, as the boys goofed off loudly and finished up the work they hadn't done the night before, and the girls quietly toiled. Instead of learning something new, I ended up helping the girl at my table, whoever she was that time around, and getting frustrated with the inexplicable but unmistakable gender split.

For the last part of the course, I was at a table with two people who epitomized the trend. Steven was smart and extremely good at math, and I think he went on to a free ride at UCLA. He also never did his homework. Instead, he'd bring in the proof he worked out the night before. "That's great. But the homework?" I asked. Nope. He breezed through it while I worked with Stephanie, whom I hadn't known well or particularly liked before, but who turned out to be funny and nice. Calculus, however, was not her strong point. I could tell she knocked herself out on the assignments but had a hard time understanding them. Though she understood the homework by the time class was over, it took her longer and cost her more effort than it did most people. The result was that while she was perfectly capable of getting the work done, she tended to feel overwhelmed and slow. She planned on retaking calculus when she got to college.

Some good things came out of that experience. Explaining integration to my classmates probably gave me a head start when I got a job tutoring calculus in college. And Stephanie turned out to be fun to hang out with. The class as a whole, though, confronted me with fabulous mathematics and frustrating dynamics. I realized for the first time that all those statistics about women and mathematics could apply to me.

In college, I wasn't the smartest in the class anymore. I went to Oberlin College, a small liberal arts school in northern Ohio where everyone had been among the smartest in their high schools. I didn't go there for the wonderful mathematics faculty, but for the creative writing department. In the fourth grade, during my first-ever poetry class, I'd decided that I was going to be a writer when I grew up. That intention hadn't changed in the past eight years, so I expected to double-major in creative writing and physics, figuring I could be a starving poet and make my living as a starving theoretical physicist. So I enrolled in Physics 110, the first course for physics majors, and its corequisite, Calculus 2. I was sure it would be only a matter of time before I was learning about quantum mechanics and general relativity.

Physics still fascinates me today. I love reading books about physicists and the most up-to-date discoveries, and I explain articles about black holes in *The New York Times* science section to my father with great enthusiasm. But I got bored in every physics class I took in college. It was all so concrete. The numbers were so messy. And there were so many nitty-gritty details that I just didn't care about. I wanted the big ideas, not these word problems about friction. I hate word problems.

Calculus, on the other hand, was the most fun I'd had since . . . well, calculus in high school. Here, the numbers weren't messy—there were hardly numbers at all! The math was getting more complicated, so I had to work harder, but the joy I found was the same. The professor radiated enthusiasm and gave dramatic lectures that ended with cliffhangers. I couldn't wait to come back the next day. I could no longer do the homework in half an hour with hardly any effort, but that just made it more satisfying when I got the answers. At the end of the semester, I didn't sign up for the next course in physics. Instead, I signed up for Discrete Mathematics, an introductory logic and set theory course that was a prerequisite for nearly everything the math department offered. Although I didn't officially declare it until the end of my sophomore year, I was a math major.

I'm not a social misfit, but I don't always make friends quickly, nor am I good at getting forms in before their deadlines. So I didn't manage to get a roommate I knew and liked or a single room for housing my sophomore year. Instead, I found myself living in a women's collective with a roommate I'd never met. I was nervous at first, but it turned out to be a wonderful place to live. It also provided a balance to my academic life, since during that year I noticed that the further into the math curriculum I went, the fewer women were in my classes. I was naive in many ways, but I knew about the gender gap in the sciences. I knew girls tended to vanish from math classes. I'd just never seen it happen before, and I couldn't figure out what was going on. I couldn't feel any pressure, but the numbers kept dwindling. I worked on problem sets and projects with Anna and Danielle, two of the remaining few, but most of the time I was surrounded by guys.

So it was nice, though bizarre, to return home, where men (bio-boys, since the collective instituted a trans-inclusive policy that year) weren't allowed in some of the common areas. Occasionally I would see some-one's friend or boyfriend in the hallway, but for the most part I was sur-rounded by women. In an average day, I'd spend several hours working on a problem set with Anna and five or so guys and attend classes with three women and fourteen or fifteen men, then return to stay up late in the collective's lounge, talking about classes and reading *Cosmo* (for both fun and feminist criticism) with a bunch of women.

I also found myself defending each group of people to the other. One day in early fall, I happened to walk home in the same direction as one of the guys in my multivariable calculus class. We chatted amiably, but when I stopped in front of the women's collective, he couldn't let me go without having his say.

"Isn't that the dorm where men aren't allowed in? How can you sup-port that? I mean, doesn't it just separate people more? It's sexist. You'd say men-only space isn't okay; how is this different?"

I sputtered, not sure what to say, but certain he was wrong. I hadn't even chosen to live there, and wasn't sure I wanted to spend time in women-only space, but at the same time, I knew there was something wrong with his logic. I just couldn't explain what it was.

At the same time, when I worked on my homework in the lounge area of the dorm, I got a lot of "What's that? It looks hard. And weird." My dorm mates only responded with enthusiasm to my math homework when I brought down a dodecahedron I'd made as part of a group theory exam. Some women were jealous that I got to make models as part of my test. Everyone was much more enthusiastic about helping me with my creative writing classes. I regularly worked on poems and short stories in the lounge, soliciting feedback and inspiration. The short play I wrote for my introductory workshop took place in the dorm, with characters blatantly based on several of the residents. But I learned to keep math homework to myself.

Only one student living in the collective understood my ever-increasing geekiness. I met Meagan through a sociology course we were both taking; we decided to share books to save money, even though we didn't know each other well. The first night there was reading assigned, we found a quiet room so we could concentrate, since the upstairs lounge was a hotbed of dyke drama. I think I got through about five pages. We wound up talking for several hours instead. Meagan was a transfer student majoring in chemistry who could also talk about gender and sexuality in a way that the math geeks I hung out with couldn't (or at least didn't). She understood the lure of logic and science instead of dismissing them as irrelevant, as the other residents tended to. We bonded almost instantaneously. She was the first person I'd met who was as excited by an organic chemistry textbook as the latest essay by Carol Queen. She understood not only my pontificating about queer theory, but also my enthusiasm for string theory, and she thought calculus was pretty neat too.

I realized junior year that I'd made a big mistake. Maybe several big mistakes. The latest one wasn't really my fault: My schedule worked out so that the assignments for my advanced calculus class and my fiction-writing workshop were both due on Wednesdays. So each week, I started the problem set for advanced calculus over the weekend, really getting into it on Monday. I worked hard with Anna for most of Tuesday, giggling about epsilon and delta and brainstorming proof ideas, then finished it up that night. On Wednesday morning, I went to class and turned it in. I then spent Wednesday afternoon frantically writing something, anything, to bring to the workshop Wednesday night, but most of the things I wrote weren't that good. The comments I got back on my stories tended to be harsher than I could take. Even though I tried to start writing earlier every week, the problem sets sucked me in. Advanced calculus challenged me like crazy, and I really needed the eight or so hours I put into each homework assignment. I had started out taking creative writing because it was what I was going to do with my life and taking math because it was fun. But math was winning my time, no matter how much I thought I should be working on the stories. I made my final decision when I tried to pick classes for the next semester. Because I hadn't taken any creative writing classes my freshman year, based on some bad advice from my adviser and the popularity of the department, I'd have to take two workshops the next semester to finish the major. But I also had to take two upper-level math courses that same semester to finish my math major. I was all set to sign up for the four upper-level courses, each of which would require my undivided attention, when I showed my plan to Meagan. She looked at me for a long moment, then said, "Are you crazy?" I was miserable taking just one workshop and one upper-level math course. I couldn't take two of each. I'd burn out.

The last piece I wrote for the creative writing department was "Curves in Three-Space and Patterns of Mind: A Proof in Six Parts." I never picked up my graded final portfolio.

$$\infty$$

The math department had two concentrations, pure and applied, and you decided between them when you declared your major. For me there was no question; if I'd wanted applications, I'd have been a physics major. Because I avoided applied courses as much as possible, I didn't interact with too many applied math majors. My senior year, though, I tutored calculus in the same room as a statistics tutor who double-majored in applied math and classics, mostly ancient Greek. She told me that the gender split on the applied side was about fifty-fifty.

"Really?" I asked her, astonished. "Because in pure math, it's almost all white boys."

"Yup. There's more racial diversity too. Maybe even more than the school as a whole, but I'm not sure; I've never counted or anything."

"Never counted? And you call yourself a statistics tutor. Wow. It's almost impossible not to count in my classes. It's just too glaringly obvious."

She nodded sympathetically. "I wonder if maybe it's a matter of privilege. The more privileged students, the white boys, feel like they can afford to study something almost completely useless."

"Oh, because ancient Greek is going to be so handy one of these days!" I couldn't argue with her about the usefulness of pure mathematics. After all, the lack of applications was one of the reasons I loved pure math so much. Her theory sounded reasonable, but I had two problems with it. First, if social privilege was the reason people felt free to avoid real-world applications, there would be a lot fewer English and history and classics majors who were women or people of color (or both). Second, I had no idea what could be done—what I could do—to change it.

One of my favorite math professors, a brilliant woman who taught me group theory and differential geometry and led a monthlong win- ter- term class on math in popular culture, once spoke dismissively about the movement in the 1970s that argued that the language of math was inherently antiwomen. I had to agree with her, both because I and many other women have no trouble learning math, and because the idea of a subtle gender bias in things like trigonometry sounded too much like a conspiracy theory. At the same time, I'm also suspicious of people who argue that the study of math is completely gender neu- tral, so the lack of women, people of color, and queer people is due to an inherent difference in thought patterns or brain structure. Math itself, I believe, is gender neutral. I'm an unapologetic Platonist; math comes from outside us and is not a human construct. It is part of the universe, and we're discovering it. There are too many applications, too many surprises, and too many connections for it not to be. That said, humans are still shaping the study of mathematics, and humans have been socialized with certain behaviors and ideas about things like gen- der. So while math itself may be free of gender bias, the way we practice it is not. It's harder to see now, and people may not know they're doing it, but it's still there.

During the math and popular culture class, I read *Women in Math- ematics* by Claudia Henrion, which debunked some of the myths about math that keep women from succeeding in it. That book fired me up, and I'd fallen in love with my topology class. So I decided to apply to graduate school. Even though I'd considered grad school before, I had never said so to anyone. Maybe that's why my professors didn't say much when I asked them for school recommendations. I wasn't sure if I was asking the wrong questions, or the right questions in the wrong way, or if my ques- tions were fine and my professors were having trouble. After I met with a few professors and got nowhere, I stopped talking to them.

Meagan was applying to grad school in chemistry at the same time, and I couldn't help comparing her experience with mine. It seemed like she knew which schools were good, and what she needed to do, and how to write her essay. She was getting a lot of that information from her research supervisors and academic adviser. A woman visiting professor, who'd only recently finished her own PhD, also encouraged Meagan. She read Meagan's personal statement and gave her advice about things like visits to schools and ways to determine whether a school would be a good fit. I, on the other hand, applied to a hodge-podge of schools whose unifying feature was that they were almost all on the West Coast, where I wanted to live. I took the GRE, which went well, and the math subject test, which did not; wrote my essays; and mailed my applications. I listened as other students, male students, talked about the schools they applied to and the people they wanted to work with and the letters they received. None of the female students in the department seemed to be talking about applying at all. I waited, studying chaos theory and knot theory, with no idea what I would do if I didn't go to graduate school. I had come to love math, and having given up my dream of writing, I clung to mathematics. I wanted to fight against the attrition of women in the sciences by being one. Most of all, I couldn't imagine giving up the way the world fell away as I worked on a problem, and the thrill of solving it.

I cried the day the first rejection letter arrived.

I thought about ending the story there. For quite a while, it felt like the end. I didn't go to graduate school, I'm not doing math, and I'm not the only one. Danielle, my differential geometry buddy, who by then was Daniel, dropped out of the math program and majored in art. I'd had hopes for my friend Anna, who was being mysterious about her postcollege plans. She loved math even more than I did, was always looking ahead to the next thing to learn, and came up with some incredibly creative ways to solve problems. I found out late in the year that she was going to give up the pure math she loved and go to school to learn how to be an actuary, a career that entails a lot of yucky applied math and no proofs at all.

As for me, I work in a law firm, possibly the furthest from math I could go. When I first started there, it seemed like everyone had to ask where I had gone to college, and—the logical extension of that question—what

I had studied. Each time, I said, as offhandedly as I could, "Math." Each time, the person who'd asked me leaned away from me a bit and said, "Oh, really, math? I hated math. You must be really smart!" And each time, I smiled a tight little smile like I didn't know what to say and thought, *Not smart enough.*

Then one day, I was chatting with one of my coworkers about her son, who was studying to be an engineer. She said something about how he enjoyed the math he was learning because it was useful. Practical. Full of real-world applications.

"But you can't know what math will be useful or practical," I said. "Not when you're developing it or learning it. Often it's not until decades after a field of mathematics is developed that is has any applications at all. Take knot theory. Fifty years ago it was ridiculed because it had no practical purpose. Mathematicians who studied knot theory did so in their spare time, and even then they were made fun of, because it was just fiddling with bits of string. Theoretical bits of string, at that."

She had the strangest expression on her face. It was like she was trying really hard to be interested, and maybe almost caught a glimmer of what I was getting at, but it was also a little panicked, like she was evaluating escape options. I went on.

"But then, in the last five or ten years, other scientists have discovered all kinds of applications for it. In chemistry, you can have a long chain of protein that gets all tangled up. Then you can switch out a piece of the tangle—that's a technical term, actually, tangle—and you get a new knot, and knot theory helps figure out what the original knot was. I don't remember why that's useful, though, because that's not the point. You study math to learn more and understand more and because it's beautiful and exciting and fun, not because it's useful."

I stopped abruptly. She was still giving me a look—worried and confused, but also curious and grateful that I'd finally shut my mouth.

That's when I realized: It doesn't matter what I'm doing for my paycheck, or what my title is, or any of the other easy labels that come from the kind of questions people ask at cocktail parties or in other awkward social situations. I'm still a geek because I can put that look of panic on someone's face. I'm a geek because I can make a person think, *My God, she's never going to stop talking, is she?* I'm a geek because I don't care. I love math too much to let it slip by, unnoticed or maligned. It doesn't matter that I'm not doing problem sets every week or that I can't quite bring myself to do random problems from my Basic Topology or Advanced Calculus books for fun (though I've thought about it.) I'll always be a math geek because I'll always be proud of what I've learned and excited to learn more, and I'll always want to share that pride and excitement with anyone who'll stand still long enough to listen.

»»»»geek, interrupted

Jenn Shreve

If it took me nearly two decades to finally discover my passion for science and technology, it was because, up until then, I had only the vaguest idea of what these things really were.

In the fundamentalist Christian schools I attended growing up, they force-fed us not the watered-down "Intelligent Design" version of science education, but the rich, meaty Biblical variety, complete with side dishes on why evolutionists were a bunch of liars and their science full of phony baloney. It was a confusing state of affairs. One day, in accordance with state guidelines, we'd be taught the scientific method: Observe, hypothesize, predict, experiment. The next, we were being told that famous scientists like Albert Einstein had used that very method to further Satan's agenda. Science, we learned, required skepticism and critical thinking. In Bible class, however, we were informed that questioning God's ways was moral rebellion. In case you were a doubting Thomas, my early teachers supplied plenty of scientific-sounding arguments for why carbon dating and Darwin were shams. God created earth with the *appearance* of age! Duh.

The science I'd encountered had barely been science by all. No wonder it often left a strange taste in my mouth. Technology hadn't fared much better. It was viewed by many of my teachers and church leaders as the modern equivalent of witchcraft. Mess around too much with those computers, and you might wind up with some evil voodoo in your soul. ATM cards weren't just a convenient way to get money out of the bank. They harbored the underlying technology that would soon facilitate the dreaded Mark of the Beast! Select "Quick Cash" and you might as well be casting your vote for the antichrist, or so the thinking went. But when technology came to the rescue in the form of medicine or a satellite channel devoted entirely to the gospel, those around me would call it a miracle, as though God had the hottest R&D outfit in all Silicon Valley.

Mixed signals when it came to science and technology were beside the point, however, because I was a girl. Thanks to feminism, women of my mother's generation were indeed becoming astronauts, computer scientists, surgeons, engineers, architects. But as a young Missionette (a Christian alternative to the Girl Scouts), I completed detailed workbooks on proper posture and the polite way to serve dinner. Lessons from the Bible emphasized service, not success. The message was clear: Christian women were destined to serve God and husband and to bear children and raise them full-time. I had no reason to doubt it. The women who lived in the California agricultural town where I grew up were moms, housecleaners, baby sitters, secretaries, or possibly teachers. They were really into their vacuum cleaners and dried flower arrangements. They were never physicists, doctors, or even farmers.

In spite of all this, my inner geek managed to shine through in small ways. If the consistently high test scores in science and math weren't obvious enough, my addiction to *Pac-Man, Moon Patrol, Centipede, Space Invaders,* and the early, text-based version of *Oregon Trail,* where you had to type "bang!" as quickly as possible or get eaten by a bear, were dead giveaways. There was also my preternatural ability to navigate the awkward user interfaces of our 1980s-era consumer electronics without ever needing to RTFM, the blue-ribbon science fair project in seventh grade, the award in high school chemistry. When it came time to dissect the frog in sophomore-year biology, I was the first in line. Given the opportunity to do the same to a small black cat in college, I bought a scalpel and enrolled in anatomy. I remember feeling great satisfaction in knowing that the answers to my algebra and precalculus questions were correct. I caught glimpses of beauty in the steps I had taken to arrive at them. I took to computers and the Internet like a hen to its nest, clucking my tongue at the old fogies who couldn't grasp the fundamentals of Pine, Usenet, and HTML.

Yet, if you were to ask me what I thought of math or science, or whether I was interested in becoming an engineer, a computer scientist, or a doctor, the answer all the way through college and into my first job would have been a slightly exasperated no. Eager to please, I had cast my lot with the humanities, which provided my best chance of becoming what every good Christian girl dreamed of—a pastor's wife. Instead of going to Space Camp in Huntsville, Alabama, I attended a *Fame*-like academy several summers in a row. Starting at the age of eleven, I spent weeknights at rehearsals for plays. In private lessons I learned voice, musical theory, piano, ballet, jazz, tap, stage fencing, and mime. To everyone's surprise, I scored higher in math than verbal on my SATs, but nobody looked askance when I decided to pursue a degree in literature and a career in writing. I completed the minimal science and math requirements as quickly as I could and didn't look back.

Except, of course, I did.

∞

It was the early '90s. I was nineteen years old, in my second year of college, unhappily married, and rapidly losing my faith. The evidence contradicting everything I'd been taught and threatened with hell for not believing was substantial and growing with every "secular" college course I took. Psychology explained phenomena like speaking in tongues and being "slain in the spirit" better than any of my pastors had. Anthropology exposed me to other cultures and religions from around the world in a nonjudgmental way. Sociology gave me tools with which to observe and critically analyze my family, my church, and my friends. In my science classes it became increasingly clear that the evidence I was told didn't exist for evolution, the big bang, and how dinosaurs became extinct not only existed but was quite compelling.

No breakup is without its share of ugliness, of course. I rejected my Christian upbringing with a vehemence. Meanwhile, interests and proclivities that had been systematically repressed suddenly became very, very appealing. I quit my foolish marriage faster than you could say Paris, which is where I went to ride out the mandatory separation and where I took up cigarettes, red wine, strong coffee, extramarital sex, and marijuana. I transferred to a college in another state and there, in my college newspaper, I published a cheeky little essay titled "Jesus Should Have Been Aborted." I was promptly invited to join a campus group called the Secular Humanists, who promoted a rational, scientific view of the universe and morality.

What a wonderful place this godless universe was! I was no longer oppressed by demons; I was just suffering from panic attacks, for which I finally got medical treatment. Evil temptations no longer lurked behind every corner, window, and screen; there were simply choices, and we as people made them to different effect. The lust I felt was not a dire moral weakness but healthy and normal responses to visual and tactile stimuli. Life itself was a chemical process that emerged over time; your particles, not your soul, would live on after you died. Particularly exciting was the fact that science, at its core, was a process, concerned with how you had come to a particular conclusion. Coming from a strain of Christianity where there are fixed answers to everything, this was refreshingly open-minded and full of possibilities. For my long-repressed inner geek, it was a veritable coming out.

Things weren't perfect. I found the vastness and impersonality of the universe quite disconcerting. I missed the comfort of having right and wrong clearly delineated, the reassurance that a benevolent, all-powerful entity was looking out for me at every moment, that I would continue to exist after this life had passed. Still, at least now I was right, whereas before I'd just thought I was right. And I wasn't alone, either. I'd joined the sneering ranks of Carl Sagan, *Skeptic* magazine publisher Michael Shermer, and Richard Dawkins. In the latter's condescending and utterly unscientific essay "Viruses of the Mind," which describes religion as a virus and its adherents as, alternately, ignorant children or victims, I hear echoes of the defiant, angry tantrum I myself had to throw in order to extricate myself from the smothering familial embrace of my faith once and for all.

Of course, I was too far along in my education—too set in my ways—to turn back and become a scientist, a mathematician, or a doctor. To embrace my love of hard science, I would have to use the so-called softer disciplines.

I graduated from college in 1996, and the Internet was about to go big time, taking me along with it. Rather than heading off to some podunk Midwestern newspaper to work my way up the editorial ladder, I landed a cool summer internship at Microsoft cofounder Paul Allen's start-up company, Starwave, one of the first commercial producers of online content. The work was a perfect marriage of writing and geekiness. Each morning I tapped out a short-and-sassy synopsis of the day's political news for the website FamilyPlanet.com. Every afternoon, I hand-coded my words and accompanying imagery into HTML. (Dreamweaver was just a silly musical refrain in those days.) The incredible possibilities posed by the web's inherent interactivity were especially exciting to me. Before long I was hitting up project managers to learn how to code more complicated content, like quizzes and reader polls. Clearly, I had found my medium.

The underlying science and technology of the Internet would also become my muse. My calling became undeniably clear that fall, when I landed my first job at a San Francisco webzine that went by the name Salon1999.com at the time; it is now known as Salon.com.

When I arrived at *Salon* I was still in denial about the full extent of my geekiness. I figured I would write about popular culture, literature, books, and politics. Yet the stories that interested me most were the ones about technology. And at work I felt the closest personal connection not to other writers or editors but to the weird, sloppy dudes who inhabited the IT department. The aspect of the online publication I found most compelling was not its voice or point of view but its choice of medium. Eventually I could no longer ignore the facts. It was time to embrace my unique, liberal-arts-infused geekiness full-on.

I started writing articles about technology and, eventually, basic scientific research. With each story I worked on, I made up for my spotty knowledge of these subjects—courtesy of my religious and liberal arts educations—until eventually I actually knew what the hell I was talking about. In the meantime, I eagerly sought out artists who were expressing scientific and technological themes not in laboratories and serious journals but in works of visual art, new media, and writing. Eventually I would follow in their footsteps, weaving scientific and technological themes into fictional works of my own. I became a sort of translator, studying and digesting technological and scientific ideas for myself, then re-presenting the concepts in language that hopefully even the least geeky among us could grasp and appreciate. At last, I had found a bridge between my long-repressed geeky side and my aimless but passionate humanities side.

»»»»universe: the sequel

Aomawa Shields

On a cold night in the middle of winter, when you can feel the hairs in your nostrils rubbing against each other, resist the temptation to turn on the heat or dive under the covers. Instead, put on a scarf and jacket, and walk outside into your back yard. Don't turn on any porch lights. If there's a new moon, so much the better. Spread your body out onto the ground faceup. Now open your eyes, lie back, and take it all in. You are the only person in the world. The universe stands before you, baring its riches like a jeweled belly dancer, sparkling and bright. The constellation Ursa Major seems to fill the whole sky, straight up and down. Its asterism, the Big Dipper, holds the pointing stars at the end of the cup. Follow the two of them and they lead you directly to Polaris, the North Star, which kicks off the Little Dipper, the brightest part of Ursa Minor. In midwinter, the Little Dipper spills out its contents onto the constellation Draco, which snakes its way between the dippers like a python in the grass. Cepheus, the house in the sky, aims its pointy rooftop at Polaris as if to shout, "He did it!" And the beautiful queen Cassiopeia winds her W through the Milky Way's trail. Watching her, you peer through our galaxy, toward the center of it, from the tip of one of its many spiral arms, where our tiny planet lies. Tonight you don't feel like an outsider though. You are part of it all. The majesty takes your breath away. The sheer expanse of the dome above your head belies humanity's singular place in the scheme of things. There is just so much more.

My passion for astronomy is what makes me who I am and is why I had to give my life to astronomy for so long. I didn't care about the world, or politics, or even dying children. I know that sounds harsh, but I was just too busy looking up. How could the bread on the grocery list or the glance of a cute boy from across the room hold any weight at all? There were planets to be explored—in other solar systems! The universe was like a state fair—full of far too much candy, and something I could never finish exploring. But I was sure going to try.

Even today it's hard to believe I lived the life of an African American female geek for years before I bolted, betraying the sisterhood and heading for Hollywood. There is only one thing more challenging than being a female geek: being a female geek who doesn't know whether to be an actor or an astronaut. Astronomy and acting had both skated the fine edge of a penny for many years. One day in the winter of 1997, sitting in my astrophysics professor's office after a particularly grueling exam at the University of Wisconsin–Madison, where I was a PhD student, something told me it was time to stop skating.

"I think you should consider other career options."

The words hung in the air like cigar smoke, swirling around my head and burning the insides of my nostrils. Didn't this man know who I was? For God's sake, didn't he know where I'd done my undergrad degree? I'd passed harder tests than this in my sleep! I'd stayed up for forty-two hours straight to finish the most monstrous physics problem sets in history. I'd crammed for a solid-state chemistry final that was so difficult, the class average score was 16 out of a possible 100 (rumor had it the professor—whom the entire lecture hall of three-hundred sophomores loathed and regularly pelted with paper airplanes during lectures—went home the night before the final and rewrote it after a particularly airplane-filled class). I'd survived college education at an institution where almost monthly, students were throwing themselves from the twenty-story heights of their dorms to fall face flat in an IQ-rich splat on the concrete, putting an end to life with a C. I'd walked through the flames of academic hell on earth, and I lived to tell about it. And I'd survived with my perspective intact. No small feat. I'd gone to astronomy field camps at Lowell Observatory and done internships at the Jet Propulsion Laboratory and Arecibo Observatory. Did he think I was going to let him push me out of something I'd worked so hard for? I felt a stinging in the outer corners of my eyes. *Goddamnit, I'll be damned if I'm going to let this asshole see me cry. Fuck you, you piece-of-shit professor. What do you know?* He was an old, white, stodgy professor who'd published way too many papers. Was this racial? I felt nauseated. If I threw up, I fully intended to aim at his shoes.

I didn't say any of this to my astrophysics professor. I sat there deflated. I probably did cry. I probably tried to tell him that I really did remember the fusion cycle of a main-sequence star, rattled off some chemical equations and ended with the carbon core, and threw in the interstellar medium so he'd know I was halfway cognizant of its importance in contributing to the formation of stars. But the picture of me from the perspective of a fly on the wall was one of a day-old birthday party balloon, slowly simmering down to a flicker of the jazz that once was. And just like that, I left. I got on a plane and I flew to Tinseltown, determined to become the first African American actress with an MIT degree to win an Oscar.

When I was a freshman at MIT, I lived in the all-black dorm, New House, next to the black men's independent living group, Chocolate City. I lived in a crowded triple, with two other African American females, and we were truly a triple threat to confident intellectual men of all races and creeds everywhere. There was Jonna, a computer genius who was destined to get her bachelor's and master's degrees in computer science in five years on a full scholarship from Microsoft and buy her own condo before the age of thirty. And there was Shelly—a future doctor with the best handwriting I had ever seen, who would, after receiving her bachelor's degree in biology, go on to get her MD from Harvard, her first-choice hospital match at Emory University, and buy a house with her husband and her three-month-old baby before starting on the staff as a doctor of internal medicine, all by age thirty-one. And there was me.

Our dorm room in New House was the center of the universe. Everyone would crowd on the floor in the evenings to do problem sets. We were all taking first-semester freshman physics, which covered classical mechanics. But at MIT, the course wasn't called Classical Mechanics. It was known as 8.01. Courses were referred to by their numbers, not their names. In the spring, we would take 8.02, Electricity and Magnetism. First-semester calculus was 18.01. Multivariable calculus was called 18.02. Differential equations was 18.03. Complex variables, 18.04. And my favorite, linear algebra, was 18.06. The numbers didn't stop there, of course. This was MIT after all. Add a third decimal place and the sequence continued.

One night during a problem set party in our room—commonly known by its number, 312—we got into a contest to see who knew the most mathematical, physical, or chemical constants and/or formulas. It was like the pistol had gone off at the Kentucky Derby.

"The gravitational constant!"

"G=6.67 × 10^{-11} Nm^2/kg^2!"

"The mass of an electron!"

"9.11 × 10^{-31} kg!"

"Mass of a proton!"

"1.67 × 10^{-27} kg!"

"Pi to as many decimal places as you can remember!"

"3.1415926!"

"3.141592653589!"

"Damn! That's twelve decimal places!"

"Astronomical unit: 1.496 × 10^8 km. Light-year: 9.46 × 10^{12} km. A parsec: 3.26 light-years. The speed of light: 3 × 10^5 km/s. Planck's constant: 6.626 × 10^{-34} Js!"

We kept going and going, until we were delirious. This was why we had come to MIT. This was the first place all of us had found where we could finally be at home, admit what we really thought about and liked talking about, and not be called nerds for it. It was kooky. I won the contest.

I was in an a cappella group at MIT called the Muses. We had a song called "Pi," whose lyrics consisted solely of digits in that nonterminating, nonrepeating value of the circumference of a circle divided by its diameter—commonly known as pi. The song was a big hit with the campus crowd. When we went on tour to other, less technical, schools though, it didn't go over as well.

I wasn't born knowing pi to twelve decimal places. I wanted to be a Dallas Cowboys cheerleader, then a secretary. Then I wanted to be an orthopedist. When I decided I wanted to do something, I didn't horse around, and I didn't wait until I had to apply to college to get started. I became obsessed with each aspiration, planning my entire future, from schooling to private practice. I took meticulous notes while poring over my *World Book Encyclopedia,* where I'd looked up my profession du jour. And then one day, when I was twelve years old, I found myself in my seventh-grade classroom watching the movie *Space Camp.* A group of kids were accidentally launched into space. And that was it. I wanted to be an astronaut.

I decided then and there in the seventh grade that I would study astronomy at the best science school in the world—MIT. Then I would get my PhD in astrophysics. I would work for a NASA research center for a couple of years, and then apply to the astronaut program.

I went to the best prep school in the country—Phillips Exeter Academy—because it had its own observatory, and I could take astronomy courses in high school. For one assignment, we had to get up at 4:00 AM to look through a telescope and measure the period of Jupiter's moons. The cold wind at that hour of the morning was electrifying. I was awake before the rest of the world. I felt like one of the cat people who ruled the earth while humans foolishly let their guard down, lying under covers. My hands tingled as I manipulated the telescope. I aligned it using the North Star, Polaris, and then shot it up toward the sky. I put my eyeball against the cold steel of the eyepiece and used averted vision to peer through the reticle. And there it was, the planet Jupiter—a hazy circle of soft, multi-colored bands, with three white dots on either side (the fourth moon was blocked by Jupiter). I couldn't stop staring. I didn't want anyone else in my group to have a turn. It reminded me of the first time I saw Saturn through a telescope. The perfect, tilted, egg-yellow circle, with such distinct rings, looked like a sticker someone had affixed to the telescope lens. Knowing that these planets and their moons were millions of miles away and right there in front of me made my skin glow in the thirty-degree chill of night.

Back in the warmth of the observatory rooms, lit with red light so as not to ruin our night vision, I pored over my notebook. I documented the whole morning in my observer's log, sipping steaming-hot cocoa while copying the exact positions of the objects in the field of view, for comparison later with other observing sessions. I was content. The rest of the world could have the earth. I wanted the stars.

Then something strange happened during my sophomore year at Exeter. I auditioned for a play. They were mounting a production of *Steel Magnolias,* and every girl in school would have sold her right tit to get a part. Every girl, that is, except me. I just tagged along with some friends who were trying out. I had done a few plays in junior high. I still remembered my star turn as the queen in my third-grade class production of *The Rabbits Who Changed Their Minds.* But I was on a career track now. That was just kid play. *I'll humor my friends,* I thought. Once the audition was over, I never gave it another thought. That is, until I was cast.

I came alive onstage. I did play after play. I joined the drama board. I became one of those "theater people." Students submitted plays they wanted to direct, and we voted on them. Other actors wanted to work with me. Directors pulled me aside during rehearsals to ask if I'd read for their next play. I entered monologue and duologue contests and won. I won the drama prize senior year. And the astronomy prize, too.

I still had MIT in the foreground of my mind. I applied under the early-decision program and was accepted. But something had changed for me. Something had torn the taut fabric of my highly structured future and sprinkled a little spice on my tongue. I began to care about the world in a way I hadn't before. I wanted to explore the human condition, make people feel, carry the audience on a journey through many lives and worlds. It was new, uncharted territory for me. I had lived so long with math, physics, distances, and absolute magnitudes that could be measured. Throughout my college experience, I was often struck in the middle of lectures with the nagging desire to feel, and laugh, and not worry about failing a final. I kept that feeling at bay and tried to force myself to stay the course.

But here I was finally, five years later, running as fast as I could. Granted, I was running to something I'd loved for almost as long as I'd loved the stars. But I was running all the same. I ran in and out of light-years and parsecs, through the Kuiper belt, and into other solar systems. I ran past the ever-changing path of a comet, and leaped out of our galaxy, and through years and into dying stars, zooming out at the speed of their expanding outer shells, until they became planetary nebulae or supernovas. I let the Large Magellanic Cloud engulf me, and I escaped.

I took a deferment from the PhD program in astrophysics and went to UCLA, where I got my MFA in acting. I began to write. I wrote my own one-person show. I laughed in bars with my classmates after opening nights at the theater. We were creatures of the night, sleeping till noon and rousing ourselves to make it to the theater by 6:00 PM so we could stretch, warm up our voices, put on costumes and makeup, and howl at the moon from the stage. We devoured life and made it sing for everyone who came to watch and live other lives through us. I thought this was all that there was. I didn't mind that I never looked up at the stars. That was another life, a world away. I got a real boyfriend, had sex for the first time at the age of twenty-three, and after six years, got married. I settled in for a life of passionate love, boring temp jobs (I once pulled staples out of paper for a year and a half), and the daily struggle to rise out of the sea of actors to stand alone. I turned thirty. But I hadn't bought a house or made my mark in my chosen field. My thoughts turned to Room 312 as I sipped tea in the corners of trendy cafés next to actor after actor killing time talking to friends on their cell phones.

Then one day another strange thing happened. A job opened up at Caltech's Spitzer Science Center, which was caretaker, along with the Jet Propulsion Laboratory, of the Spitzer Space Telescope. The opening was for a research assistant, and required a bachelor's degree in astronomy or physics. I went after that job like it was all that was left in the world. It didn't matter if I was supposed to be an actor now. I knew I was qualified, I knew it paid more than the day job I had. And somehow, I knew it was mine.

I had been gone from the world of astronomy for seven years. Needless to say, I was nervous about returning. Could I do it? Would I remember things? I'd learned how to dress nicely and wear makeup. I cared about my appearance, and I had acquired a sense of humor, and the ability to talk about a wide range of subjects other than science. Would I even fit in anymore? An African American woman, I'd felt like I was on the outskirts of inclusion seven years earlier. But now I had self-confidence. Would the whole building of scientists go into grand mal seizures at my arrival? What would my actor friends say if they could see what I was doing? And my husband, what would he think of all this, especially if it made me want to return to this world and maybe even go back to astrophysics grad school and finish this time? I thought, *Shut up, Aomawa. Stop trying to get twelve steps ahead of yourself. Just show up and do the best you can.* So I did.

After four months at my new job we began to gear up for Cycle Three of the Spitzer observations. I learned the Perl programming language and how to load ephemeris files for comets and asteroids into the proposal-planning software, which lets astronomers see the visibility windows of potential objects they want to have Spitzer observe. Every day I feel more comfortable in this world. Every day I care a little less about whether someone tells me I'm great and I should go back to get my PhD. Instead, I ask myself if I want to. I still don't know the answer.

So for now, I'm doing both astronomy and acting. I audition and perform, and I write Perl scripts and answer observers' questions about the Spitzer Space Telescope. I come home and go to movies with my husband. We play with our cats and we laugh a lot. I'm happy.

I've begun to realize that I was scared back in Madison, Wisconsin. I got scared, and I felt alone. Something shifted when things started getting hard, and I headed for the hills. I decided that somehow, if it was my choice to leave, it wouldn't be as devastating than if I just hadn't been able to cut it. I didn't want to stick around to be asked not to return the next year. So I took the opportunity I finally allowed myself to consider, and I pursued something I'd been thinking about for a long time. There is a part of me that wonders who I'd be now if I had stayed in astronomy. But I don't wish that I had. I don't think I'd be nearly as much fun if I hadn't explored this other field, this other world of words and voices and magical lives. I wouldn't have met my husband, or gotten my first role in a feature film. I wouldn't be performing one-woman shows around the country that encourage women to speak up and ask questions, and challenge men and women to think about the world and what they want and accept all of the different parts of themselves. I wouldn't have found myself in the act of writing down the truth.

I was given a gift, an open door. I walked through it, and the sky lit up again. It was like the marine layer had cleared, and I was on the summit of Mauna Kea, Hawaii—the location of the highest ground-based observatory in the world, at fourteen thousand feet. It's always been a dream of mine to go there. I had forgotten about this place. Now it is back in my dreams. I am breathing deeply, my chest expanding out over the mountains. The view is clear for miles.

games

99.9 99.8   99   98   95   90   80   70   60   50

»»»»fantasy to frag doll: the story of a gamer princess

Morgan Romine

L ike most little girls, I daydreamed about being a princess. But unlike most little girls, my idea of being a princess involved beating up boys and climbing trees, not hosting tea parties and wearing frilly dresses. In my fantasies, I was a wild princess sanctioned by the laws of a hidden, magical realm where fairies lived in flowerpots and animals would talk to a chosen few. I felt entitled and especially well suited to being the center of attention.

Most of the other bossy girls learned to channel their type-A energy toward socially acceptable activities when they grew up. I, on the other hand, found the perfect climate for living out my dream, a world in which my fantasy could become a reality. I found video games.

My hunger for enchanted worlds could not be satisfied by Hollywood's small library of fantasy films. Movies like *Legend, The Dark Crystal,* and *The Princess Bride* only whetted my appetite. I began reading about Narnia and Middle Earth as soon as I was big enough to comprehend half the words. In high school I tried to hide the tomes of Robert Jordan and J. R. R. Tolkien on my lap during class, and I became an expert at walking with my nose in a book while on the way to basketball practice. But even the thousand-paged monstrosities of fantasy literature could not satiate me: As in-depth and detailed as they were, I wanted to get even deeper into those stories.

I was six years old when I watched my cousin play *The Legend of Zelda* on his Nintendo Entertainment System. Captivated, I must have sat there for hours, wide-eyed and forgetting to breathe. For years after that I would frequently sneak over to my best friend's house to commandeer his Nintendo until both our moms were scheming to get me back home for dinner. It wasn't until I rallied with my younger brother that our parents finally gave in and got us our own gaming console, a Sega Genesis. That fondly remembered Christmas marked the official beginning of my love affair with video games. Even while those early years of gaming were bound by limited technology and sixteen-bit, side-scrolling action, I was able to get a taste of what it might be like to interact with fantastical worlds. It's no wonder that playing as Princess Peach in the Super Mario Bros. games was always especially fun for me.

Adolescence turned my life into a tornado of social activity. I still loved my video games, but hour-long, drama-filled phone calls and teenybopper mall parties suddenly became a higher priority. My new cravings were social acceptance and the attention of boys. Most of my imaginative powers were turned toward these hallmark pursuits of the teenage girl.

Aside from the Sega Genesis, my primary access point for video games was our family's computer, so I developed technical PC skills early. As a result, I discovered the wonder of online chat rooms before most of my peers. These early explorations in the online social sphere were when I first met people (primarily boys) who loved fantasy and gaming as much as I did. I started spending late nights online geeking out and flirting with boys.

Online chat gave me many opportunities to feel like a princess again. Fantasy geeks are ultraromantic and chivalrous by default, so they are more vulnerable to female manipulation. And because solitude is a necessary element of reading fantasy books and playing role-playing games (RPGs), fourteen-year-old boys who do a lot of these things are even more ill-equipped and unprepared to deal with feminine wiles than the average clueless fourteen-year-old boy. In my case, they rarely recognized what silliness they were dealing with. Some girls break hearts by passing notes in class and whispering to their friends in the halls. I broke hearts with emotes and ASCII drawings.

When I was eighteen, my boyfriend was both an avid gamer and fantasy reader. I remember driving to his house after school one day to find him playing a game I'd never seen before. Thoroughly engrossed, he paused a few times between fights to explain that this new role-playing game was extra cool because you played it online with thousands of other people. He called it an MMORPG which I later figured out stands for "massively multiplayer online role-playing game." I couldn't wrap my brain around what this might mean until I watched for a while and noticed that conversations were going on in a text box at the bottom of the screen. People were talking to each other, and their characters didn't even have to stand in the same screen to do it. The realization hit me like a brick thrown from a five-story window: EverQuest was a giant chat room embedded in a fantasy role-playing game! I was sold.

It was lucky that the onset of my new addiction coincided with my last semester of high school. I had already submitted my applications, and a little senioritis in the form of excessive gaming wasn't going to hurt anything. Granted, my real-life (as opposed to in-game) relationships suffered a bit. My friends started wondering if I was still alive, and even my boyfriend started to resent that while I was at his house, EverQuest would get 98 percent of my time and attention.

Explaining my enthusiasm for role-playing games to my nongamer friends was nearly impossible. Either their eyes would glaze over and their faces would freeze into a contorted expression of confusion, or they'd cut me off in the middle of my speech, pat me on the head, and smilingly call me a cute nerd. Even most of my guy friends from school who liked to play MMOs (short for MMORPGs) couldn't hang with my newfound and extreme brand of geekdom. For them it was a hack 'n' slash hamster wheel of mindless fun. For me, it was about finding new ways to be the center of attention while getting my fantasy fix at the same time.

Even when I moved away to start school at UC Berkeley, EverQuest remained my favorite escape. As a freshman in college, I dealt with the wildness of dorm life and the awkward process of adjusting to a new city and a new crop of peers. As a halfling druid I got to be a social butterfly in a land occupied by elves, gnomes, dwarves, ogres, and trolls, many of whom I already knew. At Berkeley, I had tests and study groups. In Norrath (EverQuest's in-game world), there were battles and quests. Crossing campus on foot took about twenty minutes. The in-game map was so vast that it could take hours to cross from one side to the other. In real life I would find myself at filthy frat parties fending off beer-soaked pickup attempts. In my game life, pickup attempts usually involved being called "my lady."

The estrogen-starved atmosphere in EverQuest allowed me to use my online social skills to gain advantages in the game. I stumbled across this phenomenon when my boyfriend observed that I was getting more preferential treatment from other players than he had ever gotten playing a male character. At first I denied it. I was a friendly, chatty extrovert, and he was not, so the difference seemed to follow naturally. But sure enough, once he created a female character, he started getting the bonus treatment, too.

Ask anyone who plays MMORPGs. Female characters are much more likely to receive random gifts of money or items from other players. The full benefits of this arrangement aren't available right off the bat, though, since plenty of guy gamers have flirted with an in-game female only to be horrified when they learn that the player is another guy in real life. If a girl gamer is able to convince her peers that she is really female, she jumps to a whole new special status. Once I learned how to exploit this system, I was never without plenty of money, the best gear, an eager power-leveling group, and a gang of friends for backup whenever I was hunting in enemy territory.

Three years after being seduced by my first MMO, a good friend from EverQuest started telling me about another game, Shadowbane. There were many things about this game that I found enticing, but one promise hooked me. It was theoretically possible for one player to rule over all the guilds on a world server (for me, this translated to major Princess Power Potential). Shadowbane was designed so that if a guild leader acquired enough influence to persuade another guild to swear fealty to her, she would then rule a nation, and her people would call her Queen. In the rare event that a queen and her nation were strong enough to acquire yet another protectorate, the guild would control an empire and its leader would become an empress. The developers intended for empires to be extremely difficult to build and almost impossible to maintain, so naturally emperor was the most coveted title for power-hungry players. After all those years of mental preparation, after reaching so many decisions by asking "if I were Princess Peach, what would I do?" I felt I owed it to myself and my fellow gamers to give it a shot.

I started following Shadowbane one and a half years before the game was released to the public, and by that time the online community forums were already a hotbed of political activity. It was obvious from the start that success was going to require copious amounts of charm and social savvy in addition to extensive knowledge about the game world. Diving into the fray, I aimed to learn as much as possible about my future friends and enemies. My socializing rapidly branched from the forums into Internet Relay Chat and instant message (IM) conversations, and my maneuverings took place on multiple levels. Because the early stages of guild recruitment were based on reputation, I crafted my guild by becoming a diligent student of the community soap opera. I studied forum posts to detect weaknesses and tension. I noted the names of those who had previously been with other guilds, and those who were friends in real life. I collected email addresses and IM screen names and built bridges—all while creating my princess persona, Talvor Ravensong.

I intended for my character's name to sound gender ambiguous, decidedly kick-ass, yet still RPG cheesy (for fantasy realism, of course) because a woman leader walks a fine line when asking gamers to follow her. She gets benefits from being female, but it's also possible to lose respect by being too girly. Luckily, though, I discovered that the same feminine charm that had worked so well in EverQuest easily carried over to Shadowbane.

Many male egos found it easier (and often more exciting) to swear fealty to a woman, and some were enamored with the idea of flirting with a queen, though they were consequently prone to being more jealous of my attentions. I didn't flirt with all of them, but when I needed a particularly juicy piece of information, some favor done, or the trust of an important friend, I was shameless about how I used implied promises and subtle suggestions to get my way. The cyber equivalent of brushing up against an arm, a light touch to emphasize a point, and mischievous giggles all were my political weapons of choice, well honed from my years of chat room and EverQuest chatting. I even reached a point where I could tailor my flirting techniques to each specific target, although I tried never to use this power maliciously. Part of this was good diplomacy, but it was also partly trouble in the making. In hindsight I shouldn't have been surprised by the drama that started to creep into my guild life. Little did I know then that this was only the beginning of the drama that would become a constant in my guild leadership and princessing.

By the time the game was launched, my guild, the Corvus, had grown to fifty active members—mostly guys whom I got along with smashingly. I would represent their interests, mediate their disputes, and favor them with girly attention. They would raise money for our city, crusade against my enemies, and favor me with their collective attention. My unique diplomatic methods won us friends in several large and powerful guilds, and where these geek factions did not get along with each other, my feminine charms could again be thanked for eventually making our neutrality possible. Ours was one of the first cities raised, and within a few weeks a smaller guild planted its city tree near ours and swore fealty to the Corvus. Becoming the queen seemed almost too easy.

Not long after the glow of this accomplishment faded, I realized that governing my guild had turned into a full-time job. Maintaining our place in a world that was becoming gradually more hostile was difficult enough without the guild's own growing pains. When the novelty of being ruled by a woman started to wear off, and my guild members began expecting more of my attention, I had to adapt my management techniques. I was able to hold everyone together by relying less on my female advantages; instead, I cashed in on a backlog of respect points. I earned a new appreciation for the "tough love" approach when the drama frayed my nerves and made my hold on charm tenuous at best. By the time we had two hundred role-players displaying the Corvus guild crest, I had morphed from a flirtatious fantasy geek princess into a no-nonsense, high-efficiency queen.

In May 2003, just over two months after the launch of the game, the Corvus became an empire, which was an astounding accomplishment by all accounts. This coronation ceremony, however, represented something different to me than what the one before it had. Earning the title of queen felt like the culmination of all my daydreams and girly desires to be loved for being special. Becoming empress guaranteed that Talvor Ravensong and the Corvus would forever be a part of the game server's legend, but ultimately it felt like a heavy responsibility. Earning the game's highest honorific had required me to sustain an intense level of focus and involvement as I found myself answering for the gaming experience of two hundred other players (people can take their recreation very seriously). Playing at princess went from fun and games to sweat-and-tears work.

When my royal burden was taking its heaviest toll on me, there was no way to explain to my friends and family what was going on. I had years of practice juggling my gaming habit and my schoolwork, so I couldn't help them decipher this particular geeky obsession from my previous ones except to point out my seemingly erratic emotional state. Sometimes I would be ecstatic and ramble nonsensically to them about Rank 5 Archer Captains and pacts with Amazons. The next day I might be quiet and brooding and prone to angry outbursts. Many hardcore gamers play their favorite MMOs for years, but my relationship with Shadowbane burned bright and hot for only eight months. The big thing for me was that once the Corvus became an empire, I no longer had an overarching goal to motivate me. When I had lived out my princessly ambitions, I finally let myself see that I was burned out.

Completely extracting myself from Shadowbane was a painful process, and though I have always been enthusiastic about playing new MMORPGs, my relationships with them have never quite been the same. My desire to rule a gaming group was forever changed as well. The alpha female tendencies were still intact, but the adolescent girl need for attention that originally defined my gaming habits no longer drove me. Where the impossibly proportioned fashion models of teen magazines once had me seeking acceptance, I now had a well-developed sense of accomplishment and purpose. After all, six months after my retirement, the server I played on was permanently closed, and my guild's city was the only one standing that had remained under original ownership since its naming day. I had worked hard to establish myself as a princess among geeks, I had succeeded with a flourish, and I couldn't have done it again the same way even if I wanted to.

Underneath it all I was still that bossy little girl, and I wanted to find a good way to use my special online gaming social skills. After majoring in anthropology, I was faced with the difficult task of finding a practical application for my degree in a job I might actually like. All the connections I made in the Shadowbane community ended up being useful when I decided that I wanted to be a community manager (CM) for Shadowbane's publisher, Ubisoft. Through the Shadowbane forums, I had come to know two CMs (both Ubisoft employees) whose responsibilities included administrating the official game website, overseeing forum moderators, translating community feedback for the developers, planning fun in-game events, and wrangling gamer geeks (which was a task I felt especially well qualified for). After some determined nagging, months of waiting, and a lot of luck, they hired me as their first female CM, which really meant that I became their first professional gamer princess.

I was assigned to communities other than Shadowbane, but the skills I learned through my years of social online gaming came in handy everywhere I went. Early on, I found that the guys in these online communities were more open to being called out by a girl. My male CM counterparts often had to be more hard-nosed in their enforcement of the rules, where I could politely ask someone to cease and desist. And once my communities found out I was an avid gamer too, the brown-nosing rate skyrocketed. As a girl gamer among many guy gamers (there is almost always a skewed male-to-female ratio in most gaming circles, with a few exceptions), certain things stay the same no matter the circumstance. Females who like games represent a mind-boggling manifestation of a mythological creature who usually dwells only in the imagination of the gaming male. These guys are used to being yelled at by their mothers and girlfriends for wasting time playing video games, so the girls who actually share their passions are fabled entities. This often means that gaming communities are easy pickings for any enterprising girl gamer, which is a surprisingly beneficial situation for all involved. The girl finds herself at the center of attention and the guys find a much-needed corrective to their otherwise *Lord of the Flies*–like existence.

Within the first couple months of interacting with communities from my new professional perspective, I devised a peacekeeping strategy. The first element of it was to be clear about my sincere wish to help the gamers. All CMs intend to represent the best wishes of their gamers, but all too often a community of jaded gamers believes it's being thwarted at every turn. By favoring a select few dedicated gamers with personal attention and demonstrating my desire to help them, I cultivated a small group of outspoken and loyal followers who would support me in any firefight. Bitching in the forums could then be met with as much levelheaded reason as I could muster, and I wouldn't even need to acknowledge any negative response before my small army would neatly nullify and ostracize the complainers. This arrangement let me be a bossy, helpful, and admired princess type, all without the messiness of flirtation.

As the only girl and youngest CM, I was like the little sister of our group at work. Having been such a gamer geek tomboy for so long, I fell into this role happily, and my new big brothers were tickled by my unorthodox management tactics. "You're a cute girl," they said. "They'll do anything you tell them to." I couldn't find a way to explain that I had actually worked hard to develop my remarkable knack for communicating with gamers.

Granted, these gamers were not quite the same ones I had spent years playing with in Shadowbane and EverQuest. There was no opportunity for me to manage an MMO community, so instead I spent my time with fans of military action shooters. I had played enough *Counter-Strike* and *Splinter Cell* during college to know the lingo, and the gamers themselves weren't so different from my old online friends. The most useful similarity to me was that these first-person shooter (FPS) gamers were captivated by the idea of a girl who loves video games. In fact, when I began regularly playing the Tom Clancy games on Xbox Live, I wondered whether there were proportionally fewer girls playing shooters than MMOs because of the shock I would encounter whenever my female voice transmitted through the headset.

My gaming coworkers loved to hear about the funny reactions I would get from guys after kicking their asses online, and as these stories circulated, a few people at work got to thinking more about it. If these guys were so excited about playing with one girl gamer, how receptive would they be to a whole team of them? The marketing logic was good enough to justify a test run, so I was tapped for assistance. Looking back now, it's funny to remember that I hesitated. After so many years of being on the consumer side of the industry, I had a knee-jerk cynical reaction to that kind of marketing-driven initiative. Gamers are notoriously skeptical of anything they see as a marketing ploy, and I was no exception, even as a young employee of a game publisher.

But ultimately, I had to help. As the only girl gamer in the vicinity, I couldn't very well let these guys stumble around by themselves trying to figure out how to run a team of girl gamers. Besides, I was excited by the prospect that this team could become more than just a promotional tool. Maybe we could help create a world where my local game-store cashier wouldn't assume I was buying a game for my boyfriend. It seemed to me that a team of talented female gamers with the support of a large game company could have the visibility to demonstrate that girls do, in fact, play games. I also admit that the idea of leading another group of gamers, especially one so different from my guild, was a fascinating challenge.

Before recruiting team members for the Frag Dolls, my experience with other girl gamers was as modest as that of the average gamer. In Ever-Quest, I made a couple of girl friends, and we would call each other "sis" and "hon" and whisper gossip, but these were merely online friendships. We got along fine in-game, but we had no real connection outside of Norrath. There was a handful of women in my Shadowbane guild—some I liked, some I didn't—but our interactions were scant and superficial. From afar I observed only two other females in positions of power. I had a bare few polite exchanges with each, long enough to size them up, and then we went back to scheming within our own spheres of influence. If someone had asked me during Shadowbane why I knew so few girl gamers, I would have simply guessed that there weren't many playing the game. But once I started thinking about it, this lack of interaction seemed odd.

The Entertainment Software Association (ESA) claims 43 percent of all gamers are women, and I was perplexed about why I hadn't crossed paths with more of them before. My nongaming life had a normal amount of women in it, so how was it that my game life was so strikingly devoid of them? Given the ESA's stats, I supposed that it must have been my doing, but this was confusing too: I had never made any conscious effort to avoid other girl gamers.

Through interviewing candidates for the Frag Dolls and meeting other girl gamers at our first few events, I concluded that the girl gamer demographic was like a cross-section of girls from any other walk of life. There was a decent number of them, too, because they were coming out of the woodwork to support or protest the Frag Dolls.

The team we finally put together was as diverse as the pool we pulled from. Some of the girls were hardcore *Halo* players, others were Nintendoholics. Some were defined by their role-play conquests, others knew about every game but were masters of none. The common thread was a delicate balance of traits that let us fill our professional roles as spokeswomen while also staying true to our gamer roots. The fact that we got along so well with one another was more a stroke of luck than by design, though this was undoubtedly aided by the fact that none of us was under twenty-one (making us notably older than many of the gamers with whom we frequently interact). We were intrigued and amused by the prospect of turning our hobby into a job, but fundamentally we were all inspired by the desire to help bring about a future in which gamer girls were no longer the exception.

Observing other girl gamers in their natural habitat allowed pieces of the game-femme isolationist puzzle to fall into place. There are more gamer princesses in the overall gaming population than I would have ever guessed before becoming a Frag Doll. Certainly not all lady gamers come from the princess mold, and in fact I can think of several who would vehemently protest if I dared to claim they had princess tendencies. It's undeniable that there are girls who just like to play, and they don't care if their opponent or teammate is male or female as long as they're having fun. There are also those who actively seek other gamer girls as friends or fellows in the feminist cause. For me, looking at women gamers as a social group highlighted patterns that resonated with my own experience. In seeking those who shared my predilections, I answered my own question about why the girl gamers of the universe often don't know about one another. It's because we all want to be the princesses of our own domains.

There are several community forces that enable gamer princesses to thrive. The simplest part of the equation is the girl-to-boy ratio. Of the 43 percent of gamers who claim to be female, many play online through services like Yahoo! Games, so in the social games I'm talking about (MMO, popular FPS, and real-time strategy games), there are still many more guys than girls.

Game content itself is also responsible for the unusual conditions that help girl gamers hold such positions of honor in gaming communities. Female game characters' physical design often embodies a worshipful attitude toward the female form. Big boobs, big guns, and battle skills on characters like Lara Croft create a loose but positive association between women and games. Add this to the perceived rarity of girls who like games, and you have an instant recipe for female idolatry among the male gaming population (especially potent if you factor in the chivalry that role-players carry in their pockets). It's ironic to think that what some call sexual objectification of women in games might actually, under certain circumstances, have contributed to the empowerment of women gamers.

The isolationist phenomenon among gamer princesses is a result of the fact that their successes in games and in the community haven't been dependent on other girls. A gamer princess might be perfectly willing to play games with other females, but there are so many guys wanting to be adopted by a lady gamer that we have often ended up establishing our own happy little niches. Again, there are plenty of girl gamers who seek out other girls to play with (the Frag Dolls are an example), just as there are girl gamers who refuse to play with other females for catty or territorial reasons. But whether it's a fundamental preference or habituated state, we girl gamers are used to being special. We are appreciated as unique even when surrounded by other girls like us, and it is possible that many of us have learned to cultivate this admiration to the exclusion of each other.

The Frag Dolls occupy a strange area of limbo in the gaming community. We are a promotional group working for a corporation, but we are also the ideal demographic for communicating with our audience (gamer princesses talking to gamers). But as a group of girls working together for our own purposes, raising awareness about girl gamers by being in the spotlight together, we break the standard gamer princess mold. We've been pleased to discover that our eccentric approach has helped us to better communicate both the company and team messages, and now that we've settled into our roles, guy and girl gamers alike have shown their support.

Like any culture built around a fast-growing industry, the gaming world is changing. Every day, more women are playing games, and as this fact becomes more commonly accepted, the special status held by existing gamer girls will shift. It will be years before the game industry routinely designs and markets popular games with women in mind, but we have taken important steps toward recognizing one another as we exist and play games today. In my case, understanding the motivations of princesses like me has given me the tools to reach out to them. If we girl gamers learn how to identify one another, others will start to identify us, too.

»»»» fatality!

Paula Gaetos

My fondest childhood memory is of playing video games with the neighborhood boys. From the moment those little guys handed me the original Nintendo console controller, gaming consumed my life. Every day after school, I'd go over my neighbors' houses and play video games until I had to go home for dinner. After months of gaming with my guy friends, I begged my parents for a console of my own and ended up with a Sega Saturn with only five games: *Virtua Fighter 2, Cyber Troopers: Virtual On, NiGHTS into Dreams, Daytona USA,* and *Virtua Cop.* I played these games until I knew every level and every fight better than many real-life hangouts. I never really mastered all the super moves or learned every little strategy, but I made it through somehow.

It didn't bother me that I was the only girl among a bunch of guys, because physical differences weren't that apparent at the ages of six through eleven. The only difference I ever noticed was that I felt an attachment to Chun-Li from *Street Fighter II* and Sonya Blade from *Mortal Kombat,* maybe because they were the only female fighters. I told myself I'd never play a male character if a female was an option. Playing male characters just didn't feel right to me, because I couldn't "relate." It didn't matter to me whether the female character was weaker or harder to learn—I wanted to prove to my friends (and to myself) that she could still kick ass.

I was at home with video games and guy friends until I was eleven, when puberty struck. It wasn't just a normal strike either—it was a freaking critical hit, a multicombo double-forward-rotation-plus-punch Super Move. I could almost hear it growl a triumphant "Fatality!" On the fateful day puberty KO'd my ass, I was on vacation in the Philippines. My mom took me upstairs in the middle of a family party and realized I'd started my period. In a matter of minutes, *whoosh,* I was surrounded by what seemed like *every* female relative I had, gushing and celebrating my entrance into womanhood. There I was, right in the middle of all it, bawling my eyes out at the embarrassment and the uncertainty. *Kill me no*w, I thought, but it was just the beginning. When my classmates back home found out through a small accidental bloodstain on my gym shorts, I was mortified. From that moment on, my male peers and friends avoided me and, on worse days, made fun of me. Who wouldn't? I used to be a talkative, clever gamer kid, and I turned into an introverted, awkward tween with giant '80s-style pink glasses, growing hair in weird places and bleeding between the legs. This felt punishingly cruel after having tasted acceptance. There was no way I could fight back like the female characters I played in my games because of how self-conscious I felt. Besides, games never showed them going through *their* periods. I started to hate my female body. *Why do I have to be so different?* I thought.

With the boys rejecting me, I had no choice but to try spending time with other girls, who were going through the same thing. In that world, there was no punching, no shorts underneath skirts, no video games, but we tried on makeup and read *Teen* magazine. I felt really awkward around girls talking about cute TV actors and looking pretty. My mom was pleased that I was spending more time with girls than guys by the time I reached junior high. At least it was a learning experience, and I told myself to accept that nothing would change the fact that I was female and this was what females did. I guess you could say my feminine side grew with each experience I gained shopping for clothes with the girls, doing each other's makeup, and reading fashion magazines. But I never understood the gossiping, the need to be perfect, and the "drama" that came along with it—for example, being friends with one person meant you weren't friends with another. Or if you liked a guy, you were enemies with any other girl who liked him too. I couldn't help thinking, in a corner of my mind, "If I wanted to play games, I'd play them with a console, not other people."

But that was when my mother decided to take my console away, seeing the feminine changes in me. She gave my Sega Saturn to my cousins in the Philippines, and I had to give up video games temporarily. With the Saturn gone, no guys to hang out with, and the need to stay away from drama as much as possible, I immersed myself in reading young-adult books and watching television. While my book tastes varied, when it came to television I only liked science fiction, fantasy, and Japanese animation. The TV shows I watched had strong feminine roles, especially *Xena: Warrior Princess* and the animated show *Sailor Moon*.

Like my video game avatars, Chun-Li and Sonya Blade, these girls were female and *kicked ass. I want to be just like them,* I thought, though I hardly knew how.

And then it came. . . .

The summer before I started high school, my parents bought a personal computer. With it came a fifty-six-kilobit-per-second modem and (cue choirs of angels) the Internet. I mostly used the computer to look up fan sites for anime and science fiction shows. I loved looking through web pages and getting information way faster than I could using libraries. By the time I entered high school, I was eager to make my own fan site. I started off using the WYSIWYG webpage builder available from Geocities, then started learning basic HTML and Java from other sites, plus chats with other newbie web designers on AOL Instant Messenger. When Blogger came along, well, crap, there was no way to get me off the Internet from the time I came home from school until I had to go to bed at 11:00 PM. My parents complained about the phone bill and the fact no one could ever call the house. I'd kept a journal since I learned how to write, so blogging came naturally to me, and Blogger allowed me to customize my blog using HTML and simple Javascript. The Internet became my haven, my realm. In chat rooms, blogs, and forums, I could talk about anything, and it wouldn't affect my life at school.

As an added bonus, a brand-new PlayStation arrived with imported games from the Philippines. I forget why my parents got this for me, but it was there and I loved it. *Dance Dance Revolution* came with my PlayStation, and it was the most innovative game I'd come across since my Saturn's *NiGHTS into Dreams.* I spent hours every day trying to master the complex steps to a song and pestering my friends to "dance" along with me. I was never that great at keeping a rhythm, but it was the most fun exercise I ever experienced. Before long, I was hooked on other games for the PlayStation, like the role-playing game *Final Fantasy VIII* and the platformer *Spyro the Dragon.*

My parents sent me to an all-girls' private school once I graduated from junior high. Being around girls wasn't a problem for me anymore. I still couldn't care less about prettifying myself or trying to get dates, though by then, it wasn't a problem if I really wanted to do it. Getting to the next level in *Final Fantasy* or remembering to add a hyperlink in my blog was more important than finding a date for the dance. Besides, if I didn't have a date, I could always dance with my girlfriends or volunteer to work the soda bar. By the time I was in my sophomore year, I'd gotten comfortable with my femininity. Monthly cycles are much easier to bear when you have other girls sharing their pains and frustrations and offering spare emergency pads. Over time, I traded the '80s pink-rimmed glasses for thin, black Armani ones (adding +5 to my Charisma). My clothes fit around my curves, and I could wear sleeveless shirts without feeling embarrassed. I was a blossoming teenage girl on the outside and a nerdy Internet and gamer geek on the inside.

But the same way my early guy friends hadn't understood my physical changes as a girl, my girlfriends didn't fully understand my fascination with the Internet, video games, and weird TV. My personality, mentality, and interests really set me apart from my female friends, since none played video games or watched anime on a regular basis. A few girls here and there in my class knew about that stuff, but those girls weren't talking to me for one (dumb) reason or another. Thank goodness my friends and I were old enough not to completely shun each other for our differences, but the gnawing feelings of *I don't belong* and *I am different* slowly surfaced in my heart like a virus-laden Trojan horse.

I hadn't made close friendships with guys since elementary school, and though I already dated sporadically, the only people I was really close to were my high school girlfriends. It wasn't like I was trying to avoid guys. My introverted personality and conservative parents hardly gave me a moment to meet people outside my school. Early in my junior year, I took classes at a local church with my best friend at the time. She introduced me to an old friend of hers from elementary school, and one of the first things I asked him was, "So, do you play video games?" I will never forget the shock on his face and the double shock when I told him I also watched anime and sci-fi television. He'd never heard of a girl even knowing about such things, let alone *enjoying* them. I soon accumulated a new circle of guy friends to match my circle of girlfriends. The only difference was the guys appreciated my video-game-loving, science-fiction-watching side.

Unfortunately, I wasn't just the only girl in two circles of guys, I was also the one with the least experience with and knowledge of the geek and gamer worlds. They were better and more knowledgeable than I was because they had more resources than I did. They were already running on broadband while I turtled along on dial-up. Their parents were keener to take them to video game stores and arcades and let them watch action movies than my parents were. Speaking of my parents, they were much less happy about me being the only girl in a group of guys now that I was teenage girl instead of an asexual six-year-old. But I wanted to expand my video game prowess and geek knowledge, and where else was I going to turn? I felt camaraderie with these guys and, like in my early childhood, I wanted to prove to them I was just as strong. I expanded my video game prowess thanks to the guys taking me along to arcades and letting me play their various consoles. They gave me the incentive to take the after-school A+ computer hardware and networking class (taught by a wonderfully eccentric Cuban man) because *they* knew how to build PCs and network cables, and I wanted to know too. They knew about all the awesome Japanese and Hong Kong action movies I'd missed out on. They gave me a steady supply of anime, because I lacked a broadband Internet connection. They became not my equals (like the male friends from my early childhood), but my superiors—my geekdom *depended* on them, and I really resented it.

I felt that if I hadn't grown up female, I would have been more experienced with the Internet, video games, and action flicks. Once a month, my period seemed to remind me that I was smaller, different, and *female*. I couldn't share that feeling with my girlfriends because, hell, none of them was having similar experiences. My girlfriends and guy friends were from different places and hardly interacted. In the geek world, the only females I encountered lived in video games that I seemed to never master. I brooded over feeling different, and ended up like the girls featured in Dr. Mary Pipher's book *Reviving Ophelia* who had problems with their self-esteem because they were trying to fit to media's standards of beauty or dealing with harassment—except I was probably the only one who owned a PlayStation 2. I was going through my own phase of self-doubt and low self-esteem because of how different I felt.

But like someone casting a successful saving throw in a Dungeons & Dragons game, I could feel awareness grow deep within me. I took the A+ class in high school that trained high school students to be able to become A+ certified through the Computing Technology Industry Association (CompTIA) as a computer technician. I learned Microsoft operating systems and PC repair, and after completing this class, building a PC in a matter of an hour (assuming everything ran smoothly) wasn't a problem for me. And thanks to my teacher, I learned to make connections with computer hardware wholesalers. Soon I found my family and classmates turning to me for all their computer needs. By the time I entered college, relatives and my friends' family members would pay me to come and build or repair their PCs. I was advising my younger (male *and* female) cousins on the latest anime and gaming facts. By the time I turned nineteen, I'd developed into a web-comic-reading, PC-building, web-page-making, forum-trolling, anime-loving, gamer fan girl. But I still felt inferior: *How can I be this great geek when I'm not even close to competing with the guys I learned most of my stuff from?*

Or so I thought.

When my guy friends and I played fighting games, we'd each take on the winner of the previous game. Depending on the game and who seemed to be "in the zone" at the time, one person would usually stay the winner for a while, and the rest of us would go through the painstaking process of knocking him off. When the controller was passed to me, I usually lost in every fighting game I played. Until one day, the unthinkable happened: I kicked ass and I *kept* kicking ass.

The game: *Guilty Gear XX Reload*

The character: May, a cute sailor girl with a cheerful disposition and an anchor three times her size.

I ruled the game for two to three rounds until someone finally knocked me off my pedestal in an intensely close game. I looked at the boys around me.

Holy shit, their faces said.

What the fuck just happened? my face said.

Then it happened again: When matched against one of my friends, the most hardcore gamer of them all, in a puzzle game—*Magical Drop 3* for the Neo-Geo—I defeated my opponent with unbelievable ease. I even switched controllers with him just to see if it wasn't some sort of glitch, and it happened again.

Holy shit, their faces said again.

Well . . . crap, my face said this time.

There were finally games that I was actually *good* at, and at least one that I was *better* than anyone else in. Even if *Magical Drop 3* was an obscure and rare puzzle game, I was ridiculously good at it. I was shocked, proud, and left thinking these were the moments that would end up appearing as my life flashed before my eyes during a near-death experience.

After that, there was just no excuse for my inferiority complex. In the months that followed, I took a hard look at myself in the mirror and reflected every day on the person I had become. *I am different,* I told myself. I've got curves and soft features. I looked around my room, filled with Hello Kitty gear, anime posters, books and manga that barely fit into my shelves, my PlayStation 2 and its games, cosmetics, and most of all, my customized PC that I built myself. In my closet, I saw pieces of Japanese street fashion, cosplay (or costume play), Urban Outfitters stuff, and raver pants. I could put on hip-hugging jeans and makeup, but match it with a baby doll T-shirt that said, NO, I WILL NOT FIX YOUR COMPUTER, or WILL WORK FOR BANDWIDTH, and ADIDAS (because they're the best shoes to play *Dance Dance Revolution* in). Without realizing it, I'd developed my own unique blend of geekosity.

Now, at twenty-one, I realize that even though the guys in my life helped me expand my geek knowledge, my creative web design and PC-building skills and my confidence about winning video games are all my own. I stopped resenting my femaleness and hating my monthly cycle. They're just part of who I am, like my geekiness. I don't need a penis to do the things I do. Each time I see the shock on guys' faces when they see me play (and win) at video game arcades, I'm reminded of that fact. And when I see little girls watch with wide eyes as I play only female characters and win, I'm glad that I can remind them, too.

»»»»dreaming in unison

Quinn Norton

By the time we set up camp, I knew there was no way it could work. They'd seemed fine when I met them, and they'd handled themselves well in the brawl, even if they'd been pissed about it. It was just that they never let up! It was: "Tas, you bitch," "Tas, put that down," "Tas, that's not how we do things," and "Tas, you're late." The take was decent—I mean, we could all kill things. But most of the time they were just rude.

I admit I can be pretty rude, but they started it. These men were just stupid and mean. I hadn't done wrong by them, see? I'd fought hard, and I hadn't ever been late. No, these men were nasty as sewer rats and half as smart. I sighed and tried to think of what to do. I'd kept my gold on me, so that was safe. But sneaking off would be hard. Several of them were faster than me and trackers to boot.

There I sat, lost in thought, when the party leader yelled at me again. "Tas!" he said, "You have second watch!"

I stared at him. "Me? You want me to take a watch?"

"Fuck you, Tas, you're not getting out of work," he replied. They really were dumber than sewer rats, unless they were up to something. Still, they could have been up to something, right? I waited through first watch, holding still like I was sleeping and trying not to get too stiff. No one spoke to me or came for me until second watch. One of them shook me roughly and when I'd gotten up, he went over and lay down to sleep. I waited for a while. No one stirred. I lost some time just staring at them sleeping. I did some stretching and wondered how they'd gotten this far in life.

Briefly I considered just vanishing into the forest. Then I looked around at everyone's pouches. *Oh hell,* I thought, *no one misses sewer rats.* I took out my dagger. Carefully, quietly, I went to each sleeping form, found his throat, and made a quick cut, just deep enough to do the job. I grabbed pouches and weapons, as much as I could carry. I strapped them to a couple horses, but there was still a lot left for the kobolds. Somehow, I always leave something for the kobolds. Fair enough: They've left plenty for me. I started leading the horses back to Waterdeep—I had a few months' relaxing to do.

A men's dormitory, UC Santa Barbara, 1993: Five physics undergrads are staring at me. "What?" I say defensively, "I told you she was Chaotic Neutral."

"You just killed everyone," one of them replies.

"I told you this character was Chaotic Neutral!" I exclaim with some frustration. "I warned you!" One petitions the Dungeon Master: "I think that was more evil. Chaotic Evil."

"No," I explain, "She only did it because you were being mean to her. If you hadn't been mean to her, she would have been your best buddy."

Nevertheless, they are all pissed. I grumble to myself. There's a reason they call it Chaotic Nutty. The DM is amused. He's never inviting me back again, but he's amused.

∞

My mother's house in Los Angeles, 1980: I can remember opening a box—the basic set—and seeing the dice and a crayon. You couldn't read the numbers on the dice; you had to rub the crayon into the numbers to see them. I was so proud of myself when I worked that out. I read mythology exclusively and had it read to me when the words were too hard. (Many elements of role-playing games were lifted from mythologies from around the world.) My great grandmother read me the Reader's Digest version of *The Odyssey* and got me hooked on adventure for life.

Mom helped me with various books of medieval legends, though she hated them. She thought fantasy was a waste of time. She wanted me to read stuff like *Gravity's Rainbow*. But she still read the hard bits of gaming books to me until I looked for someone to play with. I forced my best friend, but her heart was never in it. I didn't really meet someone fun to play with until I was twelve. Her name was Katayna Jansen. I was off and running, but no one had warned me this was a boys' club. Kitty and I played for a year until she moved to Canada. That's when I found out the truth about other gamers: They were boys.

∞

A redwood forest in Northern California, 1983: My dad held on to my shoulders so my little-girl body wouldn't fly up from the kick on the nine-millimeter he was having me fire into a woodpile. Like the kick, the idea of shooting felt a bit bigger than me. When I think of characters choosing to kill for the first time—which is how they get to be Level 1 characters instead of Level 0 NPCs (Non-Playing Characters)—I think of shooting guns with my dad.

Calvary Church, Pacific Palisades, 1987: In a fit of religious pique I promised to burn all my first-edition books. It hurt like hell, but I did it. After all, we're talking about my soul and the devil. Despite the setback, Dungeons & Dragons outlasted Jesus in my life. To this day I'm annoyed about losing those books, including the original *Deities and Demigods.* Damn! Within a month I bought new books. Within two years, I lost my virginity, which marked the end of my Christianity.

Los Angeles gaming convention, 1989: I walked into the huge open gaming room. I started hunting for a table to join and heard "Oh look, it's the girl." I've always been the girl. Not a girl, not one of the girls, not a woman on her own, not a career woman. Just the girl. It's always been the guys, and the girl. Before I was the girl anywhere else, I was the girl in gaming.

It was the first group that accepted me because I barreled my way in, and I belonged, except for the part where I was the girl. I played hard and worked to prove myself, but that never really worked. I remained, and am to this day, the girl. The girl is often ridiculed, sometimes ignored, occasionally respected, but always just a little bit feared.

We had conversations about the alignment and character class, stats and skills of the people in our lives. Gaming requires that you fit a whole person on a sheet of paper. I made a character sheet and tried to answer truthfully. We all did, and when we looked at each other, it was with brutal honesty. This turned out to be a useful skill, to be able to evaluate people according to objective and qualitative criteria. We applied the technique for documenting a game character to looking at ourselves in real life. We evaluated each other's choices and made suggestions and criticisms. We took entire complex backstories and knocked them down to a few stats. We made choices in our role-play according to the backstories, but we rolled the dice to see what would happen to a character based on the hard stats, not the stories behind them.

Here's me, à la my game of choice, *Advanced Dungeons & Dragons (AD&D):*

> **Character Sheet**
> Name: Quinn Norton
> Race: Human
> Class: Scribe
> Age: 32
> Gender: Female
> Deity: Eris
> Alignment: Neutral Good (Chaotic Neutral)
> Height: 62 inches
> Weight: 135 pounds
> Level: 2
> THAC0: 20
> Strength: 7
> Dexterity: 9
> Constitution: 6
> Intelligence: 14
> Wisdom: 15
> Charisma: 16
> Weapon proficiencies: .22 Rifle, Quarterstaff. Kinda.
> Nonweapon proficiencies: Pottery, Swimming, Reading/Writing, Ancient History, Direction Sense

∞

The San Fernando Valley, 1991: My gaming group was up all night, every night. We played just about everything; we sampled it all. Nothing beats Hero Game's Hero System RPG for rules lawyering (finding ways to structure characters to give them advantages the creators of the game never intended). I don't think we ever got to much playing because we spent so much time coming up with undefeatable characters through loopholes and number shuffling. It was an advantage/disadvantage system. Given a flat number of points to work with, you spent points on powers (advantages) and recouped them by disabling your character in some way (disadvantages). The greater the disadvantage, the higher the point value, but also the more interesting the backstory. You could to a lot with the "Has no physical body" disadvantage.

Good character generation could take all day, people arguing back and forth about careful wordings to squeeze out interesting interactions of advantages to give a character limitless power, plus a backstory to justify it. We rarely lasted long into a game because we'd pass out from pure exhaustion. The guy who liked Hero the most went on to develop income tax software. I still think of people in terms of Hero System—it's the best character description ever made in gaming.

Still in Los Angeles, 1991: All I did was game. It was like I was in some sci-fi movie about virtual reality addiction. We all worked our day jobs to support the minimum life requirements to game. We spent all our time together gaming. I worried occasionally, briefly, about not being connected to reality, and about how the guys were constantly testing me and never really liking me, because I'm the girl. But this was my world, best I could do, so I did it. My best skill was telling stories.

San Fernando Valley, early 1992: The men had a quorum. There were four in the group, not counting me; two had been my lovers and two had asked me for a relationship. They told me I had to choose just one of them, so they wouldn't end up fighting over me. Without pausing I picked one, the one with whom I'd fallen in love. The conversation ended, but everyone looked unsatisfied. Me making the choice hadn't given them the closure they'd thought it would.

A few weeks later they asked me to leave. I had created too much strife between them. But what did I ever do? I pleaded to stay. They said I knew what I did, and they were right. I had sex with some of them and turned down the others. They had been at each other's throats for months. They identified me as the problem. Get rid of the girl, and the fights can go back to being in-game. I left in pain and humiliation. I learned a rough lesson: People behave according to their natures. Don't go behind enemy lines and expect to make friends easily.

I'll never again have that kind of closeness with a gaming group, and I'll never again spend so much of my life focused on something with any group of people. It's an intimacy I've pined for for years, and I have never really recreated it.

Central Los Angeles, April 1992: My world was literally stolen and destroyed. Over the course of eight years, I'd created every detail of a whole world. I made tectonic maps. I drew it. I wrote a book full of races, cultures, mythologies, strange gods, and fantasy medieval cities. The entire thing was in the car when it was set on fire—I found little tiny charred bits of it when the car was recovered. Soon the whole world was on fire. My workspace went up in the riots following the Rodney King verdict, during which I ran for my life and at one point was engulfed in flames. Tanks rolled up the I-5 freeway into my hometown. Real life looked disturbingly like a game.

Orange County, 1993: I began the first of a long string of jobs where I was "the girl." It could have been devastating, and the crap I got as a geek girl at the time still astounds me. Internet and web, systems administration, and the Silicon Valley boom: all boys' games. The things I learned in gaming turn out to apply beautifully to real life. Here is a helpful list:

>> Expect fights in bars and taverns.
>> Go on, check the door. It's unlocked more often than you'd think it would be.
>> When all else fails and all hope is lost, it never hurts to choose to disbelieve.
>> Sometimes in life, narrative trumps all the other rules.
>> The dice favor style.
>> When you're hopelessly lost, the right-hand rule will get you out.

∞

Orange County, 1995: Live-action role-playing (LARPing) of Vampire: The Masquerade hit big. All the rules lawyering was gone because the White Wolf system that governed how Vampire was played focused on role-play above all else, and I could role-play like a motherfucker. I had one main character called Chaot. She was crazy, barely hanging onto enough reality to stay "alive" as a vampire. Crazy I could do. I took her on the road and played her in Vampire games all over the United States. She was the bomb; she was the one and only character who was part of my identity. I liked many characters over the years, and I tried out ideals of ethics and behavior with many of them, but Chaot was the one and only character who was actually a bit about me.

Maybe that's because it was the first time I was in a safe enough place to ask questions about myself in-game. Chaot was a part of me that was crazy, delicate, and couldn't survive exposure to the rough world. When I played her, I asked, what happens when your disconnected, empathic, wondering self is all you have? What's it like wandering around the world totally defenseless? My answers were heartening: Everywhere I took her, other characters tried to protect her. Chaot confirmed to me that many people do value an inner delicacy.

One night I was wandering around downtown San Juan Capistrano early in Chaot's career. I hadn't run into any other players, and I was getting a bit bored. I thought I heard my fellow gamers' voices above me in a parking garage and decided to join them. Instead of the stairs, my little trench-coat-wearing Malkavian took to the trees. I climbed up and over to the second floor of the parking garage and threw myself quietly over the wall, coat flying behind me. I landed surprisingly silently. Turned out the voices came from two families of moviegoers—parents talking while young kids ran in bored orbits around them. I, in all my weirdness, appeared out of nowhere and walked quickly by them. The parents never noticed me, but the kids did. They looked at where I'd come from, and then at me. They crouched close to their parents and clutched one another. I looked over at them, opened my eyes wide, and gave them a slightly snarled smile.

They followed me with their eyes as I walked down the stairs. They never saw Quinn; they never even saw Quinn playing Chaot. All they ever saw or knew was Chaot, mad vampire, coming from and going to nowhere. With a mysterious grin, Chaot had given the lie to the boring world their parents described, where everything stays the same in the dark as it does in the light. I knew whatever make-believe they played next, I was going to crop up.

That moment is why I gamed.

∞

An after-LARP dinner in San Juan Capistrano, 1996: The GM raised a toast and spoke about my ability to role-play. He said I helped make the game more real for the others. I was thrilled. It was strange after all this time to be recognized as skilled in something that no one really has a place for. Everyone nodded happily, and I noticed for the first time in my life that the girls weren't so rare. The GM ended: "But next time, Quinn, could you say your character runs at the moving train, rather than actually running at the moving train?" We all laughed, but I said no. That's just how I play.

It's hard to describe skill in gaming. It's about narrative, and playing the character you've made. It's almost the opposite of acting because you need to think of what the person would say in the moment, rather than repeating and interpreting words someone else has written. But it's also about memorization, being able to recall the rules well enough to not interrupt the flow of the story. Starting with character generation, you make what you want to play, and you play it accurately, but you also weave the narrative in with all the other characters. I never really played male characters. It felt like there were enough boys, so why be another?

Part of my skill appeared to be putting up with a ton of harassment directed at both my characters and me. At the time, I had to be able to handle abuse and sexual innuendo in huge doses. It was a requirement.

I wasn't a total innocent, mind you. I slept with a lot of gamer boys. I mean, I could, couldn't I? Here they are, in chronological order: Jason, Art, Troy, Billy, Shelby, Jeremy, Dan, Arjun, Edward, Shannon, Mike. I had a lot of sex, I ran at trains, I played with swords, but I made a terrible princess. Being with the boys in a fantasy life mainly without girls confused people, even the well intentioned. I was generally asked, "Are you a slut, or something else?" I always said I was something else.

The biggest issue for me with being a slut is that you are still just a woman to be either saved or shunned. I wanted to be seen as a really good gamer, but I didn't want that to mean I had to give up sex and relationships. The boys certainly didn't think they had to. I was doing this for fun, and sex is fun. I tended to have sex with people I wanted to have sex with; some of them were people I was in love with, some of them just looked like they'd be fun. Everyone was confused: the boys by my sexuality, and me by what a big deal people made out it. To this day I'm still not clear what the problem was.

San Jose, 2001: My grown-up gamer friends and I tried a couple of games but never really kept it up. Eventually, our gaming slowed to a small trickle, and the other gamers moved on.

Sure, we got too busy, but there's more to it. The hit wasn't enough anymore; I wanted to make it real. But did reality ever live up to the expectation of gaming? Are the anecdotes from real life ever quite as good? We made and destroyed universes in our heads, we accessorized with strange dice and accounting. And, let's be honest, we escaped from our real lives. Gaming wasn't as attractive when my life went somewhere I wanted it to be. Partly I stopped gaming because life became better.

But gaming also inspired me to make my life as interesting as the games had been. I learned to seek out the beginnings of adventures. Life moves in story arcs, and I try to make reality as interesting as the stuff we used to daydream about. It's a challenge that's taken me across deserts, through dodgy border crossings, and around the basements of castles.

Games are exactly as complex as stories. But, like life, they are stories that immerse you. And you can change them as they are unfolding.

∞

San Francisco, 2006: When I sat down to write this, I asked both men and women what they thought about gaming. I was told, "Most women view gaming as an infection boys get." It's true, too. I was always an invader in the secret life of boys, and worst of all, the secret inner life of boys, where they are badass heroes or the voice of God. I wanted it too; I wanted a secret life of Bone Dragons and talking swords. They told me I couldn't because I was a girl, and besides, I was crazy to want it. I spent years being beaten and wooed, and I had no idea why until years later. In gaming all the boys wanted me because I was a gamer girl, but they also wanted me the hell out of their fantasy lives.

Boys get better fantasy lives. Go steal them.

Sometimes I'm still back in 1996, in Florida, playing Vampire in the middle of a dark park. I'm walking around with a steaming mug, tail end of a tampon hanging out. I'm grinning. I explain to the horrified boys: It's tea.

»»»»why *BMX XXX* sucks

Mara Poulsen

alt met my eyes maybe twice in all the time I worked under him. When we first met, he shook my hand and smiled at his shoes. I later heard he called me Lilith (after the uptight psychiatrist wife of Frasier Crane from *Cheers*) behind my back when I was interviewing because I'd worn a stiff pantsuit with my hair in a bun. A short guy, Walt had been at Acclaim Studios, a game-developer subsidary of Acclaim Entertainment, for five years. He was leading a programming team for the first time. He clearly wasn't expecting a Lilith type to join his team of programmers. My hiring at Acclaim had been a quick process: From the time I submitted my résumé to the time I began work was roughly three weeks, so I don't think he was prepared. I wondered, later, what his bosses had told him about me, or if they'd bothered to tell him anything at all.

Our team had a three-month deadline to port a new game from PlayStation 2 to Gamecube: an excruciatingly short schedule for a team of four, especially considering that our engine team had yet to finish the Gamecube version. I expected to miss Thanksgiving, Christmas, and New Year's entirely, emerging red-eyed in March to stare at the yellow ball in the sky and think, "What *is* that thing?" So I was more than a little surprised when Walt assigned me the opening credits and menu—what game programmers derisively call "the fluff." The original PS2 code had been thrown together by a kid right out of high school with no formal training.

Let me preface the moral crisis I faced with the facts that I'd just left my last job after an extended period of crunch time, I was newly married to a man who hadn't seen very much of me since our honeymoon, and as much as I would come to like my team, I didn't want to spend all my waking hours—as well as a few during which I shouldn't be awake—with them. Walt may have been a sexist Rodney Dangerfield type, but he was also giving me an out. If I complained about my lack of workload, there was a chance I'd end up with, well, more work. I hated the obvious lack of respect in the assignment, but at the same time, it was like getting paid to scratch myself.

Gloria Steinem would not have approved, but I kept my mouth shut. I never stayed at work past midnight, and most nights I went home about 10:30 PM. By the week before Christmas, I had the credits and menu running, while the rest of my team had yet to coax the game to load or display. While they slogged away over the holidays, I used up my vacation time for the year to take the week off. I suppose I should have thought about them, my team members, slaving under those awful fluorescent lights, all times of the day and night seeming the same for lack of windows. I didn't.

Maybe because I was such a traitor to feminism, the ruse didn't last. No one could miss the fact that I was out of the office for a full quarter of the month—not even Walt, who wouldn't speak to me without fixating on the space to the right of my head. I admitted to him that I had no more work to do. He did comment, uncomfortably, on how, um, good it was that I had turned my project around so quickly. "So," he said. "Have you done this kind of work before?"

I was forced to bow my head in shame. "Walt," I said in the attitude of confession, "I have a computer science degree from Bryn Mawr College. I worked at Saffire Corporation for two years on three different games, including one for which I was technical lead. My specialties are physics and AI."

For a minute there, Walt's face actually turned bright green. I turned my lips up in a sympathetic smile. We talked a little bit more at that point about what kind of work I had done in the past and with that conversation, my free ride ended.

I don't want to make Walt out to be a bad guy (I certainly didn't help the situation by not confronting him from the beginning), or even to imply that most of the men I worked with during my three years in the game industry were anything like him. Walt just didn't seem to know what to do with a girl in his office space. One day I wore the rare skirt to work. Walt fell all over himself trying to find a way to compliment the outfit without straying into sexual harassment territory. Watching him fidget and sputter and spout embarrassing things like, "Well, now, don't take this the wrong way . . ." and "How are you supposed to know how to say something like that without offending . . ." would have made a good stand-up act. I let it go on for about three or four minutes before finally cutting him off with, "Walt, all you have to say is, 'That skirt looks nice on you.'" He mumbled something to that effect before fleeing back to his office to watch a Mario Twins Flash movie.

But Walt was, really, an uncommon specimen of adolescent sexual awkwardness lingering in a grown man. My office mate, Jay, treated me as an equal and a friend from my first day, as did the vast majority of my coworkers. I would like to say that it was hard being the token female programmer (I was in fact the only one at Acclaim, and one of just three at Saffire), but in truth it was easy. My teammates were good people and respected me. We talked collision detection and pathfinding algorithms. We moaned together about the obtuseness of Sony's microcode. We tested each other's modules and embedded stupid jokes in the comments of one another's header files.

I've come away with the impression that men who are uncomfortable with women in the office are uncomfortable with women in general: like Nick, a project manager at Acclaim who dyed his gray hair an overdone brown and who had pictures of himself posing with "booth babes" from video game conferences like E3 all over his office. My first week at Acclaim, he bizarrely insulted my husband after looking at the wedding picture I had on my desk, as if he needed to inundate me with alpha-male pheromones at his first chance. He went on to make several stupid comments to me over the next year, almost all embarrassing and seemingly Tourettic. His eyes would bulge in fear, his mouth would open, and out would pop something offensive. He just couldn't seem to help himself, even after I asked him, "Do you practice being an ass, or does it just come naturally?"

Not every repellent man behaved like Nick, who at least had the decency never to proposition me. One of my managers at Saffire, Russ, made the mistake of professing his love for me after hours, and asking if he could come stay with me should his wife kick him out of their house. Was it harassment? Simple stupidity? Should I have reported him? By the next day, he seemed to have realized what he had done and from then on avoided me assiduously except for the horrible moment about a month later when he tried to apologize. He eventually got fired for some other reason, and I would go on to tell only two coworkers about the incident, much, much later. It wasn't that I was afraid to "rock the boat" or concerned that my job might be endangered—they likely would have fired him much earlier had I reported him. It was more that I was proud of the fact that I had achieved a certain androgyny in my job, that I'd reached formal geek status with the men who surrounded me. I didn't want to ruin that by reminding everyone that I had boobs.

How sad, then, that boobs were ultimately what did in my career as a game programmer. Sex is like bad air freshener at a development studio, pervading even the spaces where it wasn't squirted. Not real-life hetero-sexual sex, where adults engage in the mutual goal of satisfaction, but Beavis-Butthead-adolescent-male sex—where women are scary and tremendous; where great, bulbous breasts bound along ahead of women like enormous warning lights; where viewable but untouchable T&A makes the user feel safely titillated. You have to expect that kind of thing in an industry targeting the teenage boy, but I was surprised at how even the most stoic of programmers can be reduced to simpering perverts by just the sight of a few polygons fashioned into breast shapes.

My first project at Saffire was a four-person fighting game in which many of the ass-kickers were women. So far so good. Near the end of the project, one of my coworkers took on the job of—to put it in geek-speak—"soft-body dynamics." In other words, he had to create hair and clothes that shift with movement. Oh yeah, and boobs. His first attempt at realism was to make the aforementioned items bounce in proportion to the amount of space the character had crossed within one game loop. This might have worked all right, if not for the fact that at the end of each fighting round, the winner zoomed to the center of the arena for a special camera spline (a series of points that an animated camera follows) and tri-umph animation (an animation played on the character model at the end of a round if the character has won). Sometimes they crossed the equiva-lent of a football field. These poor women should have been knocked out by the force of their breasts writhing and recoiling around their torsos like John Hurt's worst nightmare.

It was just a bug that needed to be fixed, but not before a group of my teammates had gathered around one computer to bound the women around the arena in the hopes of making the best, most hilarious breast octopus. After awhile, I started throwing things at them. "Break it up, you losers!" The team lead eventually had to order them to slurp their tongues into their mouths again and get back to work. And these weren't even Walt- or Nick- or Russ-type jerks—they were ordinary geeks like me who worked in games because games were their passion, not because they had hoped to pilot a giant, gyrating hooter one day.

Most of the time, though, the sex pressure came from the publisher. My second project at Saffire was another fighting game, one in which the artists had wide latitude to design characters. My favorite was a female knight in full armor. She looked like Joan of Arc, only more likely to chop your head off than pray for you. She would have made a very striking figure in the game, broadsword swinging, light reflecting silver off her shield. The artists also created a female assassin dressed in full black—down to the face wrap that exposed only her eyes. With the inclusion of both males and females, each with a unique backstory and skills set, Saffire's artist pool turned out a complicated, rich character array. Then the publisher had a turn at them. "Not sexy enough" was the word that came back. What did that mean? Essentially, the women were wearing too many clothes.

The knight character was dropped and they were forced to turn her into a "warrior princess," replete with chain mail bikini top and little leather skirt. The assassin character stayed, but her curve-covering black was replaced by a long ribbon of material that managed, just barely, to cross all the important bits. The artists hated the changes; it limited their creativity to confine them to juggy women in skimpy clothes. Not to mention the great conundrum of the video game heroine: Why, if she's out clashing with bad guys, would she be wearing an outfit that exposes most of her vital organs? Bikini in a beach volleyball game? Makes perfect sense. Bikini on the battlefield? Moronic—like the female Klingons from *Star Trek: The Next Generation*, with the armor cutout right at cleavage height. Might as well post a sign stating STAB HERE.

There's no moral to this story. The game was published with the new character set, itsy-bitsy battle outfits included, but I stopped working on it at the point where they were forced to drop that magnificent knight. I told our programming director I was going to quit if this was the kind of crap I had to look forward to. He steered me onto a new project that had robots in it—no chain mail halter tops in sight.

At Acclaim, there was a drawing posted on the wall near the artists' corner of a girl in fantasy regalia. I never did decide if it was facetious or not. Around the girl was a list of instructions with helpful pointers on how to improve her: Make the eyes bigger, make the hair fuller, pout the lips more, increase the breast and hip size, decrease the waist. I never saw an artist looking at it, but I was often mesmerized by that poor sod in her little tunic and boots. *You look too much like a normal woman,* I used to think to her. *And that's intimidating, I suppose.* Contrast her with the "danger girls" that at one time occupied half my office—the half that wasn't mine. I shared space then with an artist, Zack, who was a very decent guy and yet had an obsession with extreme-proportioned superheroines in nonexistent clothing. I did my best to be a good sport about it. After all, I had my own poster of *Final Fantasy VII* on the wall. Even the men who saw it commented on the fact that Tina's chest, as depicted, was so over-inflated that it looked ready to burst and shower the other characters in flesh-colored polygons. Zack called me out on the hypocrisy of the poster when I tried to explain to him once why his "danger girls" could possibly be considered offensive. "I like the game," I told him, "but I would never have made her like this if I had the option. Even you have to admit she looks ridiculous." His answer: "I like her."

All these things were exasperating, but never deal breakers. I came to the industry expecting a certain amount of it. What did finally end my career was a game I would never actually see. I take some pleasure in the fact that a majority of teenage boys never saw it either. The content caused several companies, Wal-Mart the giant among them, to yank it from their shelves, though who can say if it was really worse than games that actually made it into their cases, like the Grand Theft Auto series.

A game with a glut of sex is one thing. A biking game that just happens to also have naked women in it for no apparent reason—that's just pandering. Evil marketing-team pandering. I am, of course, talking about *BMX XXX*, which Acclaim published in 2002 to a few offended newspaper articles and a resounding upturned nose by the public. It had Acclaim Entertainment heads smacking their lips and rubbing their palms together with such glee, they actually sent someone from New York City to our little Utah office just to tell us how young boys would be calling each other while their parents slept to gasp about the naughty stripper content. "It's funny," the New York executive insisted. "It's so funny!"

Funny, but its lack of success was one of the reasons the company would close its Salt Lake City studio, laying off my friends and teammates, only months after I quit. But I quit before I knew whether or not the game would succeed. I have tried to identify what it is about *BMX XXX* that pisses me off so much. Is it the fact that biking and strippers seem a bit incongruous? Is it Acclaim's in-house admission that, although the game was supposedly only for the eighteen-and-up set, they were really hoping adolescent boys would get their hands on it? Is it that I could easily imagine forty- and fiftysomething men sitting around a conference table in New York saying, "We need a hit. What game can we put some naked women in?"

I'm sure it's all of these things, but what really seems to irritate me is this notion of women as a foreign species, that we need to liquefy a woman's brain and inject it into her chest in order to make her interesting. Listen, boys, do you really feel better being alone with your TV and PS2 controller and watching pixilated body parts jiggle? Isn't that a little sad? Go outside. There are real women there. Lara Croft cannot be your girl-friend, so turn the game off, take her calendar down, and go meet some-one with a personality.

This was how I felt standing in front of Walt that first day: like the alien character Kang from the *The Simpsons* extending my tentacle to be shaken. The man had a wife, but he clearly was not expecting a female-type unit to enter this domain. I blame this on the failure of every enter-tainment designed to appeal mostly to men: Where are the women, the real women, who aren't strippers or prostitutes or blank-eyed babes with huge melons? I call future female first-person shooters to arms: Invade and infiltrate the industry! And maybe people like Walt will learn to deal or fade away, and the reign of the Big Bouncing Breast will end.

I, for one, welcome our new girlie overlords.

superheroes

»»»»sidekicks

Devin Kalile Grayson

write comic books for a living, which is apparently a novel thing for a female to do. I had no idea that was the case until I created the first ongoing Batman title to be developed and written by a woman. Of course, I didn't do so because I was female; I did so because I have a hard-on for Batman and the characters surrounding him. But once the book came out, people started asking a lot of questions about me that I found pretty uncomfortable. I am, after all, a geek. And I thought I was going to get to talk about Batman.

I love to talk about Batman.

But how's this for irony? I would never have discovered, let alone integrated myself into, the masculine cultures of comics, sci-fi, or role-playing games if not for my quest to express the most feminine, trusting, loyal, and submissive facets of my nature. How could I have guessed that finding the perfect fictional expression of my own self-censored fidelity and desire to serve would lead to being photographed in superhero-icon T-shirts and asked on an almost daily basis, "How does it feel to be a female in a male-dominated industry?" In hindsight, I guess I should have known I was in for it the first time I noticed that my male alter ego wears tights. . . .

But let me back up. As much as I hate to admit it, this all started a long time ago in a galaxy far, far away. Peeved as I am with the now-soulless merchandising juggernaut of the *Star Wars* franchise, I prefer not to dwell on a past once brilliant with nonself-referential plotlines and tender characterization, but that's where it all started for me, and that's still the clearest model going: Luke Skywalker is unquestionably the protagonist, the hero, of *Star Wars*. Nevertheless, Han Solo kicks his ass.

I don't mean literally in the plot of the movie; I'm talking cool factor. I knew it when I was seven years old, and I'm just as sure of it now. I can still remember standing with a tree-branch light saber, squinting in the sun, outside of Zach Brogan's house in the summer of '77. Zach wanted to be Luke, and we were in his yard, so that was fine—that was a given. But

Jacob and I had the entire rest of the cast left to argue over, and the results of that brief and amicable quarrel defined much of the rest of my life.

"We need Han and Leia," Zach decided.

"I'll be Han," I said, tossing aside the long branch I'd been holding.

Jacob's jaw dropped. "Uh . . . but that would mean I'm Leia. . . ."

"Right," Zach confirmed, as I found a shorter, more blasterlike stick a few feet away.

Jacob's voice rose to a slightly panicked whine. "But I don't *want* to be Leia!"

I spun toward Jacob, brandishing my new stick, and gleefully mimicked a Harrison Ford–like sneer. "Well, I sure as hell ain't gonna do it, sweetheart."

I remember my throat tightening as Jacob then turned to Zach, desperate to impute femininity to me. "But *she's* the *girl!*" he protested.

Zach stood behind us, arms folded, and nodded thoughtfully before delivering his final verdict. I saw him look me up and down with a small frown of confusion, then shrug as he turned back to Jacob.

"She *is* kinda more Han, though," he admitted. And so began my conscious life.

The thing is, it was totally true. I don't know why, and I in no way mean to impugn Jacob's manhood, but at age seven I was already ten times the Han he'd ever be. And at that moment, with a great, big thud of affirmation from my heart, I knew two things. First: There's no point in huffing around with a bad attitude and buns on either side of your head when you can drink heartily, pilot kick-ass spaceships, and get away with calling starry-eyed do-gooders "kid." Second: For that simple act of recognition alone, my Han would follow Zach's Luke anywhere, cheerfully killing any storm trooper foolish enough to cross his path. My true nature and value had been seen, and with my masculinity thus avowed, I was free to worship my little heart out.

Now, technically, Han Solo would not be considered a sidekick. Chewy's a sidekick, as are R2-D2 and C3P0 (the droids actually being sort of über-sidekicks, given that they're literally designed to assist the main characters, both structurally and in the metareality of the film, and then also manage to sidekick for one another), and Han is a rogue archetype, a swashbuckler—a whole different breed. But in looking strictly at *Star Wars's* dramatic narrative as a hero's journey à la Jung, Campbell, or

Vogler, one could make the case that Luke is the story's protagonist and Han is one of the allies who helps him through his trials.

In any case, that's an academic argument. I'm using the term "side-kick" very loosely here, to define those who devote themselves to the well-being of someone else, even when doing so is somewhat against their better (and/or normally self-serving) judgment. And I'm so defining it for wholly personal reasons. I've long since moved on from Han, carefully sifting through an ever-expanding roster of fictional entities in search of the very best fits, and it is this adoration of sidekicks that has led me to my geekdom.

Growing up, I read detective novels because of Sherlock Holmes's Watson and Hercule Poirot's loyal Hastings (on whom I had quite the fictional crush). I watched science fiction because of Han and the original *Battlestar Galactica*'s adventurous Starbuck and read "vampire genre" fiction because of the reckless but nonetheless munificent devotion Anne Rice's Vampire Lestat lavishes on every one of his acolytes, from Nicki to Louis to Armand. In my twenties, I discovered, devoured, and forged a career in comic books because—and only because—of Batman's devoted not-quite son, Robin. I still play pencil and D10 RPGs at least once a week so that I can be various tragic heroes protecting—with sidekicklike devotion— their doomed loves (my favorite gaming character being an extrapolation on a grown-up Daigoro from *Lone Wolf and Cub,* another archetypal sidekick). And although some tanks will argue that they're leaders, I play computer games for the sheer joy of jumping in front of a friend's avatar to dutifully pull and pound on whatever MOB they've directed me toward on TS. I'm also enough of a geek not to want to stop and explain what "tank," "RPG," "IRL," "pull," "MOB," or "TS" mean. Even novice geek vocabulary is as carefully guarded as a secret handshake. What sounds modish and eloquent in the context of online gaming is all too quickly demystified when linked back to the programming abbreviations and acronyms used by game developers and testers. Besides, you have to earn your geekdom comprehension. For me to just tell you would go against the dictates of male camaraderie.

I learned that from the first clerk I ever approached in a comic book store. When I asked how to find comics that featured Robin, he frowned at me like I was some strange interloper and mumbled something about a wizard (it took me two more years to realize that he had been referring to

Wizard, a flashy "trade magazine" devoted to comic books). The second guy I asked was a close friend, and his perplexing answer, "which Robin?" only drove the point home. You can't become a comic geek overnight. To be misunderstood by the mainstream is easy, but to become truly incomprehensible to all but your self-selected peers takes a great deal of practice and devotion.

While my "real life" friends patiently upgraded, twinked, power-leveled, and long-boxed me into shape, my fictional mentors worked with me on my internal life. Han taught me that though I'd frequently be mistaken for a princess, I would always be, at heart, all rogue. Along with Nicki, Armand, and Louis, I followed the Vampire Lestat into the darker realms of fandom, earning, for my troubles, an extraordinary card from Anne Rice herself, who was kind enough to respond to a letter I'd written her and encourage me in my creative endeavors. It was Dick Grayson, though—first appearing in my life with his feet up on the dashboard of the Batmobile in an episode of *Batman: The Animated Series*—who finally led me all the way into the deep end of fandom APAs (Amateur Press Associations) and fanfic. He was also the one who showed me that I'd never become fully autonomous until I learned to serve someone else.

Though I'm currently so obsessed with Joss Whedon's Firefly series/*Serenity* movie character Jayne Cobb that I'm speaking in futuristic frontier slang, TiVo-ing every Adam Baldwin movie ever made, and waking up singing the "Hero of Canton" ballad, the first and most quintessential sidekick in my life will always be Dick. Dick Grayson, as any good comic geek could tell you, was the first Robin in Gotham City and now—being in his late twenties and generally too proud to go out wearing little green shorts—goes by the superhero moniker Nightwing. Nightwing is one of several Batman-related monthly comic book series published by DC Comics, thirty-nine issues of which I've been fortunate enough to write. Yes, that's right; my fictional obsession pays my bills. Perhaps I am suspended in the perpetual adolescence that the mainstream media forever accuses the geekier members of my generation of being unable to escape, but Bruce Wayne does pay my mortgage. Shiny.

As a character, Dick embodies loyalty. Batman is a tragic hero whose misfortune and heroism both stem from the loss of his parents, who were shot to death in his presence when he was only eight years old. Bruce grew up under the watchful eye of the family butler, Alfred, but understandably experiences himself as being very much alone in the world. By contrast, although Dick also witnessed his parents' murder before he was ten, he grew up with Bruce. In my work, I imagine him as a young trapeze flyer transplanted into the home of a mysterious billionaire, achingly lonely until the bottom falls out of Wayne Manor to reveal a world every bit as thrilling and dangerous as the one he left, a secret confessed that demands even more maturity and dedication from him than the self-contained, itinerant community of the circus. Energetic, physical, and effusive by nature, Dick—now called Robin—flourishes. Maybe there's even a point at which he stops wanting his old life back—can't, in fact, imagine any other destiny than the one he now knows as the "laughing, darting ray of sunshine" fighting beside Gotham's Dark Knight. The mission Batman experiences as atonement and obligation, Robin expresses as gratitude and devotion. And although it's difficult for most of us to imagine being so driven that we dedicate our entire lives to a single, fundamentally unattainable goal (such as ridding an entire city of crime), who among us cannot imagine the blissful coincidence of meeting up with someone we believe in so much that we dedicate our bodies and being to his or her cause?

Note that I said, "imagine." Many people simply aren't predisposed to be followers. I know because I'm one of them. Perhaps not surprisingly, my obsessive adoration of sidekicks and allies thrives in the tension between my inherently loyal nature and my learned inability to trust or delegate. I would give anything to give myself over wholly to another person, but I don't know how. So far, I haven't even figured out how to pick people who are actually available, let alone assess their true worthiness of my devotion. Like a CEO paying a dominatrix to relieve him— even if only for an hour and only in an erotic context—of the burden of control, I use both work and play to attach myself to fictional entities who embody allegiance. In real life (which I can't help but mentally refer to with reductionist gaming term "IRL"), I'm judgmental, intolerant of incompetence, and so intent on moving things along efficiently that I usually find myself taking over any project in which I participate. I have no patience with convention when it is not effective and so am often considered an iconoclast and a pioneer—not the usual starting profile for a sidekick. According to the Myers-Briggs Type Indicator, I am, along with less than 1 percent of the population, an INTJ: introverted (as opposed to extroverted), intuitive (as opposed to sensing), thinking (as opposed to feeling), and judging (as opposed to perceiving). This type has been called the Architect, the Visionary, and the Systems Builder, but never the Sidekick, Ally, or Acolyte.

The Myers-Briggs Type Indicator is often used by businesses for profiling and placing potential employees. Of the sixteen possible types, I am one of four that no attentive supervisor would ever place in a subservient or deferential work position. I've spent the last eight years of my career writing Batman and Batman-related comics, and I can state with utter certainty that Bruce Wayne, an exceptionally attentive supervisor, would never allow me to follow him across the Gotham rooftops at night. Physical incompetence aside, he would find me far too argumentative and would have difficulty appreciating my frequent assertions concerning the ultimate futility of his mission. I'm not saying that Robin obeys every order that comes his way without question. He does not. And as for arguments—Bruce and Dick have had some doozies (conflict, of course, creating the best drama). But Dick Grayson is obedient by nature, as, I would argue, are Armand, Daigoro Ito, and even the formidable but cuddly Jayne Cobb. Some of them, like Armand, subscribe to dogmatic religious beliefs. All of them have faith.

Faith, after all, is the fundamental glory of the sidekick. Our heroes are forced to act decisively, but we allow them—carrying, as they do, the burden of advancing the plot—doubt and reservations as they move through their trials. The sidekick has no such concerns. Whether a sidekick is mercenary, pragmatic, or gorgeously loyal, his course of action is clear: assist, protect, and obey the hero. Jayne believes that Mal will lead him to fortune. Armand believes that Lestat is a prophet of the future, Daniel its embodiment. Robin believes that Batman is the greatest man ever to live, worthy of almost any sacrifice. Even when entirely devoid of romantic subtext, all sidekick decisions are made within a context of electively narrowed options, so that being a good sidekick is, in the thick of things, a lot like being in love. Imagine making a decision with decisiveness, conviction, no regard for practicality, and the absolute certainty that if you prove wrong after all, someone has your back. Imagine how much of yourself you could find if you were able to give it all away.

This is one of the main qualities I have compulsively circled in my work and in my play, and it has not escaped my notice that most of the media that brings me closer to these traditionally female values of devotion and self-sacrifice are discovered in the traditionally male bastions of comic books, sci-fi, and online RPGs. I have no trouble expressing empathy, tolerance, open-mindedness, or affection in my day-to-day existence as a biological female, and I think both my family and friends would consider me loyal, devoted, and even surprisingly socialized in feminine acquiescence. But something essential is missing, some attribute of unreserved commitment and passionate abandon (whether for love or bloodshed or the cause du jour) that I can only experience from a male point of view. This is part of the difficulty in answering a question like "What does it feel like to be a female in a male-dominated industry?" I have nothing to compare the experience to, having never been a female in a female-dominated industry or a male in any industry at all. But truthfully, most of the time I'm not sure I *am* a female in a male-dominated industry, since when alone writing I channel male characters and when in meetings with my colleagues I am "one of the guys." Only the question itself—usually posed by a well-meaning fan or member of our small comics-industry press—relentlessly keeps me aware of my gender. After working so hard and successfully to become an industry insider, the question pulls me out of the professional collective of comic book writers and positions me as an outsider in a small, still woefully underpopulated subclass.

Speaking from that subclass, I can easily enumerate examples, both positive and negative, of the impact my sex has had on my work environment. Early on in my career, the novelty of my gender probably helped open some doors. It also spawned a baseless and nasty Internet rumor that I'm sure would be familiar to successful women the world over about how I, being female and therefore apparently incapable of possessing either skill or talent, supposedly got that job. Later on I was overjoyed to be invited to serve on convention panels shoulder-to-shoulder with my male colleagues, and frustrated later in the evenings during convention-related social events when I was suddenly expected to socialize with the wives and girlfriends of those same colleagues while the boys talked shop (and to be fair, it is rarely a matter of exclusion on the part of the men, but rather an effort toward inclusion on the part of the women that nonetheless takes me out of some important industry conversations). I've never known what to say when a male comic fan, caught off guard by the gender ambiguity of my first name, approaches me, wide-eyed, at a convention signing table to inform me, "You're a girl!" Once I glanced down, astonished, at my breasts before knocking my chair over backward and leaping to my feet with a scream, but usually I just nod blandly and try to muster up a smile. The line between selling your work and selling yourself has become so thin in this celebrity-crazed culture that introverted writers and artists must learn the extremely extroverted art of self-promotion, which includes a solid understanding of the "whole package" you are striving to present. I generally try to avoid *"Female!"* as a selling point, but then, of course, my being female *is* the most socially relevant characteristic of my work. The best way to persuade someone that my work is unique is to have them read it. Barring that possibility, though, I'm stuck either describing it ("I write primarily about relationships") or describing my place in the industry ("I'm the first woman to . . .").

Often, the choice of whether or not to advertise my femaleness is taken out of my hands by the very framework of the setting in which I'm doing the selling. I'm frequently invited to participate in panels and sometimes even conventions dedicated to highlighting the work of females in comics. Sometimes I participate, sometimes I don't. Obviously, it's helpful to bring attention to the work my female peers and I do, but I also bristle when I glance around an all-female panel and find no interest or quality linking the work of the people sitting on it other than their sex. I recently had someone try to coax me into participating in just such an event by mentioning that Ramona Fradon would be in attendance. Fradon is a wonderfully talented American comic book and comic strip artist who worked on Aquaman in the '50s and '60s (among other notable accomplishments). She's a great addition to any comic convention and someone I'd definitely enjoy meeting, but the only possible question you could ask both of us with any chance of mutual relevance would be along the lines of, you guessed it: "What's it like to be a female in a . . . ?" She's a visual artist; I'm a writer. She was in the fortieth year of her career when I started mine. We have never worked on the same project, or even, as far as I know, on the same characters. But we're supposed to sit on a panel together because we're both "women in comics." What would that panel really be about? How much of a chance would we have to move the conversation away from gender politics and into a discussion about our actual work, the kind of conversation our male peers have all the time? How different *would* my experience in this industry be if I were male? Would I even have been interested in writing about superheroes?

By now it should be clear that one of the main attractions of this work for me is the chance to slip into powerful male psyches long enough to tell stories using their perspectives and voices. I love imagining moving around the world in one of those bodies, seeing the world through different sets of eyes. I have friends who have taken that a step further, living their lives in self-defined "male" drag or arranging for sexual reassignment surgery. I admit to having flirted with this idea but have proved too vain. Unless I could be a guy who looks like Dick Grayson or Jayne Cobb, what's the point? With my double-D chest, long eyelashes, and addiction to organic cosmetics, it would almost certainly take more effort than it would be worth to make me into a physical male. Besides, then I'd just be stuck with another incomprehensible set of expectations. I don't relate to the male stereotypes any better than to the female ones. I have never met any of the people the stand-up comics love to joke about; the stereotypical laconic, farting, butt-scratching, beer-swilling, football-obsessed guys are just as foreign to me as these supposedly ubiquitous chocoholic, shoe-fetishizing, histrionic, red-rose-and-diamond-tennis-bracelet-obsessed ladies. Those aren't gender archetypes; those are idiots. And because they are idiots invented by the same industry (advertising) to be consistently represented in mutually dependent pairs, we should all feel equally irritated with stupid generalizations about both males and females.

Fortunately, I am not at all alone with this discomfort. Almost everyone resists being stereotyped, and geeks in particular have become very good at finding ways to become who they truly are without worrying overly much about social conformity. So I join their ranks in a female body with a male heart, a sidekick bereft of a mentor, and a compulsively efficient and desperately loyal enthusiast in an age of incompetence and passivity. Unlike gender, geekdom is knowledge based and therefore not so easily stripped away. Because it suggests passionate erudition on any one of so many impenetrable subjects, geekdom can function as a societal warning sign: DANGER, DO NOT ASSUME YOU KNOW WHAT'S GOING ON IN MY MIND. It is also, unlike gender, possible to hide.

Though considering the determinations society will make about you based on just the available physical evidence, why you'd gorram bother is beyond me.

»»»»neville-mania

Michelle Villanueva

1. Beyond Character Sheets

I pretend I'm a fictional character on the Internet. In real life, I'm a Filipino American woman on the brink of her thirties who lives in Northern California, but I write a blog in the persona of a nineteen-year-old male who lives in the United Kingdom and teaches at a prominent school there. I guess I also should mention that he used to be classmates with Harry Potter.

Yes, *that* Harry Potter.

I'm a journal role-player. I don't care about stats or quests or bringing my character to the next ability level; I care about storytelling and interactivity. I'm part of a world of free-form online role-playing. We call ourselves character bloggers.

The Internet is tailor-made for creative anonymity. Look at the countless numbers of so-called celebrity blogs and LiveJournals and MySpace accounts that fill up every corner of the web. Are most of these real? Not by a long shot. Most of the famous-people blogs are thought up by bored nobodies who want to experience the illicit thrill of pretending to be someone else without the baggage of not physically looking like the people they're portraying. People like me.

2. Rampant Fan Speculation

For many fans of the boy wizard, the Harry Potter books just aren't enough. A voracious fandom has sprouted around those soon-to-be-seven novels. Many people write their own stories featuring the characters from the books. Most fanfiction writers and readers seem to be female. Maybe women are more willing to explore the "what-ifs" that fanfiction makes possible. We're more open to playing with and stretching the characters, writing them into scenarios the original author wouldn't touch. And it seems we're more open to sharing our own works and supporting each other.

The only problem with fanfiction is that it's static. Once you send a story to fanfiction.net or post it on a LiveJournal community, it's done. The story has an end, and apart from other people speaking with the original author, the ideas and plots contained within the story have been locked away. But what if you don't want the story to end or be static? What if you want to immerse these characters into an ongoing, interactive, serial story while exploring ideas that won't ever show up in the original books? That's where online journal role-playing comes in.

Search any popular journaling site (like LiveJournal or its code-cousin GreatestJournal) and you will find hundreds of accounts of people claiming to be Harry Potter, Ronald Weasley, Hermione Granger, and the rest of J. K. Rowling's dramatis personae. Explore further, and you'll notice nearly all of these accounts are connected to journaling communities. These characters gain new life when unleashed upon the Internet in the hands of capable players. Just like fanfiction writers, the vast majority of Harry Potter role-players are female, and many of them play male characters. Not every girl can portray Hermione. Someone's got to be Harry. Or Ron. Or Snape. Or Remus. Or Neville.

3. Gaming in Drag

I'm a heterosexual female in a healthy relationship, but I still feel a need to satisfy my curiosity about the opposite sex. I may have a boyfriend, but that doesn't mean I understand the way his mind works. Portraying a male character gives me the freedom to explore what it feels like to be a guy. It also gives me the freedom to experience how the world treats a man.

Once I log in to my account, everybody treats me like a man. Whenever I interact with another user, we both stay in character, whether we're male, female, or inhuman. (Some people play centaurs, house-elves, giants, and other magical creatures.) As long as I believe my male character is speaking with another user's male character (even if both of the users behind the keyboards are female), then it's true.

Although I haven't told my boyfriend that I role-play a male character, I doubt it would bother him. He already knows I write fiction with male protagonists, and I consider journal or blog role-playing as an extension of writing fiction. The only reason I haven't told him is because he finds Harry Potter boring.

4. Neville, the Boy Who Lived (Nearly)

When I read the books, one character stood out for me. It wasn't Harry or Ron or even Hermione. It was that poor, forgetful, clumsy kid whose luck was so bad he kept misplacing his own pet. I didn't like Harry. You're supposed to like Harry—he's the hero, for God's sake! And yet Neville Longbottom fascinated me. I wanted to know more about him, and when the books didn't deliver those crucial facts, I decided Neville needed an advocate.

Neville's online "birth" came in the autumn of 2003, when I was bored and a little sick and needed a distraction. I went through a long labor, forging a complete biography of a character whose background is barely touched on in the books. I really enjoy the challenge of pulling hints out of the main text and building on them. It's as if J. K. Rowling gave me a rough sketch of the character, and I needed to add colors, shadows, and highlights in order to create a believable character. Applications for role-playing characters generally include spots for a character's appearance, personality, and biography. After I was accepted as The Floo Network's Neville Longbottom, I worked on the character journal's user info (still available at www.greatestjournal.com/userinfo.bml?user=nev_l), which went deeper into Neville's personality. My version of Neville expresses some aspects of my personality, and it's exciting to watch him learn things and grow up.

Neville is timid, shy, and a bit of a pessimist. He has the tendency to worry about the most inconsequential things, though he gets pleasantly surprised when events turn out well. He gets nervous when in a new situation and then tends to stammer over his words. He's more comfortable when talking to his friends, however. He has a slight aversion to being touched and will noticeably flinch (or blush, or try to flee) if hugged or caught by an impromptu physical greeting like a hand on the shoulder. He's been known to trip over his own robes if he's not paying attention, but he always gets back up. He may not fit the profile of the average

Gryffindor, but Neville does have his own type of courage. Though slow to anger, he'll fight against anything that threatens those he loves.

After creating this character, I still needed to wait and see if the game's moderators were willing to take a chance and accept me to portray this role. Once the welcoming email came, I had in my possession a beautiful seventeen-year-old boy.

I plan to extend his life well past the reach of the books he sprang from, as J. K. Rowling has stated she won't carry on writing them after the seventh book. In a way, role-playing gives her characters a certain type of immortality. The Neville I portray has finished his schooling at Hogwarts and now teaches Herbology there. He has found meaning in his life, while in the original books he's still searching. I want to give him a happy ending, some amount of closure without having to worry about war or battles. Mostly, I'd like to see him content. And I'm going to make damn sure he gets that. I'm such a proud "mom," and I often joke that my boy has done quite well for himself.

5. "Slash" Stories

You can't discuss portraying a character of the opposite gender without focusing the spotlight on sexuality. "Slash" stories, where two characters get together sexually, are common in Harry Potter fanfiction—especially gay slash. Female fans love to see these boys get into relationships with other boys. Harry/Draco pairings are popular in fanfiction as well as role-playing, even though the books have Harry dating Ginny Weasley. Sometimes game moderators limit the number of gay relationships in their communities because they can become so overwhelmed with same-sex love stories.

Neville's sexuality is hinted at in the books but never mentioned outright. He asks Hermione Granger and then Ginny Weasley (after Hermione turns him down) to the Yule Ball. He seems to hold some sort of attraction (though the reader never knows if this goes past regular friendship) for Luna Lovegood. It's pretty clear that he likes girls and enjoys their company. He might also have some issues with the opposite sex because he was raised not by his two parents, but by his overbearing grandmother. He loves and respects her, which is reflected in the way he usually treats girls, but sometimes his grandmother terrifies him, too. She compares him unfairly to his father, and Neville feels inadequate in all relationships because of that.

In a way, it's simpler to portray this aspect of Neville (his inability to follow his heart and find a girl he likes) than to act out a self-confident male character, ready to take on all flings as they come. Neville is shy and awkward. He has an unbelievably difficult time asking a girl on a date and prefers concentrating on his greenhouse plants to romance. I don't have to think about how he would react to a kiss because Neville would try to dodge it at first. That's not to say that he'll never fall into a romantic relationship. I, along with one of the other players in our RPG, once imagined a future where Neville and her character (a female friend) finally get together and raise a family. The stories were adorable, and we were very pleased with the result, instant-messaging each other about how wonderful and cute the future would be. As you can see, the right heterosexual pairing can create as much insane, dorky fan-girling as the gay slash!

6. Neville and Me

I see a lot of Neville Longbottom in me, namely my own insecurities about being an only child and shy, and being more than a little clumsy and forgetful. Careless is probably the word that most people would associate with me. I try to build on those real-life experiences and plug them into the character. Since I identify a lot with Neville, as I bring him to more new experiences, it's like I'm growing in the process as well. If this fictional boy whom I adore can stumble through his world and survive after all of the things he's seen and gone through, then there must be some hope for me too.

»»»»when diana prince takes off her glasses

Annalee Newitz

On the suburban lawn outside our condo, I imitate the way Diana Prince becomes Wonder Woman every week on television. I pretend to pull my hair out of a tight bun, take off my imaginary glasses, and spin around until I explode like a star going nova. When the light withdraws, I'm wearing her lasso of truth and her bulletproof bracelets. The glasses have disappeared.

For the rest of my life, I find myself thinking occasionally about that transformation. In my thirties I buy the DVD box sets of the *Wonder Woman* TV shows to see if the show holds up over time. Unfortunately, the plots are silly, and Wonder Woman's self-effacing heroism ("Oh Steve! It's just little old me lifting up this tank!") is wince-worthy.

Still, the moment when Wonder Woman takes off her glasses is burned into the retinas of my unconscious. She's a geek until she takes them off, but afterward she's a fantasy—not because of her super strength and invisible plane, but because she's smart, commanding, and sexually appealing at the same time. As anyone familiar with mainstream U.S. culture knows, such a woman is not supposed to exist.

My first lasso of truth is a Kaypro 4 with two floppy drives and a tiny green LED screen. It has a modem, which my friend John explains is for logging in to a thing called a BBS, or a computer bulletin board system. He knows a good one called Wiznet, where up to a dozen people can chat at the same time. Every night, I log into Wiznet and talk until all hours of the morning with people whose bodies are lines of glowing text. I pick a gender-neutral handle: Shockwave Rider. Everybody assumes I'm male, and I don't bother to correct them.

I write my first story about high-tech outlaws in high school. It's about my best friends, who recently cracked a piece of software. "Cracking" means breaking the copy-protection scheme that prevents people from making free copies of the program. I sit with them while they go over dot-matrix printouts and get them to teach me about assembly language and how to turn Apple's graphics program MacPaint into something that anybody can download for free. Later, they teach me about phreaking, a way of hacking the phone system so you can make free phone calls. I sit at my Kaypro for days, composing a tale about geeks who are romantic outlaws, liberating software for the benefit of humanity.

My English teacher isn't crazy about the story, but I gain a reputation among the computer nerds as a strange and unexpected ally. One of the phreakers uses a version of my name as a password to his BBS. I am honored.

Two movies about science change my life while I'm in high school: *Real Genius* and David Cronenberg's remake of *The Fly*. Both of them are about heroic geeks who break the rules in the name of scientific freedom, and both have strong female characters who work alongside the men as equals.

Real Genius is an antiwar story wrapped in a teen comedy. Young Caltech physics student Mitch discovers that the mysterious project he's helping his respected mentor complete is in fact a dangerous, space-based weapons system. As he struggles with the morality of what he's doing, Mitch meets the hyperactive engineering geek Jordan, whose cute-dorky look and constant experiments with bizarre equipment make her the first vaguely realistic female geek I've ever seen represented on film. With her help and the aid of some friends, Mitch finally exposes the true nature of his professor's research in a creative hack that involves taking over the weapons system and training its laser beam on the world's hugest container of Jiffy Pop—which just happens to be in the professor's house. As the house explodes under pressure from the popcorn, Mitch's shamed professor is arrested. Score one for justice-loving dorks!

My friends and I journey en masse to watch *Real Genius* in the theater, bopping along to the Tears for Fears soundtrack, thrilled that at last there's a movie that makes us look cool. But I'm especially thrilled, because Jordan offers me a place in the narrative for once. I don't have to go through the trouble of identifying with the male characters, a psychological sleight of hand that gets a little old after you've done it every single time you read a novel or watch a movie about nerd stuff.

The Fly, which seduces me immediately with its disturbing images of transfigured bodies and technical innovation run amok, is the first movie I've ever seen where a science journalist is a major character. Veronica meets the elusive genius Seth at a party and comes back to his lab with him to see an experimental device he's developed. It turns out to be a set of teleportation pods, and he invites her to document it for an article. She becomes as involved in his research as he is and falls in love with him before she realizes that he's been doing teleportation experiments on himself.

As anyone familiar with the oft-retold plot of the film knows, the result of Seth's self-experimentation is that he accidentally gets fused at the genetic level with a fly that's trapped in the teleportation pod with him. Slowly his body rots away, piece by piece, revealing a horrifying, insane human-fly creature who wants nothing more than to take Veronica into the teleportation pod with him so that they can be "together" as one genetically fused entity.

At sixteen, I watch the action unfold with a sense of nauseated enlightenment. It isn't just the graphic fly-barf scene that makes me queasy for days afterward. It's the realization that this is some kind of monstrous allegory for what can happen to women in science. If we are attracted to men in our fields—which is understandable enough—the result may not be the partnership we seek. Instead, our male colleagues may try to absorb us, to turn us into functions of themselves, and in the process eradicate our existence. To me, *The Fly* isn't the story of Seth's tragic experiments with science—it's about Veronica's tragic experiments with a scientist.

There are an equal number of men and women in the graduate program where I'm studying the relationship between mass media and American culture. The year I receive my PhD in English and American Studies, most of my colleagues—of both genders—graduate without getting academic jobs.

I stop using contact lenses while I'm in graduate school, and instead wear cheap, horn-rimmed frames that make me look like a nerdy boy from the 1960s. These are the same kind of glasses I am wearing when I leave academia with my PhD and go searching for a full-time writing job. I've been publishing a magazine online called *Bad Subjects* for several years, and designing a few websites on the side. Weirdly, I don't think of myself as interested in computers, even though I'm more computer obsessed than most of the humanities and social science types in my circle of friends.

I joke with my friends that having a PhD in English means I'm the sort of doctor you call when you have a cultural emergency. But my very first cultural emergency as an adult turns out to be my lack of science education. How was I able to go for so long without ever learning how computer networks operate? Without learning basic chemistry, physics, and genetics? In what way does an encyclopedic knowledge of 19th-century naturalist fiction and postmodern discourse make up for not understanding turbine engines and the quantum behavior of light?

Luckily, this particular problem is overshadowed by yet another cultural emergency: the dot-com boom in San Francisco. Plunging straight into the high-tech economy, with its plethora of short-lived publications, gives me a chance to learn computer science on the job. Whenever I want to find out about some new aspect of programming or computer hardware, I propose a story about it. Since this is the boom, everybody has money to fund my personal research projects.

I write about the Linux operating system, computer hackers, and the first generation of multimedia handheld devices. I attend scientific and technical conferences and take copious notes like a student. Eventually, I get a science journalism fellowship at MIT, where I have a chance to immerse myself in geek culture for a year. My books on the history of film and literature are replaced by ones about ENIAC, the first electrical computer, and evolutionary biology.

It's 1999, and I'm at a press conference for a company whose business model is to sell services to companies using Linux. I have no idea where this company is now—it probably fell off the NASDAQ with all the rest of the nice Linux companies from that era.

I'm talking with another tech journalist, a guy who favors the same cheap engineer's glasses I do, and he's congratulating me on an article

I've just published in the *San Francisco Chronicle*. It's about a group of Linux enthusiasts who spend most of their weekends at trade shows doing "installfests." They'll help anyone install and start running Linux on any computer. It's their way of challenging the Microsoft Windows hegemony, one box at a time. A primary source in my story is the elusive head of a semiunderground group called the Linux Cabal.

"So how did you manage to get him to talk to you?" the journalist asks, narrowing his eyes. "He won't ever talk to me."

Maybe I'm paranoid. Maybe I'm sensitive. But suddenly I realize that I'm the only woman in the room except for a few marketing droids who look like they were paid mostly to look good in heels and lipstick. And I hear a barb in this guy's query. So I tell him exactly what I think he's implying.

"I flirted with him," I say. "Yeah, it's lucky I'm a girl because geeks always want to talk to me." Then I stalk away. To the journalist's credit, he looks confused and a little shaken.

Why didn't I just tell the truth? I could have explained that I spent a whole weekend at the trade show, sitting at the installfest table and getting to know everybody who came. I watched install after install, saw kids and retirees get excited at the sight of a command line, learned the pros and cons of different Linux distributions, and even talked to the gadfly trying to interest people in FreeBSD. I made Cthulhu jokes and admitted that Data is my favorite character on *Star Trek: The Next Generation*.

I could have said that if you actually go out and pound the pavement and take the time to get to know people, they'll talk to you. I could have explained to him that this is my philosophy of good journalism. But I didn't.

∞

A few months later, I do an experiment. I decide to write an entire article about biotech using only female sources. I call scientist after scientist, getting amazing information about how to compare mouse and human genomes with small number-crunching programs and constantly growing databases of genetic information. Each source refers me to several other top-notch women in the cutting-edge field of computational biology. One builds her own data-mashing computer clusters; another wrote the software that allows people to browse the fruit fly genome.

It's one of the coolest articles I've ever written, and every name in it is female. Nobody seems to notice that almost every other article in the science and technology press cites all-male sources.

∞

At the turn of the century, there's a resurgence of pop culture aimed at geeks of various sorts. Trend spotters call it "geek chic." Suddenly there's all this college rock sung by people in glasses who use words like "cavalcade" and "arrears" in their lyrics. Movies like *Hackers* glamorize the tech underground, and computer geek character Willow on *Buffy the Vampire Slayer* becomes a smarty-pants sex symbol. Hipsters start wearing bulky glasses, chunky shoes, awkwardly fitted granny dresses, faded T-shirts with obscure slogans, and too-short pants that look like the kind of Wranglers that got my dorky friends in junior high ostracized.

None of it makes much difference to real geeks, especially women. We're not worried about mainstream acceptance because we're too busy writing and researching until all hours of the morning. Being deemed fashionable by a bunch of New York magazine editors doesn't make it any easier for us to make our male colleagues respect us.

In fact, it makes things harder. Some of these new hipster geek images are borne in teen comedies like *She's All That,* which is the kind of hit movie that could occupy the same place as *Real Genius* in the consciousness of a young geek like I once was. It's the story of Laney, a nerdy outcast girl with the requisite thick glasses and weird clothing who makes sculptures out of circuit boards. On a dare, popular boy Zach tells his friends he'll ask her out and turn her into a prom queen in just a few short weeks.

Laney undergoes a real-life version of what Veronica is threatened with in *The Fly.* Her body and identity are completely eroded after she's teleported into Zach's presence. She begins wearing the Gap clothing all the other girls wear, replaces her glasses with contacts, and discovers the joys of being conventionally attractive. We are supposed to cheer her along as she undergoes this geek-into-beauty transformation, to applaud her enthrallment to a boy rather than her mad scientist art.

The flick is so popular that it spawns a whole mini-genre: In *Ice Princess,* a young physics nerd chucks her Harvard scholarship for a career as an ice skater; in *The Prince & Me* (directed by Martha Coolidge, who directed *Real Genius* nineteen years before), a premed geek drops her studies to marry a Danish prince; the lawyer geek heroine of *In Her Shoes* exits her promising career to become a dog-walker and marry a nice Jewish boy. Why don't geek boys ever toss their test tubes aside for lower-status jobs or for the opportunity to raise babies for their high-powered wives?

∞

In early 2005, Harvard's soon-to-be-ex-president Lawrence Summers gives a now-infamous speech at a conference about women in the sciences, where he speculates that the lack of women in these fields might be the result of problems with female neurology. Women, he argues, are intrinsically more interested in raising kids than they are in becoming engineers. I'm so pissed off about his speech that I pore over countless statistics on women in the sciences and engineering, looking for patterns that reflect cultural—rather than neurological—differences between the sexes. What I find is astonishing, and highly underreported.

Women are actually graduating with more science and engineering bachelor's degrees than men. In 2000, 56 percent of sci/tech degrees go to women. But only 25 percent of them get jobs in the fields they spent four or five years studying. Obviously, women's aptitude for science is tremendous. It's the job market that has a problem, and I'll give you a little hint about that—it ain't neurological.

∞

"Get up, Trinity. Get up."

I hear a version of those words in my head all the time. They come from the opening scene of geek cult movie *The Matrix,* and they're uttered by female hacker Trinity after a particularly harrowing gunfight. She's just thrown herself through a window and landed in a crouch, guns at the ready. Though she's evaded her enemies for the moment, her muscles remain locked in place. She has to talk herself out of that defensive stance, pushing herself to stand up and return to safety.

I think of the scene often partly because Trinity is a fantasy version of Jordan from *Real Genius*—she's a hacker girl on par with her male counterparts, skinny and pale, whose first encounter with hero Neo goes exactly the way you'd expect. "You're Trinity?" he asks. "I thought you were a guy." Of course she goes on to save Neo, and to save the day. But not without having to push herself in a way the male characters never do. Not without having to pull herself together, to give herself the hard guidance that the men get from each other.

Trinity's words are tough self-comfort for me one morning when I see my name on a popular geek blog called Slashdot. An article of mine has been featured, and the long discussion it inspires includes a spirited debate about whether I'm too fat to be considered attractive. Several months later, another article of mine is Slashdotted, and I'm described as a "gorgeous nerd" rather than a journalist. Needless to say, none of the male authors on Slashdot are evaluated for pulchritude. I'm so enraged that I can't pull my eyes away from the screen. I want to kill those fucking boys. Where are my goddamn blaster rifles? My muscles are locked and my face is burning.

"Get up, Annalee," I have to tell myself. "Get up." Only then can I pull myself out of my chair and get back to researching innovations in gene-sequencing technologies.

Those of us who are successful in male-dominated geek fields have to rely on our own psychological resources far more than men do. We're often forced to work alone and to find role models and mentors in the world of fiction rather than in our everyday lives. Understandably, many women are discouraged by this. Policy wonks are constantly insisting that we need more mentors for women if we ever want to right the gender imbalance in the sciences. But of course these mentoring relationships are impeded by the same media images and social presuppositions that made the Slashdot geeks debate my rack rather than my ideas.

I call it the "girl takes off her glasses" myth: Women are viewed as either smart or sexually appealing. As a corollary, it's understood that a geeky woman hides behind her glasses until contact with a man strips her face of its shield and turns her into a cute baby-maker. This myth is one of many impediments preventing the current male-dominated nerd establishment from mentoring young women. With some exceptions, men fear their colleagues will assume they're sexually infatuated with the women they advise. At the same time, women fear that they'll be accused of using their feminine wiles to win male mentors. So many walls of culturally sanctioned suspicion and fear have been raised between male and female geeks that it's almost impossible for them to share labs and projects.

But if women are to make inroads in male-dominated fields, the genders will have to work together. For that to happen, we need to demolish the idea that there is some kind of contradiction between female intelligence and sexuality. We must insist that women can be sexual without that affecting their ability to work with men—and vice versa. Possibly we'll do this by creating new myths of strong women whose mentors and sidekicks are male. And possibly we'll do it by inviting men to attend geek women's mixers and mentoring events, thus laying the foundations for a gender-neutral Old Nerds Network.

Either way, we'll be heading in the right direction if we acknowledge that this is a gender problem, not a women's problem or a men's problem. We all need to get over our fears and prejudices if we're going to invent a quantum computer that works, if you know what I mean.

When you're buried in a field, busy with running gels and hacking code, you don't always have time to sit back and ask big-picture questions about gender balance in your lab. You may *feel* those questions—they may be beating you over the head with their obviousness—but you're never going to become first author on that article in *Nature* if you spend all your time answering them.

I know this because I'll drive myself insane if I think for more than a few disgusted seconds about how one of my editors—a nice guy, one of several nice guy editors at a glossy sci/tech magazine—tells me that "women work harder on their articles, but men are the real geniuses." If I ponder that for too long, if I let it seep into the same part of my brain where Wonder Woman fights for justice, I'll never write another word.

It's been a whole day, and I'm still letting myself smolder over that stupid posting on Slashdot. Finally I decide to write an email to a few geeky women friends about it, just to vent. I start filling in the CC: field, adding name after name, thinking to myself: "Oh yeah, she'll want to know about this too," and "She'll totally understand." I've added about a dozen recipients when I realize that the very act of addressing this email is already making me feel better.

My friends' replies have me giggling: They advise me to wear high heels on spaceships and throw lemon wedges at the annoying boys during techie mixers. But some of the replies are more serious, containing stories about male colleagues who openly admired my friends' asses while they crawled under desks to do computer repairs. It's not just what these women say that helps. It's also being reminded that I know a ton of female nerds. Some are friends; many others are colleagues. We swap science fiction DVDs, read each other's blogs, and follow each other's research. We're writers, scientists, engineers, lawyers, professors, and wonks. You know what? We fucking rule.

And our numbers are growing. A recent Pew Internet & American Life survey found that women under the age of twenty-nine were more likely than men of that age to go online. If you look at statistics over the last forty years, the number of women pursuing careers in science and engineering has gone from close to zero in the early 1960s to 35 percent in some areas, such as the life sciences, in 2004. That's a huge leap in one generation, and I expect the next generation to take it even further.

I still love Wonder Woman and Trinity, but it's hard to live on fantasy alone. Right now, I'm hearing the words of real women in my head. They're telling me to be strong. Oh, and they're also asking if they can borrow my copy of the New X-Men comic book collection.

acknowledgments

several people helped us out in the early stages of creating this book by talking to us about our ideas. Although their names don't appear in the table of contents, their influences do: Thanks to Liz Henry, Pagan Kennedy, Cecilia Tan, Katie Hafner, and Esther Dyson. Also, thanks to the excellent sites BoingBoing.net and StarWars.com for getting the word out about this book when we announced our call for submissions. Thanks to Erin Raber, our amazing editor at Seal Press. And most importantly, thanks to all the female geeks out there—we are not alone.

about the contributors

KRISTIN ABKEMEIER earned a PhD in experimental condensed matter physics before working in information technology development. She is now a writer and artist.

VIOLET BLUE is a best-selling, award-winning author and editor of more than a dozen books on sex and sexuality, two of which have been translated into French, Spanish, Russian, and Turkish. Violet is a sex educator who lectures at various UC campuses and other community institutions and writes about erotica, pornography, sexual pleasure, and health. She is a professional sex blogger and femmebot, a celebrity forum moderator at Stockroom.com, an author at Metroblogging San Francisco, and on the Gawker payroll at Fleshbot.com. She has also presented at Dorkbot, worked ten years at Survival Research Laboratories, and is a Geek Entertainment TV correspondent. Her podcast is Open Source Sex and her website is tinynibbles.com.

THIDA CORNES is the mother of a four-year-old daughter who loves to "work on the computer" and an eighteen-month-old son who loves to bang on computer keyboards. She and her family live in the Silicon Valley, where her husband works as a software engineer for a start-up company. She can be found online at www.mandalay.org.

JESSICA DICKINSON GOODMAN is a native Californian and honor roll student at Harker High School ("The Geek School"). She is currently in her junior year and looking forward to testing for her black belt in Shito-Ryu Karate.

NINA SIMONE DUDNIK is a PhD student in molecular biology at Harvard Medical School. There she divides her time between studying fruit fly genetics and collecting used laboratory equipment to send to developing countries. Prior to entering graduate school, she worked in international agricultural development in the Ivory Coast and Italy.

SUZANNE E. FRANKS is a chronically educated (BS, MS, PhD, Women's Studies graduate certificate, MEd) engineer/scientist/feminist geek. She has conducted cancer research in the United States and Germany, written new drug application documents for FDA review in the pharmaceutical industry, and created a flourishing garden from scratch on the Kansas prairie. She was the founding director of the Women in Engineering and Science program at Kansas State University. She now writes Thus Spake Zuska, a witty and informative engineering/science/feminism blog at http://radio.weblogs.com/0147021.

Born in Quezon City, Philippines, **PAULA GAETOS** moved to the United States with her family at the age of six. Her Filipino roots and multicultural American upbringing give her an appreciation and love for other cultures and especially for history. She is currently a third-year student at Mount St. Mary's College in Los Angeles, double-majoring in history and philosophy with a minor in political science. Her interests lie in video games (particularly puzzle games), computer software and hardware, action movies, web design, web comics, and anime.

DEVIN KALILE GRAYSON is delighted to count herself among the dwindling number of former English majors to be gainfully employed in their chosen field. She is particularly grateful to DC Comics for letting her hide a burgeoning personality disorder behind the facade of "work" for the last eight years, and absolutely tickled to have penned a few novels. Devin currently resides in Oakland, California, with three frogs, four computers, a feline muse, and her wonder dog, Cody.

DIANA HUSMANN is a physics major at MIT. She loves reading books and articles about everything from Bose-Einstein condensate to the big bang and enjoys hiking in the beautiful mountains of Washington State.

QUINN NORTON is a freelance journalist and busy mom. She recently acquired a set of first edition AD&D books and an interested group of people.

MARA POULSEN spent three years as a video game programmer, first at Saffire Corporation and then at Acclaim Studios in Salt Lake City. Some of her published titles include *Xena Warrior Princess: Talisman of Fate* and *Jeremy McGrath Supercross World* for Nintendo Gamecube. She now writes full-time and has just finished her second science fiction novel.

CORIE RALSTON holds a BS in physics from UC Berkeley and a PhD in biophysics from UC Davis. She is currently a staff scientist at Lawrence Berkeley National Laboratory. She has published half a dozen science fiction short stories and is on the editorial staff at the *Internet Review of Science Fiction* (www.irosf.com).

ROOPA RAMAMOORTHI holds a BS in chemical engineering at Indian Institute of Technology and an MS and PhD in chemical engineering with a minor in biology from the California Institute of Technology. Her postdoctoral work was conducted at University of Washington in molecular biotechnology and at MIT in biochemical engineering. She currently works as a senior scientist at a biotech company in the San Francisco Bay Area and is working on a collection of interlinked short stories.

MORGAN ROMINE fell in love with video games when she was six years old and has been playing them ever since, with online games being her current passion. Better known as "Rhoulette" in the video game online community, Morgan helped found and build Ubisoft's all-girl gaming team, the Frag Dolls. As captain of the team, she serves as spokesperson, gamer, and road manager, and has participated in several panels discussing gender and games. As an undergraduate at UC Berkeley, Morgan studied anthropology and music, and during her senior year she coordinated and led a class about the anthropology of online gaming communities. After graduating from UC Berkeley, she entered the game industry. Her introduction to Ubisoft was through their MMORPG title, *Shadowbane*, where she led a clan of more than two-hundred players. Currently a community manager for Ubisoft, Morgan interacts directly with their core video game audience and serves as a communication hub between the gaming communities and dev teams. In her personal gaming life she is currently playing games such as *World of Warcraft, Ghost Recon Advanced Warfighter, Halo 2, Guitar Hero,* and *Oblivion*.

JAMI SCHOENEWIES is an art teacher, writer, and visual artist who is currently working toward a Master of Fine Arts degree in St. Louis. Her husband, Michael, is also an artist and a fellow nerd who works in exhibit production for their local science museum.

WENDY SELTZER teaches Internet Law and Information Privacy as a visiting assistant professor of law at Brooklyn Law School and writes about online free speech. Previously, she was a staff attorney with the Electronic Frontier Foundation, specializing in intellectual property and First Amendment issues. As a fellow with Harvard's Berkman Center for Internet & Society, Wendy founded, programmed, and led the Chilling Effects Clearinghouse, helping Internet users to understand their rights in response to cease-and-desist threats.

ELISABETH SEVERSON is an unrepentant math geek who enjoys reading feminist critiques of cyberpunk, pop-culture biographies of famous mathematicians, and science fiction with humor and strong female characters. She and her equally geeky girlfriend, a chemist, live in Seattle with two cats that show no interest in the sciences. Her favorite constant is e.

AOMAWA SHIELDS holds an MFA in acting from UCLA, and a BS in earth, atmospheric, and planetary sciences from MIT. She has published two papers in astronomical journals and has done research at Lowell Observatory, the Jet Propulsion Laboratory, and Arecibo Observatory. She appeared in the recent film *Nine Lives* and continues to tour her one-woman show, *Goddess. Divided.* Aomawa lives in Los Angeles with her husband, actor/director Steven Shields, and has just completed her first book of poetry. She is also on the Science User Support Team at the California Institute of Technology's Spitzer Science Center and helps to support the astronomical community in its use of the Spitzer Space Telescope.

JENN SHREVE's love of science and technology makes its way into both her fiction and nonfiction. Her work has appeared in *Slate, Seed, Wired, Ready Made,* and the *San Francisco Chronicle,* among others. She lives in San Francisco and can be found online at www.jennshreve.com.

ELLEN SPERTUS is an associate professor of computer science at Mills College, where she directs the graduate program in Interdisciplinary Computer Science. She is also a part-time software engineer at Google. She has numerous technical publications in computer architecture, information retrieval, and online communities, and has also written for *Technology Review, Chronicle of Higher Education, Glamour,* and *Odyssey.* She lives in San Francisco with her husband.

MICHELLE VILLANUEVA is a freelance writer living in the San Francisco Bay Area. Apart from her Neville Longbottom geekiness, she also finds video games very difficult to resist. She is an avid anime and manga collector. Her website is www.neville-sam.com.

A native Tennessean, **KORY WELLS** directs software development for Specific Software Solutions, a Nashville-area Fortune 50 business. Her novel in progress, *White Line to Graceville,* was a finalist in the William Faulkner Creative Writing Competition, and she has published several short stories. Her mother, Judy Lee Green, is also an accomplished writer.

about the editors

ANNALEE NEWITZ is a nationally known technology and science writer. She is a contributing editor at *Wired* and also writes for *New York* magazine, *Popular Science, Salon, New Scientist, The Believer,* and *The San Francisco Bay Guardian.* Her syndicated column, "Techsploitation," deals with all things geeky and runs in newspapers throughout the U.S. and Canada. In 2002 she won a Knight Science Journalism Fellowship that allowed her to spend a year at MIT doing research. She is the author of *Pretend We're Dead: Capitalist Monsters in American Pop Culture,* the editor of the anthology *The Bad Subjects: Political Education for Everyday Life,* and coeditor of *White Trash: Race and Class in America.* She is also the cofounder of two indie magazines: *other* and *Bad Subjects.* Annalee has discussed her work on CNN, NPR, CBS, the Discovery Channel, BBC, and the CBC, as well as in *The New York Times* and *The Wall Street Journal.* She holds a PhD in English and American studies from UC Berkeley.

CHARLIE ANDERS is the author of the Lambda Literary Award–winning *Choir Boy,* which was a finalist for the Edmund White first novel award and was named one of the top ten fiction titles of 2005 in Richard Labonte's Book Marks column. She also wrote *The Lazy Crossdresser,* a feminist style manifesto for transgender women struggling with body image and gender stereotypes. Her writing has appeared in *McSweeney's Internet Tendency, Salon, The San Francisco Bay Guardian, The Wall Street Journal, ZYZZYVA, Tikkun, Fresh Yarn,* Pindeldyboz.com, the *San Francisco Chronicle, Publishers Weekly, Punk Planet,* the *New York Press, Kitchen Sink,* and *Watchword,* among others. She's also contributed to various anthologies, including *Paraspheres: Fabulist and New Wave Fabulist Fiction* and *Pills, Chills, Thrills and Heartache: Adventures in the First Person.* Charlie cofounded *other* magazine with Annalee Newitz and organizes the award-winning reading series Writers With Drinks.

Selected Titles from Seal Press

For more than thirty years,
Seal Press has published groundbreaking books.
By women. For women. Visit our website at www.sealpress.com.

Dirty Sugar Cookies: Culinary Observations, Questionable Taste by Ayun Halliday. $14.95, 1-58005-150-2. Ayun Halliday is back with comical and unpredictable essays about her disastrous track record in the kitchen and her culinary observations—though she's clearly no expert.

What Would Murphy Brown Do? How the Women of Prime Time Changed Our Lives by Allison Klein. $16.95, 1-58005-171-5. From workplace politics to single motherhood to designer heels in the city, revisit TV's favorite—and most influential—women of the 1970s through today who stood up and held their own.

Pissed Off: On Women and Anger by Spike Gillespie. $14.95, 1-58005-162-6. An amped-up and personal self-help book that encourages women to go ahead and use that middle finger without being closed off to the notion of forgiveness.

Reckless: The Outrageous Lives of Nine Kick-Ass Women by Gloria Mattioni. $14.95, 1-58005-148-0. An entertaining collection of profiles that explores the lives of nine women who took unconventional life paths to achieve extraordinary results.

Stalking the Wild Dik Dik: One Woman's Solo Misadventures Across Africa by Marie Javins. $15.95, 1-58005-164-2. A funny and compassionate account of the sort of lively and heedless undertaking that could only happen in Africa.

The Risks of Sunbathing Topless: And Other Funny Stories from the Road edited by Kate Chynoweth. $15.95, 1-58005-141-3. From Kandahar to Baja to Moscow, these wry, amusing essays capture the comic essence of bad travel, and the female experience on the road.

Without a Net: The Female Experience of Growing Up Working Class edited by Michelle Tea. $14.95, 1-58005-103-0. A collection of essays "so raw, so fresh, and so riveting, that I read them compulsively, with one hand alternately covering my mouth, my heart, and my stomach, while the other hand turned the page. *Without a Net* is an important book for any woman who's grown up—or is growing up—in America."—Vendela Vida, *And Now You Can Go*